GODDESS
Aloud!

ABOUT THE AUTHOR

Michelle Skye (Massachusetts) is a Pagan Priestess. She teaches classes, leads workshops, and founded the Massachusetts Pagan Teens and Sisterhood of the Crescent Moon. Her articles have appeared in *Circle Magazine, SageWoman, Llewellyn's Herbal Almanac,* and *Llewellyn's Magical Almanac.*

MICHELLE SKYE

GODDESS
Aloud!

TRANSFORMING YOUR WORLD
THROUGH RITUALS & MANTRAS

Llewellyn Publications
Woodbury, Minnesota

First Edition
First Printing, 2010

Cover illustration © 2009 by Wen Hsu
Cover design by Ellen Dahl
Editing by Nicole Edman
Interior illustrations by the Llewellyn Art Department

Llewellyn is a registered trademark of Llewellyn Worldwide, Ltd.

Library of Congress Cataloging-in-Publication Data
Skye, Michelle.
  Goddess aloud : transforming your world through rituals & mantras /
Michelle Skye. — 1st ed.
      p. cm.
  Includes bibliographical references.
  ISBN 978-0-7387-1442-4
  1. Goddess religion. 2. Goddesses. 3. Mantras. 4. Rites and
ceremonies. I. Title.
  BL473.5.S597 2010
  203'.8082—dc22
                              2009031527
  ISBN: 978-0-7387-1442-4

Llewellyn Publications
A Division of Llewellyn Worldwide, Ltd.
2143 Wooddale Drive, Dept. 978-0-7387-1442-4
Woodbury, Minnesota 55125-2989, U.S.A.
www.llewellyn.com

Printed in the United States of America

OTHER WORKS BY MICHELLE SKYE

Goddess Alive!
(Llewellyn Publications, 2007)

Goddess Afoot!
(Llewellyn Publications, 2008)

Llewellyn's Magical Almanac
(contributor, 2000, 2002, 2004, 2006, 2008, 2010)

Llewellyn's Herbal Almanac
(contributor, 2006, 2007, 2008, 2009, 2010)

Llewellyn's Witches' Datebook
(contributor, 2009)

Llewellyn's Sabbats Almanac
(contributor, Samhain 2010 to Mabon 2010)

FORTHCOMING WORKS BY MICHELLE SKYE

Goddess Magic
(Llewellyn Publications)

This book is dedicated to all the men in my life:

To my Dad, Rui, who first helped me find my voice and encouraged me to use it.

To my husband, Michael, who supported and challenged my voice in so many ways. You are my greatest teacher!

To my ritual-mates, Gene and JD, who listened to my voice with compassion and mirth.

And to my chihuahua, Muchacho, who reminded me that it's important to bark at the big Husky down the street, even when you're only two and a half pounds!

Thank you all! I love you guys!

CONTENTS

CHAPTER ONE

Finding Your Voice

In the beginning God created the heavens and the Earth.
The Earth was formless and void, and darkness was over the surface of the deep,
and the Spirit of God was moving over the surface of the waters.
Then God said, "Let there be light"; and there was light.
—NEW AMERICAN STANDARD BIBLE, GENESIS 1:1–3

I begin with the most recognizable example of the power of the voice as expressed by the Divine. Yahweh, the God of the Christians, created the world simply by talking. He called for light, and light came. He called for the sky, and the sky appeared. He called for water, Earth, stars, plants, and animals, and guess what? They all manifested before him through the power of his voice.

The Feminine Divine, which has been historically subjugated by male-dominated religious philosophy, has equally powerful examples of the voice in stories and legends around the world. These, however, have been forgotten over time, condensed and covered over by the weighty words of the monotheistic God. With this book, I seek to bring the stories of the Voice of the Feminine into the light of day where their messages can be read, understood, and implemented in everyday life. Behold the power of vocal confession with the Aztec goddess Tlazolteotl! Hear the mighty magical words of the Egyptian goddess Isis! Feel the depth of emotion in the cries of sorrow from the goddess Demeter and the shouts of joy from her daughter Persephone. The Great Goddess is here to guide each of us in the recovery and the strengthening of our individual voice. Through her example and with her love, she will aid us in manifesting our dreams on this Earth, helping us heal so we may finally recognize our true inner self. The journey waits before you. All you need to do is take that first step. Make the choice to honor yourself, to open your voice, and to begin to change the world around you.

IN THE BEGINNING

This book was conceived out of my own personal needs. You see, in the past, I have had a hard time accessing the power of my voice. Even now, after a year of writing this book and working to strengthen my voice, I still find myself, at times, retreating into silence. Silence is so much easier, after all. You don't hurt people's feelings. You don't need to defend your ideas. There's no confrontation, no "situation," no issues, no conflicts. It's just you, in the quiet, by yourself—which is, of course, the root of the problem. Silence isolates the individual from the world. It also isolates the individual from herself. If you don't express your thoughts, concerns, and philosophies, you disavow their intrinsic worth. Your great ideas, kept locked up tight in your mind, affect nothing. Change nothing. Connect with nothing. By refusing to use your voice, you deny your right to be an active participant in life. In *your* life.

And I *know* this truth on an intellectual level, but I sometimes find it so hard to get the words out of my mouth. I worry that I'll hurt people's feelings, that they'll verbally attack me, that they won't like me. So, out of fear, I keep quiet. And then I get angry. I take that anger home with me and lash out at the people I *do* feel comfortable around. I attack my family and friends who I know will love me no matter what I say or do. And they didn't do anything wrong! This is not healthy behavior. It is not the way to build relationships. So what's a girl to do?

For me the answer was simple: turn to the Goddess. My journey to find my voice began in 1999, when I first started to teach Wicca classes at local metaphysical and New Age shops. My first teaching job was at Women of Wisdom in Easton, Massachusetts, a cute, purple-accented building with a lovely warm energy. The owner of the shop agreed to allow me to teach an Introduction to Wicca class, and she specifically asked me to include songs and chants in the six-week workshop. She said that women hid their voices too much and she hoped that my class could address this issue, if only briefly. I was terrified! I did not always trust my speaking voice, forget about my singing voice! But I included a song and chant section in the class on Sabbats and ritual work, even though I didn't really want to. As the class loomed ever closer, I began to do copious amounts of research in an effort to "gloss over" what I considered my singing "defects." In my research travels, I found a powerful poem in the midst of a Virginia Slims ad for their regular light 100s. I will share it with you.

The
   mysterious
      power
Of my voice
         Endures.

My essence glows.
        My heart
   Dances.
  My Voice
     Sings.

        The eyes
Are the messenger of
      The Soul,
        But the
          Voice
     Reveals
      The Spirit!

To this day, I still have the glossy, full-color ad, replete with sensuous, energetic women and this powerful, thought-provoking, voice-enhancing poem. It just goes to show, you never know where you'll find inspiration and Divine guidance.

Years passed, during which time I continued to sing a few Pagan songs and chants in my Wicca classes. And then I had a baby. My daughter trundled into my life, all chubby independence and, as a brand-new mama, I tried all sorts of ways to form a connection with her. One of my more brilliant ideas was to purchase the video, "Baby and Mom Post-Natal Yoga," a forty-five-minute foray into the practice of Kundalini yoga with noted yogini Gurmukh. When I bought the video, I did not know it was a Kundalini practice. I figured all yoga was the same (HA!) and, having done some Hatha yoga, thought that a yoga exercise regimen that included my baby girl would be fun and enjoyable. And it was! But the absolute best part of the video occurred at the very end when all the moms rubbed their babies and moved their little chubby Buddah-bodies around while chanting. Chanting! I had never done chanting in a yoga class before. I loved it! I still love it. It made perfect sense to craft a more flexible voice after creating a more flexible body. My chanting connected to the Divine without, the Divine within me, and the Divine within my precious baby girl. This was awesome!

The chanting of the Kundalini mantras helped me to feel more comfortable with my voice. As my daughter grew up, I willingly sang lullabies and nighttime chants to her while we gazed out at the darkening star-strewn sky. I began to create with my voice. I made up songs to soothe my daughter, encourage her, and connect her with other members of the household. (These are now staples in our household that we often sing to each other.) I began to sing more and more in my classes, more and more at home. My voice was finding wings!

I was so excited. I had found my voice! Huzzah! I figured that I no longer had any issues related to my voice. I was cured, whole, complete. What I didn't realize was that once I had found my voice, I had to use it. Outside of my house. Outside of my well-constructed, safe, and secure environment. With adults who, unlike my daughter, did not love me unconditionally.

So, in an effort to bring my voice into the world around me, *Goddess Aloud!* was formed. When I first started writing this book, I didn't know it was meant to help me with my own voice-enhancing process. I simply wanted to explore the possibility of accessing the vocal energy of the Goddess in the creation of ourselves, our lives, and the world around us. Through the exploration of goddess myths and legends around the globe, I have recognized the truth of the power in the feminine voice. It is different from the male voice, which is why, I think, many women have problems accessing that power. The voice, as it is commonly utilized in modern society, is strident and true. It must be physically expressed and, for it to have impact, it must be heard. The voice has a lot of male qualities because it is not necessarily consensus-driven. It is your truth at that one moment in time, and it often resonates with staccato energy.

There are many heroines with strong voices in classic literature. The two that leap to mind are Katherina from Shakespeare's *The Taming of the Shrew* and Jane from Charlotte Brönte's *Jane Eyre*. Katherina, as you may remember from high school English class, is labeled a shrew because she speaks her mind in a very masculine way. She does not try to sugarcoat her words and, thus, her family believes her to be unwomanly. In truth, she is not very pleasant and doesn't care what men or women or family members think of her. She is mean and cutting and biting. She is a woman trying to access her voice through a masculine conversational structure. She imitates the dictatorial attitude of the men of her family and of her society, and her choice to emulate a societal voice— rather than to find her own feminine voice—causes her to lose her voice entirely. By the end of the play, Katherina is married to Petruccio. He is a powerful, willful man who completely transforms Katherina into the subjugated woman, voiceless in public. Yet, Katherina allows herself to be so transformed, believing there are only two choices for the use of the voice: the powerful, strident masculine usage, or no usage at all. She does not even conceive of a third option.

Jane of *Jane Eyre*, however, does realize and utilize that third communication option for the voice. Jane is another spirited woman who ends up married at the end of her novel. However, Jane does not lose her voice. Her forthright manner becomes less abrupt as she gets older, but she still speaks her mind. Her relationship with her employer Mr. Rochester is fairly equal, and he treats her with respect and esteem. Jane's voice is her own, feminine and full of meaning and inspiration. She does not try to overcome others with her voice but, rather, to engage them. She seeks to form a connection with others in an effort to express her personal point of view. There is never a need to overwhelm others in her conversational tone. Instead, she chooses to express her own truth, whether it is agreed upon or not. Jane forges a new and different pattern for her voice. I call it the Voice of the Feminine; however, this force is neither male nor female, but intrinsic to all life on the planet.

The Voice of the Feminine gives us the ability to be open and honest with ourselves and with others in the world, without the need to conquer and command. In essence, it is a communication style, a voice pattern true to the self. With the Voice of the Feminine, it is not necessary to convince others of our viewpoint. It is enough to know our own mind, state such thoughts clearly and succinctly, and then continue about our daily existence. The lesson that Katherina and Jane teach us is *not* that women should be silent. Rather, they teach us that women have a completely different vocal communication style than men, a feminine communication style that is often not expressed or accepted in the popular culture of the day. The Voice of the Feminine is alive and always has been, but, like much of female history and spirituality, it hides in out-of-the-way places and can be difficult to find. Yet, for our sake and the sake of our daughters and sons and future generations, we have a responsibility to unearth these hidden truths. The time for confrontational use of the voice is over. The old masculine paradigms are at an end. It is time to utilize the voice for connection, for understanding, for bridge-building. It is time to use the voice to create, rather than destroy.

The Voice of the Feminine has the ability to craft and construct. It can unify people, cultures, and even philosophies and ideas. The Voice of the Feminine is not about changing people's minds to "our" way of thinking but about understanding other ways of thought. This style of communication is not uncommon, new, or radical. Women have been doing this for centuries in the home and around the hearth fire. Yet, the Voice of the Feminine is revolutionary in its possibilities. It is time for all people on this planet, whether female or male, to embrace the use of their voice for connection, rather than control. It is time to wrest the Voice of the Feminine out of the home and into the spotlight of the world to effect positive change.

Altering our speech patterns from control to communication begins with the knowledge of the intrinsic worth of the self. We each have the right to state our own truth. Once we have accepted this right, it leads to the understanding that just as we have intrinsic worth, so too does every other person on our planet. Their intrinsic value does not vary by region or age or race or sexual orientation. Each one of us is valuable and powerful. Therefore, all people have the right to state their individual truths. We need not agree with everyone's beliefs, only accept that those beliefs are right for that person. We may engage in thought-provoking, meaningful discussion about the differences between our truths but the point is not to alter each other's viewpoint; instead, it is to understand those differences and accept an individual's truth.

The Voice of the Feminine is very empowering for the self as well as for all those you meet. It gives you the right to own your thoughts and ideas. It places value on your individuality and your ability to express yourself to others. It allows you to act based on your true self. Yet, the Voice of the Feminine is not egotistical or demanding. The true Voice of the Feminine does not force others to believe or act against their will. Instead, it accepts and loves others for their differences. Imagine a world where all people—men, women, and children of all races and cultures—could express themselves freely without censure or fear. Imagine making choices based on your own personal beliefs rather than on societal mores. Imagine stating your truth and acting upon it, with the welfare and well-being of all in mind. This is the true value of the Voice of the Feminine: the ability to realize our individual dreams side-by-side with the hopes and dreams of others in the world. The Voice of the Feminine creates community while honoring and valuing the individual. The time has come to embrace the Voice of the Feminine in all aspects of our lives. To do otherwise is to undermine the very truth of who we are, as individuals, on this planet. And to begin, we need to embrace the idea of the mantra.

MANTRAS

Mantras are important spiritual tools of the Hindu and Buddhist religions. They are used to connect to the Divine through the mind (meditation and vibration) and through the body (words and sounds). They are repetitive sounds and words that are said (usually, although not always) aloud to honor a specific deity. Often, the characteristics of the deity are considered when choosing a mantra. For instance, if you were wishing to increase your prosperity, you might intone the mantra "Om Shreem Om," which is the mantra for Lakshmi, the goddess of abundance and prosperity. A mantra differs from a prayer because you are seeking to welcome the energy and guidance of the Divine into your life by actually connecting to their energetic presence. In other words, the mantra helps to lift you out of mundane reality and into the reality of the universe and of the spirit.

I chose to use the mantra as the vehicle for accessing and expressing the Voice of the Feminine because, in the Hindu and Buddhist religions, mantras are already linked to the Feminine Divine. There are mantras currently in use around the world devoted to such goddesses as Lakshmi, Sarasvati, and Green Tara. Since they are already associated with feminine Divine energy, mantras seemed the natural choice for our work in connecting to the Voice of the Feminine through the Divine. There are numerous other spiritual alternatives to the mantra—prayer, affirmation, incantation—yet each of these has a specific usage that does not flow with the ultimate purpose of this book. The goddess mantras in this book are not spells or affirmations meant to create change. They *will* effect change and help welcome positive manifestation in your life, but their primary goal is to connect you with the Divine. By chanting the mantras continually, you access a frequency and vibration higher than that of the earthly plane. You become more than the words by connecting with the universal energy. In short, your life changes because you no longer are the same person.

Through the repetition of the mantra, you access the Divine and shift your perception of reality. You are not pleading with the Divine (as in prayer) or cajoling Him or Her (as in incantation and affirmation). Rather, you are merging with an energy that is ancient and modern and universal. You are becoming one with Goddess energy, worshipped in distance lands, across oceans and deserts, and right around the corner.

Mantras are much more intimate than prayer, incantation, or affirmation because the goal (peace or love, for instance) is just a side-benefit of that wonderful connection with the Divine. So, while the goal is still important, the focus is on the Goddess, both within and without.

This book does not utilize traditional Hindu or Buddhist mantras. It is not meant to replace or devalue the mantras that were created in the Eastern lands hundreds or thousands of years ago. Traditional Hindu and Buddhist mantras were specifically crafted by talented seers and holy men to connect to the gods and goddesses of their spiritual path. Being neither Buddhist nor Hindu, I cannot hope to replicate the power of those spiritual vibrations in relation to Eastern thought and philosophy. Yet, as a spiritual tool, the mantra has value across cultures. In my mind, it need not be relegated to Eastern religions only. Connecting to the Divine—whether you call it God, Goddess, Buddha, Allah, or Yaweh—has value and power. Therefore, the mantras found in this book connect to goddesses from all over the world. They were crafted to represent the culture of the specific goddess as well as to relate to modern goddess spirituality. If you are familiar with Hindu and Buddhist mantras, you will find the goddess mantras to be completely unlike their Eastern cousins. They are meant to be different. And, indeed, they *should* be completely different. After all, the goddess mantras here were created for goddess-worshippers in the twenty-first century who are trying to find their true selves though the reclamation of their voice and a connection to the Feminine Divine. Our spiritual goals, needs, wants, and issues are dissimilar from those who follow Eastern philosophy. Neither is better than the other, just different. Therefore, it is important to approach the mantras in this book knowing that they are not the same as traditional Eastern religious mantras.

CHANTING THE MANTRAS

In traditional Eastern religions, mantras are counted out with the aid of mala beads, Buddhist prayer beads. Mala beads generally consist of 108 beads strung together, with a larger mother/parent, guru, or Buddha bead serving as the place to begin the recitations. While you repeat the mantras, you move your fingers across the beads, one bead per repetition. Often there will be placement beads throughout the string to let you know how many times you've said a specific mantra. Many mantra practices require that you recite the same mantra twenty-one times in a row. Therefore, some mala beads have a spacer or placement bead to acknowledge the end of one mantra recitation and the beginning of another. Also, in some traditions, it is considered bad etiquette to recite the mantras twice in the same direction. In other words, if you have recited your mantra for one revolution of the mala beads and returned to the Buddha bead, you would need to turn the mala beads around and recite them in the opposite direction, rather than skip over the Buddha bead. The Buddha bead is the beginning and the end. To skip over it and continue your practice is considered a sign of disrespect.

The number 108 is quite consistent in relation to the length of mala beads. In Tibetan Buddhism, the number 108 is divided into the numbers 6 x 3 x 2 x 3 = 108, with each number having a corresponding meaning in relation to Buddhist spirituality. The number 6 represents the six senses of a human being—sight, sound, smell, taste, touch, and thought. The first 3 represents past, present, and future. The 2 corresponds to the two states of the mind, heart, and soul: pure or impure. The second 3 signifies the three disturbing states of emotion: like, dislike, and indifference. In the Japanese culture, the number of beads also equals 108 but their number corresponds to the 108 worldly desires, confused thoughts, and passions that the follower works to relinquish in the course of spiritual discipline.[1]

There are numerous reasons for the use of the number 108 in relation to mala beads. Some enthusiasts claim that since 9 and 12 are highly spiritual numbers and 9 x 12 = 108, that the beads relate to a numerological principle of wholeness, spirituality, completion, and the Divine. For Western astrology lovers, there are 12 houses in a natal chart and 9 planets, which, of course, correspond to the number 108. (Pluto still counts in astrology, if not in astronomy.) In India, a predominantly Hindu country, there are 54 letters in the Sanskrit alphabet and each letter has a masculine and feminine quality, thus bringing the total to 108 (54 x 2 =108). It is said that 108 energy lines converge on the heart chakra, the energy center of the body related to relationships, love, and self-love. If so, perhaps each bead represents one of these energy lines.[2] In short, the number 108 fits into numerous spiritual pursuits and religious philosophies around the world.

For modern Goddess worshippers in search of connecting to the Feminine Divine, I think it is important to pay attention to the way the number 108 is divided. The number 108, when divided in half, becomes the number 54. When the number 108 is divided into

---

1. Sakura Designs, "What is a Mala?"
2. Bharati, "Meaning of 108 Beads on a Mala."

thirds, it turns into 36. When quartered, 108 becomes four sections of 27 and, when divided into twelfths, is twelve sections of 9. Now, take the individual numbers—108, 54, 36, and 27—and separate them into their individual parts: $1 + 0 + 8$, $5 + 4$, $3 + 6$, and $2 + 7$. What do you find? They all add up to the number 9, which represents the highest spiritual attainment and the ability to access the highest level of spiritual vibration. "Nine represents attainment, satisfaction, accomplishment, and our success to achieve an influence in our circumstances. Nine beseeches us to recognize our own internal attributes, and extend these abilities out into the world to make a positive, influential difference."[3] The power of the number 9 works with the spiritual goals of connection to the Feminine Divine through the mantras. Yet it also corresponds exactly to the attributes of the Voice of the Feminine. The number 9 transcends time and space, linking the spiritual with the worldly, the individual with the Divine. For this reason, I believe that the number 108 should be used in relation to the beads used in reciting the goddess mantras.

When chanting mantras, mala beads help to hold the place of the individual, aligning the physical (the hands) with the mental (the chant). They are a tangible object for one to focus upon during the meditative recitation. Sometimes, during meditation, the mind wanders and begins to worry about groceries, work, clothes, or mowing the lawn. The mundane reality often intrudes upon our spiritual practice. The beads help to hold our focus so that we are not merely saying words with our mouth while our brain flies off in a million different directions. I find that mala beads are helpful in conditioning the mind to stay alert and aware of the spiritual practice at hand. You don't need to use mala beads, but they can be very helpful.

There are two traditional hand techniques for using mala beads during the recitation of mantras. In the first method, you drape the beads over the third finger of your right hand, holding them steady with the second finger and the thumb. The second finger serves to move the beads toward you after each recitation, while the thumb serves as the placeholder, resting upon the bead that is marking your current chant. In the second technique, the beads rest on your second finger and your thumb does all the work, serving as placeholder and as the mover of the beads. In both techniques, the index finger never touches the beads.

---

3. Venefica, "Spiritual Meaning of Numbers."

Your beads can be made out of any material you choose. You will find mala beads made from wood, berries, and semi-precious stones. Don't let a lack of funds discourage you in the attainment of a set of beads; there are always options! You can buy the plastic beads meant for kids' craft projects and string together your own set of beads. If you don't like the idea of using plastic, you can tie 108 knots in a length of string. You may not feel as though these options are ideal, but they will connect you to the Divine just as well as any expensive mala bead set. Spirituality can be found in the most unusual and nondescript places, so embrace your unique situation and see if you can find a solution!

Once your beads have been created or purchased, it is important to store them respectfully. Even if they are a simple knotted string or a set of brightly colored plastic beads, they are your conduit to the Divine and should be treated honorably as a sacred tool. A silk or cotton bag or pouch is an excellent storage container. Choose a style and color that suits your individuality and spirituality. Then store them in a place where the kiddies, dogs, and cats won't get to them. There's nothing worse than coming home to a tangled pile of string and a mess of loose beads!

❧

I leave you now to explore the many voices of the Great Goddess as revealed throughout time. May you find her stories, exercises, rituals, and mantras fulfilling and helpful in your search for the Divine within and without. May she grant you wisdom, clarity, and all that you seek in the fulfillment of your sacred journey upon this Earth. The following invocation is one that I state aloud before I begin any goddess mantra practice. It helps to focus my mind and narrow my goals to those that are most important for me—the reclamation of the Voice of the Feminine, the connection to the Divine, the achievement of earthly goals in concurrence with the sacred, and the growth and usage of my own individual voice. Feel free to utilize it to begin your mantra practice, or to craft an invocation of your own. After all, this is *your* time with *your* voice, in connection with the Feminine Divine. Honor her and yourself and your voice in whatever way feels most right to you. Know that you are held in Divine love every day. May you feel that love and be blessed by the Goddess in all that you do!

GODDESS MANTRA INVOCATION

My voice is sacred and Divine

For it is mine,

Mine alone.

With honor and praise

To the Great Goddess,

I express my Voice of the Feminine

To sing her praises

And receive her gifts.

I am open and receptive.

I am one with Spirit.

I am one with the world.

I am one with myself.

Namaste.

CHAPTER TWO
Goddess Mantras for Peace

PEACE: A COMPLICATED IDEA (CHAOS REBORN)

Peace. Harmony. Concord among peoples. We talk about it all the time, seeing images of little children running across green fields or splashing in the waves of an ocean beach, unmolested, unconcerned, alive and happy for it. We yearn for that sense of balance, of complete ease. We want to stop wars and bombs and bloody carcasses on the battlefield. We just want everyone to get along.

At least, that is the lie that we tell ourselves. Humanity has been fighting since the first man picked up a stick and bashed his cave neighbor in the head. There has never been an extended period in humanity's lifetime on our planet where no war has raged. It is time to admit that not everyone wants peace. Not everyone wants to play nice and get along. In fact, if we all look deeply into ourselves, far down into our inner cores and craters, I suspect we will come to the truth of peace. For the difficult reality that prevents humanity from ever attaining genuine serenity is that we are chaotic individuals living on a chaotic planet, interacting with other chaotic individuals in a constant froth of ideas, temperaments, and words.

Individuality is our savior and our curse. It gives us the ability (and some would argue the Goddess-given right) to decide what is right and wrong for us as individuals at any given moment in time. Circumstances change, experience alters, and we find that we indulge a bit in the chaos that lives within. We swear at the driver who cuts us off on the freeway. We yell at the dog who pees in the hallway. We are curt to the girl at the register after an especially long wait in line. We've all done it at one time in our lives. Perhaps now, after contemplation and meditation, we are less likely to express the chaos. Perhaps we are more likely.

The chaos lives within, and it is our choice to feed it and allow it to grow or to starve it and watch it hibernate. That chaos never really goes away. It is a part of the human experience, as we live it now. There is some evidence that small hunter-gatherer societies have less violence than our own "enlightened" Western society and all the Third World countries that emulate the rich and powerful West. So be it. But somehow, it seems contrary to human nature to go backward voluntarily, to give up electricity and indoor plumbing and cancer treatments and cars in order to give up violence. Our other option is to give up all traces of individuality, to live under the pressure and power of a superior political (and undoubtedly military) force to enforce peace. With our options limited, taken away, and dictated to us by another, our individuality fades to an inconsequential grayish haze on our horizon. We do what we do for the good of all, regardless of our own thoughts and ideas. At this point, I wonder, would we even have any ideas of our own?

Neither of these options is truly viable for humanity on a large scale. For either of these to work, every human on the planet would need to voluntarily succumb to the uncomfortable changes and adaptations of transformation. And then the old truth of individuality rears its head yet again. If even one person does not agree, the foundation crumbles. The chaos of one awakens the slumbering chaos of others and reminds us all of our true nature. So, should we all simply indulge in the chaos, creating and accepting random violence as a necessary by-product of being individual and human?

That is a question only you can answer in your bed, late at night, as you explore the darkest corners of your inner psyche. But consider this: chaos is not innately bad. It is uncontrollable, uncertain, and tempestuous, but it is not linked to evil, just to change. Chaos brings war and death but also love and birth. It is the chaotic element within each human that allows us to fall in love, to laugh with friends, to create art, to orgasm, to cry for peace. Chaos teeters within each human individual, balancing precariously, ready to bring love or war, peace or violence. The power of individuality is that we can control our own chaos. We have the power and the ability to make the choice. Peace springs from chaos just as war does. The root is the same, anchored deep within the nature of humanity. Each human is charged with making a choice, every single moment of every single day of our life. How will your chaos manifest on our planet? Will you bond, connect, and unify or will you rip, tear, and destroy? You are a chaotic individual, living on a chaotic planet, interacting with other chaotic individuals. You have the power. Make your choice.

ENERGY RETURN

It is hard to conceptualize negative consequences in striving for and actively seeking peace. But it is important to consider that peace has a stagnating quality. It holds everything still and calm, removing any shake-ups or turbulence. It stabilizes. And while stability is not bad in itself, magic to enhance and produce peace can create a block to necessary and important change. You may find relationships in your life withering or lacking verve. You might, over time, lose interest in your job or hobbies. Your interest in women's reproductive rights around the globe or archery or old chess matches could diminish significantly. You may find yourself completely content to sit on the couch or sleep in bed. You might find that struggles arise in your romantic relationship with your significant other. Your desire and striving for peace holds you in check, crystallizing your life into one set pattern, resistant to rock the boat. Your significant other, on the other hand, is continuing to grow and move with the currents of life. Therefore, if you ask for peace in your life, you may want to clarify your desire so that you are still living a full and hearty life. Peace without vital energy and activity is simply sluggishness.

Asking for peace around the world harbors the same possible stagnant ramifications, diminishing any opportunity for growth and expansion. Change is often violent and unpredictable, but necessary. Removing the element of aggression, although commendable, may limit the development of the human race and our interaction with the world. (For example, the bloody American Civil War was necessary to end slavery, and the heart-wrenching World Wars brought about great advances in medical technology.) The change will then need to re-route itself into alternative methods and pathways, possibly extending the period of violence that you are trying to end. It may, however, end the violence abruptly, funneling the energy into more positive endeavors. Who can say? You may decide that the possibility of more violence is a perfectly acceptable consequence, since the prospect of an end to war lingers before you. The choice is entirely up to you. You should, however, carefully consider all possibilities before undertaking your desire to manifest peace.

PAX
Roman Goddess of the Peaceful State

MANTRA

Peace with light, Peace for good, Peace anew
Pax ad lux, Pax et bonum, Pax de novo

There is probably no better known goddess for peace than the Roman goddess Pax, meaning "peace." We learned about the *Pax Romana* in high school history class, considered the word's usage when applied to *Pax Britannica*, and wondered at the implications of *Pax Americana*. Pax is as synonymous with the concept of peace now, in the modern world, as it was in the ancient world of the Roman Empire. During the height of Roman power and occupation and strength, Pax was a necessary and sought-after goal. After all, the Roman emperors wanted peace to prevail in their lands. Revolution and anarchy were the enemies of Roman domination, therefore the Romans worked to uphold the peace and prosperity of a unified empire.

Enter the goddess Pax, who is the personification of peace. Pax is not a widely recognized or mentioned goddess during the time of the Roman Republic. It is only after the ascension of Emperor Augustus, successor of Julius Caesar, that Pax becomes a well-known and well-regarded goddess. In the later period of the Roman Republic, Rome became embroiled in one civil war after another. The African states were attacking and killing traders; the Italian states sought more voting power. Beginning around 140 BCE and continuing until 31 BCE, Rome was constantly at war with itself. Generals fought to assert their authority and claim the role of supreme military leader, wielding martial power to the Senate's political power. However, by the end of this period (which included the well-known in-fighting between Julius Caesar and Pompey, Julius Caesar and Marcus Anthony, and Marcus Anthony and Augustus [or Octavius]), one man emerged as possessing the intelligence and guile necessary to unify Rome—Gaius Octavius, nephew of Julius Caesar.

Learning from his uncle's mistakes, Octavius (who renamed himself Augustus, meaning "the good"), allowed the Senate to remain intact. Instead of calling himself a dictator, Augustus took the title of "first citizen" and got himself elected a tribune of the Senate. In this role, Augustus was able to maneuver within the existing political structure, manipulating the politicians to get his desired end result. As the "first citizen," he held enormous power and used it to influence and make deals with the senators and other tribunes. Augustus was not only adept in politics but also in propaganda. He pulled the goddess Pax out of relative obscurity and set her up as the symbol of peace and prosperity in the Roman Empire under his rule.

In 13 BCE, after Augustus' military victories in Gaul and Spain, the Senate (with the auspices of Augustus) ordered the creation of the *Ara Pacis Augustae* or the Altar of Peace in Rome. Four years later, in 9 BCE, the altar was consecrated and erected just west of the Via Flaminia. The Ara Pacis represents the shift in Roman politics from that of a Republic to an Empire. The monument is also a symbol of Augustus' ability (and thus the ability of Rome) to bring peace and prosperity to all. The Ara Pacis is covered in ornately carved scenes, including one on the eastern side that depicts a goddess.[1]

True to form, the goddess represented is not Pax, who was just in her infancy as a deity during the reign of Augustus. The goddess is most commonly cited as Tellus, a goddess of the Earth who shares many characteristics with the better-known grain goddess Ceres. Despite the fact that the goddess on the Ara Pacis is not Pax, it is important to look at the symbols and items found on the altar, as they evolved into the Roman concept of peace as represented by Pax.

Throughout the monument, the carvings indicate the fertility and abundance of Rome. Flora and fauna abound on all sides of the altar. On the eastern side, the goddess is depicted in a see-through gown with a crown of corn and poppies, obvious connections to growth and fertility, both in regards to sexuality and vegetation. The symbolism continues with two infant boys sitting in her lap, playing with fruit. Below her feet, vegetation and domestic animals spring forth, indicating health and bounty.[2] In later years, as Pax becomes more and more established as an icon in the Roman Empire, she adopts the concepts of abundance and fertility as a part of peace through the use of her own emblems—the cornucopia, the caduceus, the olive branch, the scepter, and the *hasta pura,* a spear without a sharp point.

Pax was a regular image on Roman coins for more than 350 years. One of the earliest examples of Pax appearing on coinage is in 28 BCE, during the reign of Augustus. On one side of the coin known as the Cistophoric Tetradrachm of Ephesus, Augustus' profile

---

1. Sulzberger, "Ara Pacis Augustae."
2. Ibid.

is wreathed in laurel. On the other is the goddess Pax, holding a caduceus, a symbol for free commerce in ancient Rome. Pax is standing on a sword, indicating an end of hostilities, and she is flanked by her name "PAX" and a *cista mystica*, a Middle Eastern symbol known as the magic box. (It was common for Roman coins to adopt meaningful symbols from their conquered lands in an effort to get the inhabitants to accept the Roman occupation and government.) They are all encompassed by a circular laurel-wreath, signifying Augustus' victory over Asia Minor.[3] Other coins more commonly depict Pax with her olive branch, extending her peace and prosperity over the breadth of the Roman Empire. During the reign of Vespasian, coins from 70 CE and 75 CE showed Pax sitting and leaning back with her elbow supported by a throne. (Other leaning coins often depicted figures being supported by columns.)

The leaning pose is, perhaps, at the very heart of Pax's relationship with the ideal of peace. Pax is not an independent goddess, searching for peace by any means necessary. She is an emissary of the government, an important component of the propaganda and goals of the state. The leaning pose on Roman coinage indicates the general concept of *securitas*, a feeling of freedom and relaxation brought about by good government and a trust in the political system and the men in power within it.[4] Pax's job in the Roman Empire was to inspire the ideal of securitas. She circulated throughout the Roman States for hundreds of years on coins, lending her abundant fertility and peace to the emperors whose visages adorned the other side of her coin. With her cornucopia and her threatening (but not lethal) staff, Pax served to bring a sense of resigned acceptance to a conquered populace, emphasizing the benefits of Roman citizenry rather than the consequences.

Pax, as created and utilized by the Romans, is a state goddess who aids in spreading the benefits of a centralized government to the outer edges of a nation. She works to bring calm and peace to all people through increased abundance, fertility, and bounty. Working with Pax in the modern era would involve utilizing the societal and governmental structures already in place, rather than striving to re-work and create new ones. Pax is a goddess of security and leadership, of conservative action and legislative trust. She is not concerned with internal peace or inner issues of the shadow self. Pax wants everyone clothed, housed, and sleeping with full bellies. She wishes all to accept the cur-

---

3. Spade, "Roman History."
4. Welch, "The Sign Language of Roman Coins: Leaning on the Handy Column."

rent situation and flourish within it. Pax does not advocate rebellion or revolution. To her, these bring poverty, want, and need. Call on Pax to work within the current system to bring prosperity to all, fertilize your fields, and feed your children. Pax will help with these things. But do not call on her for your own personal ideals of peace and right, for this concept is alien to her. As a goddess of the State, she works on a universal, holistic level, for the good of all. She will bring about peace, but only through the already entrenched channels of society, culture, and government.

Pathway to Pax

There are two ways you can allow the peaceful nature of Pax to guide your life. The first pathway to Pax is through your local and national government. As a State goddess, Pax works very well within labyrinthine legislative corridors. In fact, she is a great advocate in any established hierarchal system. Feel overlooked at work? Call on Pax to shed light on your accomplishments. Want to be accepted into a members-only club? Ask for Pax to pave your way into the enclave. Want to spread abundance and prosperity to the world? Request Pax's help in negotiating the inner depths of your government. Pax understands the needs of the individual while accessing the solutions through well-established systems. She doesn't work fast, but with steadfast perseverance, Pax aids you in achieving your dreams and goals . . . just as long as they coincide with the preserved culture.

The second pathway to inviting Pax in your life is by asking for her help in self-understanding and self-acceptance. Many times, our personal angst comes from comparing our present situation to a conceptualized ideal that exists solely in our minds. The popular axiom "The grass is always greener on the other side" illustrates this mentality. Sometimes we are unhappy where we are because we believe someplace (or someone) else is better. Pax can assist us in gaining a sense of accomplishment and peace for ourselves, exactly where we are right now in our spiritual, emotional, and material development. We can be pleased with what we have accomplished, gladdened by our surroundings and the people we see every day.

In order to access this second aspect of Pax, make a list every day of ten things for which you are grateful. Perhaps you are grateful for the sun or the rain or the little blue pencil on your desk. Perhaps your daughter's smile or your significant other's kiss warms your heart. You may praise the clover in the field or the little bunny who eats the clover or, maybe, even that clover-loving, lettuce-eating bunny Peter Rabbit, who reminds you of your childhood. (I'm a fan of the Flopsy Bunnies, myself.) It doesn't matter what ten things you write down, as long as you are truly thankful for them. Save all of your Ten Things lists in a three-ring binder. After ten days, go back and re-read your lists. After thirty days, read them again. Continue making lists and re-reading them until you feel a shift in your perception, until you truly begin to recognize the bounty that is your life. Pretty soon you'll begin to realize that the grass is really quite green right where you are. Use this foundation in reality as a springboard to attain other goals and dreams, bringing them back to fertilize your already plush lawn.

OUR LADY OF FÁTIMA
Peaceful Mother of Christianity

MANTRA
Blessed Lady of Fátima,
Immaculate Heart of Peace,
Hear my Prayers.

Figure. 1: Sacred Heart of Mary

In 1917, on the thirteenth day of May, three small shepherd children experienced a visitation of the Feminine Divine. Being raised by simple families in Fátima, in the Catholic country of Portugal, the children identified the vision as the Virgin Mary. Bringing with her a cry for peace, the threat of hell and eternal damnation, and a plan for achieving lasting spirituality in the world, Mary irrevocably changed the lives of those three children, forever altering our perception of the power and might of the Christian Mother Goddess.

Lucia Santos and her cousins Francisco and Jacinta Marto were first chosen by the Divine in the spring of 1916, when an angel came to them while they were watching their sheep in a place known as Cabeco. The angel identified himself as the Angel of Peace and instructed them to pray, even giving the children a small prayer. Unlike many of the traditional Catholic prayers (which are long and often complicated), the prayer from the Angel of Peace is short and repetitive. Known alternately as the Prayer of Pardon and The Angel's Prayer of Reparation,[5] its simplicity must be attributed to the youth of the three children, ages nine (Lucia), eight (Francisco), and six (Jacinta). Reminiscent of a mantra in tone, length, theme, and style, the prayer is as follows: "My God, I believe, I adore, I hope, and I love you. I beg pardon for those who do not believe, do not adore, do not hope, and do not love you." The Angel of Peace visited the children two more times, once in the summer and again in the early fall, always exhorting them to pray.

Thus, when the Virgin Mary appeared in the spring of 1917 in the Cova da Iria fields outside the small village of Aljustrel, the children were prepared for her Divine message. Mary appeared standing on a small holm-oak tree,[6] dressed in a white gown with a gold border. She clasped her hands before her in prayer, holding a rosary. Mary identified herself as Our Lady of the Rosary and instructed the children to return to the Cova da Iria fields at midday on the thirteenth day of the month for the next six months. She asked if they wanted to accept any and all difficulties in order to convert non-Christians and bring peace to the world. The children, confronted by this visionary lady "brighter than the sun, shedding rays of light clearer and stronger than a crystal glass filled with

---

5. Catholic Youth Networking, "The Fátima Prayer."
6. The holm-oak is also known as the Holly Oak tree and the Evergreen Oak tree and is native to the Mediterranean.

the most sparkling water and pierced by the burning rays of the sun,"[7] agreed to be modern day prophets for the Virgin Mary.

Mary appeared as promised in June and July. She told Jacinta and Francisco that they would be joining her in heaven very soon but that Lucia would remain on Earth, doing God's will and consoling herself with the Immaculate Heart of Mary.[8] Throughout the summer, the children prayed the rosary daily, refused to drink water during the hot summer days, and tied rough pieces of rope around their waists as penance. They subjected themselves to these physical difficulties in the hope of bridging the gap between the spiritual and the physical. The children did not fear for their own lives after death. They agreed to do this penance for others in the world, in order to bring all people salvation and lasting peace. Lucia, throughout the years, stated time and time again that they prayed for peace and that the rosary was the key to peace within the self and around the world.

In August, as the children's story grew and circulated around Portugal, local politicians came to believe that the religious fervor surrounding the children would have politically disruptive consequences, causing rebellion and revolt against a secular state. On August 13, the children were not allowed to view the apparition at the Cova da Iria, and were instead detained in jail by the mayor of Ourem, Artur Santos (no relation). Artur Santos was so suspicious of the three shepherds that he threatened to boil them in oil if they did not reveal the secrets given to them by the Lady. The children held firm and did not share any information with him, despite his threats. After a day, Artur Santos allowed the children to go free and they received their visit from the Virgin Mary on August 19 in Valinhos. Once again, Mary's presence descended into a tree, where her heavenly perfume lingered on its branches.

By September, the children's fame had grown to large proportions. Priests and officials of the Catholic Church came to visit the shepherd children in order to ascertain all the details of their wondrous visitations with Mary. Devoted people came to see the children and gather bits of their clothing, even locks of their hair, to take home with them, in the tradition of religious relics. The children's homes were inundated with sick

---

7. Lucia Santos, as quoted in John O'Connell, "Our Lady of Fátima."
8. Ruffinelly, "The Little Shepherds of Fátima," 7.

and dying people who wished to be blessed by the shepherds who had been chosen by Mary.[9]

So, it was of little surprise that the October 13 visitation was attended by 70,000 people, including representatives from three major newspapers, officials from the Catholic Church, and the three shepherd children. From the very beginning, Mary had told the children that a great miracle would occur on the thirteenth of October and people, having observed the small miracles and religious conviction of the children, were eager to see the living spirit for their own eyes. It was a rainy, overcast day as people trudged out to the isolated fields of the Cova da Iria. Doffing their caps, despite the rain, the people looked to the sky for a miracle to occur. And they were not disappointed. The sun radiated colors other than yellow, moved forward and backward, and created zig-zag patterns in the sky. According to eyewitness reports, the unusual solar activity was visible from up to forty kilometers away. This phenomenon is now known as "The Miracle of the Sun."[10]

Both Francisco and Jacinta died within three years of the appearance of the Virgin Mary in their lives, falling victim to the 1919 Spanish flu pandemic. However, Lucia lived, serving as a nun in the Catholic Church, until the age of ninety-seven, dying in a convent in Coimbra, Portugal, in 2005. Throughout her life, Lucia wrote and discussed the visitations, outlining several secrets given to her by Our Lady of the Rosary. The first secret was a vision of hell, complete with fire, smoke, screams, and writhing bodies. (Lucia writes that if she had not already been assured a place in heaven, she would have died of fright.) This extremely disturbing image is followed by an admonishment to consecrate Russia to the Immaculate Heart of Mary and to perform the First Saturdays, a practice executed on the first Saturday of five consecutive months in which devoted Catholics go to confession, attend mass, say the rosary, and then spend fifteen minutes after mass contemplating the fifteen mysteries of the rosary. Only this, the Virgin Mary assured Lucia, would bring peace to the world. The third secret is another disturbing vision. In this image, the Holy Father (the Pope) and various religious leaders walk through a war-torn city, praying for the souls of the dead. When they get to the top of a hill, with a rough-hewn cross on top of it, they too are shot and killed. Two angels

---

9. Ibid., 9–11.
10. De Marchi, *The Immaculate Heart*, 139–150.

gather the blood of the religious men and women and sprinkle the souls of the newly dead.[11]

The images described by Lucia are often at odds with traditional views of Mary as the virginal, pure woman. As Our Lady of the Rosary, Mary brings disturbing, bloody images to three children of a very impressionable age. We, in modern society, work very hard to shelter our children from such visions and here the Mother of All is purposely exposing them to painful images! This dichotomy in Mary highlights the close relationship between peace and war, chaos and stability. With just a thought or shove or idea, humans can move into the stance of a warrior or the pose of a friend. It just takes one moment, one thought, one action. Mary knows that we, as humans, are always balancing on the precipice of war and death. Sometimes, taking a few minutes to reflect on life will change the outcome of a situation. From death to life, from war to peace. Therefore, Our Lady of the Rosary builds into her charge for us the time necessary to avoid conflict. She asks us to pray the rosary, a fifteen- to twenty-minute meditation that can relax the mind and bring clarity. She requests us to spend extra time on the first Saturday of the month in an isolated and lonely church to connect with her and, as Sister Lucia writes, to "keep me [Mary] company." Mary walks the battlefields as well as the pious church pews. She is with us every time we pray, taking time out of our busy day to access the peace within, in order to create peace without.

Pathway to Our Lady of Fátima

Having grown up in a pious Portuguese family, I was regaled with stories of Our Lady of Fátima at a very early age. She was a vision of Mary that seemed to be very accessible to my family and, thus, to me. It is this openness that differentiates Our Lady of Fátima from other visitations of Mary on the earthly realm. Our Lady of the Rosary appeared to three simple peasant children, rather than well-versed religious leaders. In order to achieve lasting peace, Mary exhorted them to pray, an action that requires neither money nor education but simply time and an open heart. Through her visions, she demonstrated her knowledge of the human race and her belief in our ability to achieve peace despite our violent natures. Our Lady of Fátima loves us, even with all our faults and foibles.

---

11. Santos, "The Message of Fátima," special insert.

Following my grandmother Laura Barboza Santos' example, I suggest putting a little Our Lady of Fátima statue in your car. My grandmother used to have to tape her car statue to her old Buick's dashboard, but now the statues come with magnets attached and are available for less than five dollars. If you can't afford a statue, print out a picture from the Internet or go to The Fátima Network web site[12] and request a free picture card of Our Lady of Fátima, then install that in your car. (Just be sure to keep your line of vision clutter-free!) Once you've got your representation of Our Lady of Fátima, memorize her mantra or make up one of your own and say it before and after you drive. In our modern world, we often spend more waking time in our cars than in our homes! Bring prayer and intention into the modern era by taking a minute or two out of your day to honor the Divine Mother in the guise of Our Lady of Fátima and her message of peace.

BRANWEN
Welsh Goddess of Compassionate Peace

MANTRA

Heart of Branwen, Heart of Peace
(The mantra continues as long as you wish, substituting synonyms for *peace*,
such as *tranquility, calm, comfort, harmony, serenity, reconciliation, quiet, concord*, etc.)

Branwen is, perhaps, the goddess who best represents our modern interpretation of peace. Having experienced war and loss first hand, she has an immense dislike for the use of battle in negotiations and politics. Branwen does not choose sides in war-torn situations. Instead, she feels the grief and mourns the devastation brought about by war. Wide-open of heart and caring for all (humanity, animal life, and the very Earth itself), Branwen wishes to stress the connectedness of our earthly family and the needless, restricted viewpoint necessary to wage war. If Branwen were here before us today, she would implore, "Can't we all just get along?"

---

12. The Fátima Network, https://secure.Fátima.org/forms/freegifts.asp. Along with the free picture card, the Fátima Network offers small vials of Fátima water free to the public.

As told in the Welsh mythological cycle, *The Mabinogion*, Branwen—daughter of Llyr and Penarddun, sister of Bendigeidfran (a.k.a. Bran) and Manawydan, half-sister of Nisien and Efnisien—is courted by the king of Ireland, Matholwch. Already Branwen's role as a lover of peace reveals itself, as the marriage is intended to unite the island of Ireland with the Island of the Mighty (Wales/England), bringing an end to discord and war. The match is arranged and a large feast is laid out with much food and drink. After a night of festivities, Branwen and Matholwch sleep together and the marriage is consummated and considered binding. Throughout the marriage negotiations, we hear nothing from Branwen. Apparently, she is content to serve as a vessel of peace for her people.

The next day, Branwen's half-brother Efnisien stumbles across the horses of Matholwch and questions the handler about them. When he hears that his sister was given to the king of Ireland without his knowledge or consent, Efnisien flies into a rage (a not uncommon state for this tempestuous man) and mutilates all of Matholwch's horses by cutting off their eyelids, ears, tails, and lips. Matholwch, understandably, is incensed at this slight against his manhood and immediately calls off all nuptial relations with Branwen (after conveniently already having had sex with her). Still Branwen says nothing.

Bran scrambles to make amends with Matholwch, to preserve the peace treaty and restore his sister's honor. (Branwen's honor is not necessarily connected to her lack of virginity. Matholwch tarnished her reputation by turning away from her. After having been joined in good faith, Matholwch rejects Branwen, thus casting doubt and suspicion on her good name.) Bran offers Matholwch a gold plate the size of his head and a silver staff as tall as himself. However, it is the magical cauldron of rebirth, in which dead warriors return alive albeit without voices, that turns Matholwch's heart. He agrees to reinstate his marriage with Branwen and sails back to Ireland with substantial booty, including Branwen.

Once in Ireland, Branwen is met with much rejoicing; she is treated well and births Matholwch's son Gwern. However, by the second year, discord erupts and old enmities between the Irish and Celtic Cymry people are remembered. The Irish people become uneasy with their "foreign" queen, remembering the insult dealt to Matholwch by Efnisien. (It is interesting to note that they do not remember Branwen's sacrifice in leaving her family and coming to live among strangers.) Branwen is banished to Matholwch's kitchen, where she has her ears boxed by the butcher once a day.

Branwen withstands such mistreatment for three years, never knowing love in any form from a human being. (Her son is fostered out to a wealthy Irish family.) However, she begins to open her heart to the natural world around her. During this time, she nurtures a starling, teaching it words, telling it of her homeland and her brother, and training it to carry a message from her to Bran. With Branwen's tutelage, the starling delivers the message and Bran immediately puts together a military force of huge proportions; only seven men are left behind to protect the Island of the Mighty.

The ships set sail with Bran wading alongside, as there was never a ship (nor a house) that could hold him. Matholwch, seeing what appears to be a forest upon the sea and a moving mountain, is confused by the apparition. He says to his messengers, "There is no one here will know anything of that, except Branwen knows. Do you ask her."[13] Here is the first time that we observe the power of Branwen, Queen of the Land, Lady of Peace. Until this time, she has been mute, appearing to accept the control of her male relations.

The messengers question Branwen at length about the vision upon the water. She answers their questions promptly and succinctly, explaining that the forest on the sea is the navy of masted-ships that Bran has amassed and that the moving mountain is her brother, angry at the injustice done her. The messengers return to Matholwch with the knowledge that war is imminent. The reasoning for Branwen's truthful answers is perplexing. Why wouldn't she give her brother the element of surprise and lie about the strange images Matholwch has seen on the sea? After all, wouldn't she want her brother to win? Of course, but Branwen is no longer simply Queen of the Britons. Her sense of self has shifted, becoming something greater than Britain or Ireland. She is all of the land, and as such, sees the beauty and sorrow of all living beings. The outcome of such a war is devastating to her either way, as living beings are sure to die. Also, having transcended her mortal prejudices and judgements, Branwen, as a goddess, cannot lie. Falsehoods are as foreign to her as to an infant. She has become pure, innocent, untainted love.

The men spar. Matholwch sets a trap for Bran and his men by building a house that can hold Bran and hiding warriors inside. Efnisien senses the trap and expertly sniffs out the hiding places and kills all the warriors with his thumb and forefinger. Thwarted, Matholwch is forced to agree to a political truce that allows Gwern, son of Branwen and Matholwch, to rule Ireland, compelling Matholwch to step down as king. At the feast to

---

13. Jones and Jones, *The Mabinogion*, 28.

seal and honor the truce, Efnisien asks Gwern to come and visit with him. For some reason, although probably out of jealousy and all-consuming love for Branwen (remember, his anger that Branwen was given to another man without his consent started this whole fiasco), Efnisien kills Gwern. As soon as Gwern comes close, Efnisien, his half-uncle, throws him into the fire, thus starting a destructive battle. (Branwen tries to grab her son out of the flames but is ushered out of the house by her brother Bran as the bloody battle commences. In her position of Goddess of the Land, she can empathize with humanity but has no control over it.) In the end, only seven of Bran's men survive. Bran also lives but is gravely wounded by a poisoned spear to his foot. He requests that his men cut off his head and carry it to the Island of the Mighty. He assures them that "the head will be as pleasant company to you as ever it was at best when it was on me."[14] Of the Irish, the only people left alive on the whole island are five pregnant women hidden in a cave in the wilderness.

Branwen, the seven men, and Bran's head sail for the Island of the Mighty, landing at Aber Alaw in Talebolion in northern Wales. Upon landing, they rest and Branwen is confronted with the desolation of both islands and the enormity of her role in creating such a situation. She looks first to Ireland and then to the Island of the Mighty and says, "Woe is me that ever I was born: two good islands have been laid waste because of me."[15] She then heaves a great sigh, which breaks her heart, and she dies. The men bury her on the bank of the Alaw in a four-sided grave.[16]

Branwen is an instrument of war as well as of peace. Bran and Matholwch circle around her like hungry dogs, fighting over a bone. They do not think of the repercussions of their actions but simply react with flying swords and bloody daggers and war and death. Branwen's message of peace comes attached to the ideal of universal love, a concept both embraced and reviled by humans on this planet. She would prefer that we all sacrifice our blatant desires in order to see the reality of everyone's situation, for every person has a position to maintain, a unique point of view. With Branwen's help, we can see beyond our provincial views to the universality of human existence on Earth.

---

14. Ibid., 31.
15. Ibid., 32.
16. Much of the story of Branwen first appeared in *Goddess Alive!*, 180–183. For more information and intimate workings with Branwen, Lady of Sovereignty, including a guided meditation and ritual, please see chapter 10 of *Goddess Alive!*

We can understand the enormity of war as a destructive force that not only affects those in the war zone but everyone in our human family. Branwen wants us to see through the eyes of others and feel compassion for their lives, their viewpoints, their cultural stances. We are all human in Branwen's eyes, and all beautiful and worthy of compassion and care. Through Branwen, we can let go of our differences and focus on the similarities of human existence. Perhaps then we can forego the battlefields for meaningful, productive discussion.

Pathway to Branwen

As Branwen is about accessing the peaceful center within and sacrificing personal needs for the good of all, she is intimately connected to clearing away old energies and thought patterns. After all, one cannot strive for peace among people while being mired in old, possibly negative ideas. We have all felt the resistance of leaving familiar patterns for new concepts and activities. We must be willing to catapult over the past in order to access the hopefully peaceful future. One of the best ways to remove past influences is by cleansing and purifying the present. After all, every action we take sends ripples forward, creating either peace or chaos in the world.

Many of us are familiar with cleansing and purifying ceremonies that occur directly before ritual. We smudge ourselves with sage, sprinkle the ground with holy water, and anoint our ritual objects with oil. But I want you to consider cleansing and purifying as a life path, as essential to the existence of life on our planet. Consider your daily actions carefully, reconstructing them with the object of purification in mind. Pay attention to the number of times you wash your hands every day. Notice the gentle swish-swish of the washing machine or the rumble of the dishwasher. Feel the water gurgle over your skin as you remove leftover bits of food from your dinner plate. Imagine the unproductive dirt and debris sluicing from your body as you take your regular shower. With a subtle change in mindset, such mundane activities become infused with cleansing power. Visit a rushing stream and watch the stream bed shift and flow. Here is the essence of peace among all peoples, the ability to look beyond our small lives to the fluid universe around us. Don't be afraid! Go forward on your path, cleansed and reveling in the amazing gift of life!

RITUAL FOR PEACE:

THE SACRED PRAYER OF PEACE

Suggested Ritual Days

January 24: World Peace Day, as declared by Lions Clubs International

June 21: World Peace and Prayer Day, as declared by the Wolakota Foundation

September 21: International Day of Peace, as declared by the United Nations

Items needed

one square of light-weight cotton material, any solid color

fabric paint

paintbrushes

free Fátima water (see page 25)

several yards of strong ribbon or rope

thread of the same color as the cotton material

sewing machine or needle

sharp scissors

common pins

birdseed

In Tibet, prayer flags are an important aspect of spiritual life. Flags are hoisted to bring prosperity, to heal the sick, and to bring harmony to a place. Wedding parties troop up to rooftops to raise flags and brides touch them to signify entering into her husband's family and departing from her biological family. Scarves or small flags, called *kata* in Tibet and *hadag* in Mongolia, are given to honored guests or friends to show great respect. They are made of sky-blue silk and express the message, "I wish good fortune to you from the bottom of my heart." Prayer flags connect you to the land while spreading your sentiments and wishes through the winds, which represent the primal psychic energy of life.[17] What better way to bring peace into the world than by creating and hoisting your own sacred peace prayer flag?

Once you have gathered all the items, cut and measure the material to the length and width you wish. If you want it to be exactly even on all four sides, be sure to add an extra 1.5 inches to one end—this end will form your casing, through which you will

---

17. Wood, "Wind Power," 28–31.

slide your ribbon or rope. Pin the material down to form the casing and sew along the bottom edge, making a tunnel at the top of your flag. If you want, you can sew miniscule rolled hems along the other three sides of the flag. (This creates a more uniform look and prevents fraying but is not necessary.)

Next, decorate your flag using the fabric paint and paintbrushes. Draw traditional symbols of peace, such as a dove or an olive branch; connect to Pax by creating a cornucopia or a scepter; or simply splash peaceful colors on your flag or words that represent peace to you. You can even try stenciling if you have some extra cash. No matter what icons and colors you put on your flag, always keep your initial intention of inner and outer peace in mind. Turn off the phones, listen to some peaceful music, find a quiet time when you'll be alone, and construct a peaceful prayer flag.

The raising of your prayer flag can be loud and raucous and can occur directly after your flag is created (once the paint has dried) or on another day. Locate an area to string up your peace flag. This could be between two trees, over a doorway, or someplace else that is unique to your residence or land. Bless yourself, any other participants, and your flag with the Fátima water and state your request for peace in the world and within yourself. Have all the participants hold onto the flag and shake it, imitating wind and activating the energy around you, within you, and within the flag. Raise the flag while chanting one of the mantras in this chapter or one that you have created just for the occasion. You can include the other participants in the chant by having them repeat after you. You: *Pax ad lux.* Them: *Pax ad lux.* You: *Pax et bonum.* Them: *Pax et bonum.* You get the idea. Once the flag has been raised, offer more Fátima water to the flag by pouring it onto the ground nearby or (if indoors) into a small bowl. Leave an offering of birdseed to honor the spirits of your land and the animals and birds who dwell with you in that space. (If your flag is indoors, scatter the seeds outside.) Give one last joyous shout of HUZZAH FOR PEACE! Then eat, drink, and be merry!

Throughout the year, as you think of it, give more offerings to your peace prayer flag. These can be as simple as a handful of cornmeal or as elaborate as an intricate wood carving. On the anniversary of your Ritual for Peace, consider making another peace prayer flag and adding it to your original flag. You can even make a party out of it and have your friends over to craft their peace prayer flags. What better way to promote peace in the world than with a few laughs among family and friends?

Chapter Three

Goddess Mantras for the Environment

THE ENVIRONMENT: HOPE SURVIVES

What can one say about the environment? Environment, good; toxic waste, bad. Clean water, good; air pollution, bad. Recycling, good; greenhouse gases, bad (although not always). There is a current trend in our society to see environmental issues in black or white, but I'm not sure they can be so easily defined. Greenhouse gases provide an atmosphere for our planet that keeps in the heat of the sun. Like a greenhouse (hence the term), the gases let in the light and heat of the sun and trap some of that energy, allowing our planet to be a horticultural hothouse for plants and animals alike. Without greenhouse gases, we'd be living on a ball of rock. And we'd be cold, besides.

This is not to say that spewing massive amounts of CO_2 into the air is a good thing. Obviously, as we have seen in current years, it is not. Ask our polar bear brethren if they're psyched that their snow-bound climate is shrinking, giving way to the next Club Med, and I'm sure they'd give you an emphatic "No." (If they could speak human, that is.) The inhabitants of the Polynesian island Tuvalu, on the other side of the globe, would undoubtedly concur with their neighbors from the north. Their island is experiencing severe flooding, thanks to global warming. If the warming trend continues, their island nation will sink into the sea, becoming a modern-day Atlantis.[1]

So what does this mean for us, in our comfy, cushy Western homes, replete with digital thing-a-ma-bobs and automatic this-and-thats? Well, as with everything that happens on a gigantic scale, it's difficult to say. The Earth has experienced climate change before. Recall the infamous Ice Ages I and II. (No, not the movies!) Comets crashed into our planet, changing the weather drastically and ending the reign of the dinosaurs. The Northern Hemisphere was covered in snow and ice for hundreds of years at a time. And

---

1. Patel, "A Sinking Feeling," 734–736.

yet, despite these truths, mankind survived. Eking out a difficult, hard-scrabble existence, humanity did not succumb (like the dinosaurs) to the variable elements. Instead, we endured, eventually building this mammoth, global society that sprawls before us today. Here we are, reaping the rewards of the trials and sacrifices of our prehistoric ancestors, perhaps leading our planet back to that very snow-covered, destitute existence.

As a lover of mythology, I cannot help but wonder if we have done this all before. Could we have created civilizations thousands or millions of years ago only to destroy them with our own self-important power and knowledge? The names hang tantalizingly close, on the very tip of the tongue. Atlantis. Shangri-La. Llhasa. Lemuria. Avalon. The Mayan Calendar claims that December 21, 2012, marks the end of the Mayan Great Cycle of the Long Count. Some modern spiritual followers believe this date marks the coming of the apocalypse, the end of the world as we know it. And some of them link the doomsday prophesy to our environment, especially global warming. Could the Mayans have tapped into an Earth-deep cyclic wisdom related to human life on the planet? My intellect dismisses the idea as ludicrous, but my child-like mind wonders at the possibilities.

Whenever I think about humanity's impact on planet Earth, the movie *Lost in Space* pops into my mind. Unlike the kitschy 1960s television show, the movie (released in 1998) takes itself seriously, and it takes the end of life on Earth even more seriously. In fact, it is serious enough to be the main reason for the Robinsons to go gallivanting about in space. (That's pretty darn serious, folks.) The beginning of the movie, the prologue, if you will, explains that the nations on Earth have banded together to save the human race by jointly creating a "hypergate" that will allow spaceships to pass instantaneously to the only other inhabitable planet that has been found, Alpha Prime. Within fifteen to twenty years, humanity will be able to pass through the hypergate to colonize Alpha Prime, leaving behind a devastated Earth. To highlight the importance of the mission, Professor Robinson (played by William Hurt) and Major West (a young, hunky Matt LeBlanc) have the following conversation.

West: Every school child knows that our recycling technologies will cure the environment. Sending a family across the galaxy is a publicity stunt to sell computers to people of all ages.

Robinson: Every school child has been lied to. Recycling technologies came too late. All fossil fuels are virtually exhausted. The ozone layer is down to forty percent. In two decades, the Earth will be unable to support human life.

A daunting statement and one designed to get people's attention. Remember, *Lost in Space* was created about a decade before green living and environmental policies came to the forefront of public life. Before Al Gore and his movie *An Inconvenient Truth,* the only people thinking about saving the Earth were the Greenpeace activists in their boats and the hippies in their communal houses. Now soccer moms and Wall Street tycoons are looking at their actions and weighing them against the needs of the environment, against the healing of our planet Earth.

But is it too little, too late? Like the Robinsons, do we find ourselves accessing our collective environmental wisdom too late to save our planet? Only time will tell. But of one thing I can assure you: the human race is not one to lie down and die quietly. We will fight to continue our existence. Through frigid, snow-bound climates or starry-eyed space adventures, we will strive to live and learn from our past mistakes. For now, we can all pitch in by making small, everyday changes around the house—recycling plastics, metals, and glass; switching to energy-efficient fluorescent light bulbs; turning off the lights when not necessary; and conserving water. We can commute to work with others and refuse to dump toxic substances into the land.

If, as the Mayan adherents claim, our actions cannot stave off the end of the world and the environmental destruction of planet Earth, we will adapt. We have in the past; we will in the future. The message of humanity's interaction with Earth is not one of despair but one of hope. We will find a way to continue, through the difficulties brought on by ourselves and survive. Will we be forgotten in the mists of time, relegated to legendary status like Atlantis, Avalon, or Shangri-La? Perhaps. But our stories will survive and our ancestors will endure, learning from our past actions, living their own truths.

ENERGY RETURN

Sometimes, when we look at the big picture, we lose the importance of the details. We ignore the subtle brush strokes of salmon pink and lilac purple that contribute to the creation of a wonderful, beauteous whole. Beauty is minute, stored in the smallest of spaces, shining from the littlest crevices of light. So, when choosing to work, magically and mundanely, to better the environment, it is very easy to lose oneself in the giant causes and issues and concerns of the day, forgetting that sometimes the tiniest action makes the biggest difference.

And so I encourage you, as you venture forth to save the planet, to strive to live your environmental truth every day. Don't just jump on the nearest bandwagon on Earth Day and Arbor Day and Save the Ocean Day. Rather, perform small Earth-healing miracles every day. For every day that we live on planet Earth is Earth day. The universe, the Goddess, even the Earth Mama herself will view your small everyday actions through a filter of honesty and respect. These tasks, done with love over time, will add so much more to the universal environmental consciousness, because you are owning them as a lifestyle. They are not a fancy title that you strap on for special occasions and parades; rather, your actions enlighten your beliefs and buttress your words. Believe in the power of the one. Believe in the strength of the small. And you will change the world!

ASASE YAA
Akan Mother Earth Goddess

MANTRA

Asase ye dur.
Tumi nyinaa ne asase.
(Land is mighty.
All power emanates from the land.)

Figure 2: Akan symbol: Asase Ye Dur

Asase Yaa is the Earth Mother Goddess of the Akan people of Ghana, a country on the western coast of Africa. Asase Yaa is one half of a dual-deity belief system, along with her husband Nyame. Akan religious philosophy puts the God and Goddess far above earthly concerns, preferring to utilize intermediaries, such as ancestors or spirits, to access the Divine. This is not to say that Nyame and Asase Yaa are not available; they're just slightly untouchable. Nowadays, Ghana is relatively monotheistic, with Christianity and Islam being its two main religions. Nyame has morphed with the monotheistic Supreme Deity to become God of the Bible or Allah of the Koran. Asase Yaa has remained separate from monotheism and does not play an important role in the structured religious life of the people.

She is not forgotten, however. Asase Yaa, despite being outside of accepted monotheistic religious practice, still holds an important place in the hearts of the people. As recently as November 2007, a feature article for the Ghanaian Homepage (an all-Ghanaian news source on the web) thanked Asase Yaa for saving President Kufuor from a near-death incident.[2] A goddess was mentioned in thanksgiving for saving a national figure?! Amazing! But such is the case in Ghana, where organized monotheistic religions coincide with ancient folk beliefs and customs. When European missionaries colonized Africa, in the early to mid-1900s, they preached that all traditional spiritual practices, ceremonies, thoughts, beliefs, and activities were no longer necessary due to the power of God. The Ghanaians, especially the Akan, the largest ethnic group in the nation,[3] held a belief system that included a supreme masculine deity already, so the ideas of the missionaries were neither foreign nor difficult to accept. Nyame became God. However, the missionaries were not able to wipe out cultural spiritual ceremonies and rites of passage. Naming ceremonies for babies, rites of puberty (mainly for girls), traditional marriage and funeral rites "are done before their Western counterparts."[4] Asase Yaa falls into this traditional spiritual category and is still honored throughout the country.

Asase Yaa has two human-form children, both boys, and their names are Bea (or Bia) and Tano. Tano is thought to be one of the most important gods of Ashanti (a subgroup of the Akan) traditional spirituality. He is a powerful river god who sired all the small local gods of the people, especially the river gods. These "lesser," Earth-bound

---

2. Obenewaa, "The President's Accident."
3. Larbi, "The Nature of Continuity and Discontinuity . . ."
4. Yiadom, "We Believe That the Earth is God's Gift to Us."

gods serve as intermediaries between humans and Nyame, giving humans access to the Divine. Asase Yaa's other son Bea probably has something to do with the land, as his name is the Akan word for place or location. He is considered the oldest son of Nyame and Asase Yaa. Having given birth to two healthy boys, the fertile Earth Mother Asase Yaa was not yet finished. Her last child with Nyame is well-known around the world and has numerous names: Anancy, Anancyi, Aunt Nancy, Ananansa, Ananse, Hanansi, Kompa Nanzi, Nansi, B'anansi, Kweku Anansi, and Anansi the Spider.

Anansi the Spider is not a god; rather, he is considered a folk-hero, serving an important role in legends and parables all over the world. His stories spread to the Caribbean and eventually to the American South when many Africans were kidnapped during the slave trade of the 1700s and 1800s. Anansi is a trickster character who uses his wits and cunning to trick more powerful beings so he can benefit from their stupidity. His most well-known role in folktales is as the keeper of stories. When Anansi requested the knowledge of all stories from his father Nyame, he was given three tasks to complete. If he accomplished all three tasks, then he would be granted the honor of the knowledge of all stories. But the assignments given him were not easy, especially for a little spider. In the African version of the story, Anansi must capture a jaguar, a hive of angry hornets, and a fairy who cannot be seen. The Jamaican version of the story has Anansi seizing the hornets as well, but substitutes in a leopard and a python.[5]

In the American South, Anansi's struggle with the fairy who cannot be seen morphs into the tar-baby episode of Brer Rabbit fame from the Uncle Remus stories, which were derived from African-American folktales. In the African story, Anansi tricks the fairy through the creation of a baby made out of tar. When the unseen fairy investigates this strange-looking phenomenon, he gets stuck to the tar-baby and cannot get free, thus winning Anansi the knowledge of stories. In the African-American version, the tar-baby traps Brer Rabbit, the small yet cunning animal who serves as Anansi's American counterpart. True to form, however, Brer Rabbit talks his way free of the clinging tar-baby and saves himself from becoming Brer Fox's supper.[6]

As a goddess of fertility, it makes sense that the stories of Asase Yaa's children should circle the globe. After all, she is the land that nourishes each and every one of us. In Ghana, farmers often honor the goddess of the land by halting work on her special day,

---

5. Krensky, *Anansi and the Box of Stories*, 7–8.
6. Hamilton, *Bruh Rabbit and the Tar Baby Girl*, 15–28.

Thursday. When they are tilling the land, they will request special permission before cutting into Asase Yaa's soft, pliable surface. Consent is asked, once again, before digging to bury the dead at a funeral.[7] Rites are performed before trees are cut down as the "cutting of trees depletes the source of life."[8] Asase Yaa, along with Nyame and the ancestors, is called upon before any traditional spiritual ceremony or function. A libation is poured on the ground, asking for the blessings of the God and Goddess, and any spirits present. During libation, Asase Yaa is invoked as a spirit mother who can influence the lives of those gathered before her. Sometimes, these offerings are made to ritual stools made of wood, which were housed in "stool rooms." In these instances, the traditional offering was human blood, gunpowder, alcoholic drink, or spiderwebs. Today, human blood is no longer used as a sacrificial offering.[9]

Along with her all-encompassing fertile Earth Mother aspect, Asase Yaa is known as the upholder of truth. "Whenever someone's word is in doubt, he is asked to touch his lip to some soil to become credible."[10] Asase Yaa has a supreme interest in proper conduct as well, and helps to maintain traditional morals, ethics, and social behavior. As such, she is especially important for young Akan girls, who have strict rules to which they must adhere in order to stay within the moral structure of society. "In the Akan culture, women represent the beauty, purity and dignity of the society and are guarded against corruption by our traditional laws and regulations."[11] No woman is allowed to get married without first going through the traditional puberty rites, and every woman must remain a virgin prior to participation. These rules are meant to ensure that mothers have the sought-after cultural morality and will pass these values on to their children. It is important to note that many of the sub-groups within the Akan culture (the Ashanti, Fanti, Akim, and Akwamu) are matrilineal in construct. This means that children inherit through the female line.[12] Women hold strong places of power within cultural groups and are often known as "Queens" when they display wise power and knowledge in guiding their people. When viewed with this in mind, the puberty rite becomes less of a male-dominated system of

---

7. Yiadom, "We Believe That the Earth . . ."
8. Apeadu, "The African Indigenous Religion."
9. World Culture Encyclopedia, "Akan Religion."
10. Yiadom, "We Believe That the Earth . . ."
11. Osei-Adu, "Puberty Rites."
12. Afrodesign Studios, "West Africa."

control and more of a self-regulating mechanism. After all, when one holds power, one must exercise responsibility.

Asase Yaa is a part of everyday life for many Ghanaians who still practice traditional spiritual activities alongside monotheistic religious beliefs. She is the land upon which we walk every day, giving us food and nourishment, fertility and life. The land is life's sustainer, not only for the Akan but for all of us. Just as Anansi's stories have spread across the globe, so too does Asase Yaa touch each and every one of us. Queen Boakyewa Yiadom I, Queen of Adamorobe, Aburi-Akuapem (Ghana), wrote that "the distinctive feature [of African religion] is the sharing spirit."[13] And, in my mind, Asase Yaa exemplifies this idea. She is all around us, providing, giving, and returning our gifts back to us. The energy we pour forth into her returns to us again and again. As a traditional maxim from Ghana states: "The land is mighty. All power emanates from the land." Asase Yaa is mighty and will guide and aid us, if only we acknowledge her presence, recognize the plight of her people, and accept the reciprocity of our actions.

Pathway to Asase Yaa

The Akan may use ornate rituals to honor Asase Yaa, but don't worry; I'm not about to suggest you undertake a traditional Akan puberty ritual, complete with dancing and vows of chastity! After all, despite our global world view, cultural mores and ceremonies are distinct, having been created over thousands of years for specific societies. They should not be undertaken lightly and with little understanding of the history behind their meanings and implications.

Having stated that belief, however, I do think it would be appropriate to offer a libation to Asase Yaa on a piece of land that is near and dear to your heart. If you have a garden, consider following the example of Ghanaian farmers by asking for permission and giving an offering before tilling the Earth. If you don't garden, follow your heart and choose a place that means something to you. Perhaps it is a ritual space or the roots of a flowering lilac bush. Maybe you honor the sturdy trunk of a tree or the wood chips that protect your little one's feet at the playground. The exact place is incidental as all places on Earth resonate with the spirit of Asase Yaa.

Once you've picked your place, fill up a cup of water and pour it on the ground while offering up one of these traditional Akan prayers, or one that you craft yourself:

---

13. Yiadom, "We Believe That the Earth."

Nyame, we invoke your name. Asase Yaa, who was created on Thursday, we invoke your name. Our venerable ancestors, we are grateful to you for granting us health, children, wealth, love, and peace. We pray that you continue to protect us all.

The prayer goes on to include a few sentences concerning those who may wish your family harm. It is common in traditional Akan ceremonies to send away evil and blast its presence in the lives of the people gathered. In the West, we tend to not focus on evil influences, trusting instead in our positive thoughts and the power of our chosen deity. I include the end of the prayer for those who wish complete authenticity. Do not feel compelled to say anything that makes you uncomfortable or that goes against your own personal morality.

But anyone who has evil thoughts against us in the family; the one who wishes that misfortunes happen to us, we pray that the person is completely overpowered![14]

The following traditional prayer is often said at Christmas or the New Year by the head of the family:

Nyame here is drink; Asase Yaa here is drink; Great Ancestors, come and drink . . . We are not calling you because of some evil tidings. The year has come again and you did not allow any evil to befall us. We are offering you drink; beseeching that the coming year be prosperous. Don't allow any evil to come near our habitation. Bless us with rain, food, children, health, and prosperity.

May you feel a connection with Asase Yaa always!

PACHAMAMA
Peruvian Earth Mama

MANTRA
Pacha Mama
Mama Pacha
We need you.
We love you.

---

14. Starspirit International, Inc., "Akan Culture and Protocol."

Pachamama is the Incan Earth goddess who is still worshipped by modern Peruvians. She is a goddess of agriculture, of fertility, of the Earth below our feet, and of the air we breathe. Pachamama is infused with inner power and might. Her name is often translated as "Mother of the Earth," but she is actually "Mother of All." The word *mama* indicates a sacred female presence full of wisdom and knowledge, a true "mother" to us all.[15] *Pacha* means time and space, sacredness, the Earth, infinity, and the Divine. It is a word that encompasses all that it means to be alive on planet Earth, from the beginning of time to the present and even beyond, into the future.[16]

In Peruvian mythology, Pachamama is tied directly to the essence of life through her family and the trials and tribulations she undergoes. It is said that Pachamama birthed the great god Pachacamac into the world, completely on her own. Now with this birth, there were suddenly two beings in the universe—a god who animates the world and all its creations and a goddess who nurtures and provides sustenance for those creations. Together, they created a set of twins, a boy and a girl, whom Pachamama birthed. Soon after their birth, Pachacamac disappeared from their home atop White Mountain. Pachacamac and Pachamama were never to be reunited again.

Alone, Pachamama provided for herself and her children, withstanding the dark nights and the cold days. One evening, the children and their mother saw a flame in the distance. Curious and intrigued, they decided to follow the bright light. Eventually they came upon the cave-home of Pachacamac's brother, Wakon. The mother and children were elated. No longer were they alone in the world. Now they had light and company! But the good feelings did not last. When the children were out fetching water, Wakon expressed a romantic interest in Pachamama, which she refused. Incensed, Wakon killed Pachamama, chopped her up into little pieces, ate some of her, and then stored the rest of her body in a cooking kettle over the fire. When the children returned and asked for their mother, he told them she'd be back soon. But, of course, she never returned.

As the days passed, the children made friends with the animals around their new cave-home. One, a bird, told the children of Wakon's actions, informing them that their mother was dead. He instructed the children to tie a boulder into Wakon's long hair as he slept. The children did this and exited the cave, leaving their uncle behind. As they

---

15. O'Neill, "Mama."

16. Brown, "The Lessons of Juan Camargo Huaman—Peruvian Shaman."

fled, a fox offered to hide them in his den. The children gratefully accepted. Burrowed deep in the Earth, in the warm embrace of their mother Pachamama, the children listened as their uncle stomped about, looking for them. Wakon demanded the location of the children from the cougar, the condor, and the snake but they refused to tell him. Finally, the shrewd fox stepped forward and suggested that he imitate their mother's voice, calling to them from the top of the highest peak. Wakon, who had yet to notice the boulder hanging from his hair, thought the fox's idea was brilliant and he ran to the top of the mountain. He called forth with the voice of Pachamama, leaning over the edge of the cliff. The boulder attached to his hair dislodged, tumbling forward into the abyss, dragging Wakon with it. Wakon's death shook the Earth, causing massive earthquakes throughout the region.[17]

Eventually Pachamama's children climb a long rope up to the sky where they are reunited with their father Pachacamac and they become the sun and the moon. Pachamama remains on Earth, forever separated from her children, yet forever a part of them. Together, her family is the universe that surrounds the Earth. The celestial beings that were important to the ancient Incans were the Earth, the sun, and the moon. Throw in some air to breathe and you've just described Pachamama's immediate family.

As the Earth, Pachamama plays the biggest role in the everyday lives of humans. She gives us food and drink, shelter from the elements, and a place on which to live. To the Incans and to modern-day Peruvians, the Earth is a living, breathing entity with emotions, moods, needs, and desires. She needs us to love her. Juan Camargo Huaman, a modern Peruvian shaman describes Pachamama in this way:

> Her rivers need to flow, they are her veins. Veins she is desperately trying to clean out with all the rain that has been falling. Her mountains are her shoulders. Her forests are her lungs. The hole in the ozone layer is a hole in her aura, and the greenhouse effect which is raising her temperature is because she is ill and running a fever. When the Earth is ill, then we are too; because we are like cells on her body, we need to heal ourselves in order to help her heal.[18]

---

17. Lila, "Pachamama."
18. Brown, "The Lessons of Juan Camargo Huaman."

When Pachamama is sick, when she feels unloved by her human children, she is thought to take the form of a dragon deep inside the Andes Mountains. This dragon causes earthquakes and disruptions in order to help humans re-focus their attention back on the importance of the Earth and of Pachamama.

Today, as in times past, it is quite common to give offerings to Pachamama at agricultural festivals, in times of need, before cutting into her soil, during harvest season, and on her special holidays—the Tuesday before Ash Wednesday (Fat Tuesday), any Friday, or on any day during the month of August. The offerings take the form of cocoa leaves, cornmeal, unwrought silver, china, wine, cigars, cooked food, or a special Peruvian fermented drink called *chicha*. They are usually placed in a permanent sacred offering site known as an *apacheta*. An apacheta is a hole or well in the Earth that is piled high with stones. In order to make an offering, you remove the stones, drop the gift to Pachamama into the hole, and then reassemble the stones. The apachetas often resemble cairns and can be found in individual yards, in the center of towns, and even at mountain passes, so travelers can make an offering for a safe journey. Sometimes they mark energetic openings or doorways along the Earth.[19]

Such is the power of Pachamama—embraced by the universe, connected to the soil. Pachamama is the Universal Mother, giving us the light of the sun and the moon and providing us with land to stand upon and food to eat. She is infinitely grounded in the here and now, yet wise and knowing beyond all comprehension. As the old Peruvian saying goes, "Wisdom comes through the soles of our feet."[20] Pachamama is here with us every day, listening to our voices, waiting for our love.

Pathway to Pachamama

It is time to embrace Mother Earth with our bodies, to offer her love in a very physical way. It is time to give her a hug. A hug is one of those universal expressions that make people smile. It is hard not to feel connected, not to feel cared for and loved by the people around you, when embraced in a hug. Nowadays, in the industrial West, we don't hug each other enough. We stay away from intimate human interaction by e-mailing, texting, and chatting via cell phone. And many of us are lonely and sad because we miss relating with people in the flesh.

---

19. Lila, "Pachamama."
20. Brown, "The Lessons of Juan Camargo Huaman."

One man, Juan Mann, started a worldwide movement based on the idea of the power of hugs. It is called Free Hugs Campaign[21] and it works to spread love and connection around the world, through the power of a hug. From Japan to Paraguay to America to Australia, people are creating signs, checking in with their local officials, and offering free hugs to the world. Amazing! So simple, yet so profound.

Let's take this simple, profound idea and expand it to the Earth Mama under our feet. Choose a day, any day, and go outside and lie down on the Earth. Don't bring a blanket or yoga mat to lie on. Instead, allow every part of your body to come in contact with Mother Earth. If you wish, invite friends and family members to join you. And while you all lie on the Earth, giving her a giant hug, hold hands and feel your love for each other as well. I promise you, you'll sit up with a smile on your face!

ERIU
Irish Goddess of the Land

MANTRA

Eriu

(Pronounced AIR-oo, the mantra should
be chanted like *Om*, by drawing out the syllables.)

Unlike the Greek goddess Gaia, who serves as the deity for our entire blue and green planet, Eriu is the very land of Ireland—her trees, her winds, her rivers and wells. To this day, Ireland remains deeply entrenched in its reverence of the land, of the actual green plains and rolling hills of the fertile, mystical island of the Gaels and the Tuatha dé Danann. There is power in the rocks and hills, in the very soil itself, and the Irish have never forgotten this truth. Lie on her grass and feel her comfort. Step on her dirt and feel her support. She is alive and breathing every day, smiling on the children who make their way to her shores.

Eriu is yet another example of an Irish triple goddess. With her sisters, Banba and Fotla, she creates a triad reminiscent of Brigid and Morrighan. In fact, Eriu, Banba, and

---

21. http://www.freehugscampaign.org.

Fotla share the same mother as Morrighan: Ernmas. They were the first goddess triplets born to Ernmas, the she-farmer and bountiful mother. In the *Lebor Gabala Erenn*, the eleventh-century Book of Invasions or Conquests, Ernmas births two sets of girls as well as five boys, displaying her prowess as a goddess of fertility and plenty. Undoubtedly, her fertile nature extends through her female children, especially her first three daughters, since they are the very land from which abundance spills to feed the people of Ireland.[22] The fertility of Eriu, Banba, and Fotla extends past sustenance to the granting of kingship, thus giving the goddesses a larger role in the shaping of the land of Ireland and its future.

Eriu exhibits her own innate ability to grant sovereignty when she is young in spirit, unknown to the touch of man. In *The Second Battle of Mag Tuired*, an Irish saga first written down in the ninth century, Eriu sits looking at a perfectly smooth sea when she is approached (via silver boat) by a beautiful man. The man requests an hour of lovemaking with Eriu, who initially rejects his suggestion. But the man is very persuasive and, before long, Eriu and the mysterious stranger have "stretched themselves out together."[23]

This first sexual encounter becomes a monumental event in Eriu's life and underscores her role as fertile Earth goddess and kingmaker. Her lover turns out to be none other than Elatha mac Delbaith, king of the Formorians, the race of beings that lived in Ireland before the Tuatha dé Danann arrived. Nine months after learning "the ways of men," Eriu gives birth to a son who is named Eochu Bres, or Bres for short. Eventually, Bres becomes the leader of the Tuatha dé Danann, marries the goddess Brigid, and sires a son named Ruadan.

Although Bres' rule as king is short, it is important to note the power of his mother Eriu. In her first sexual encounter, Eriu conceives a child that becomes a king. The king of Tara! As the land itself, Eriu grants sovereignty to her son, having remained stable and unchanging so the current of the sea is able to carry Elatha's silver boat to her.

As the years progress, Eriu marries another Irish king, Cethor. Son of Cermait, grandson of the Dagda, Cethor has two brothers named Sethor and Tethor who also serve as the kings of Ireland, marrying Banba and Fotla, respectively. These sons of Cermait also are known as "son of" the individual gods they worship: "Mac Cuill – Sethor,

---

22. MacAllister, *Lebor Gabala Erenn*, verses 62 and 64.
23. Gray, *The Second Battle of Mag Tuired*, verse 18.

the hazel his god; Mac Cecht – Tethor, the ploughshare his god; Mac Greine – Cethor, the sun his god."[24] As the land of Ireland, it is interesting to note Eriu's connection with the sun through Mac Greine. The land and the sun work together to sustain crops and vegetation for the people of the Earth. Both are needed to create life. Since the sun and the Earth are sometimes married in mythology, they are symbiotic entities that need each other in order to create bounty and abundance. Eriu's marriage to Mac Greine and her encounter with Elatha show a goddess who is flexible, with an ability to work with others. As a fertility deity, she is comfortable with the power that comes from losing oneself in the merging of another to create something that is greater than either.

The way in which the three kingly brothers and their sister queens rule exemplify the intrinsic nature of Eriu, Banba, and Fotla. The kings share the rule of Ireland, dividing their sovereignty into thirds. The land remained whole but the time they ruled was divided up, so that each brother only ruled for approximately ten years out of the twenty-nine they held power. Every year, the crown would shift to another brother and the name of the land changed to that of the queen. So, when Mac Greine held power, the land was called Eriu; when Mac Cuill wore the crown, Banba was the name of the land.[25] All three goddesses hold the sovereignty of Ireland, yet Eriu makes the biggest impression in the ancient mythology. It is Eriu who not only makes a king through marriage but creates one from her womb. It is Eriu who is described as "generous,"[26] while her sisters' personalities are not mentioned. And it is Eriu who changes the fortunes of the Tuatha dé Danann when the Milesans arrive on the island of Ireland.

The Milesans are the last of the mythological invaders of Ireland. They arrive from Spain to avenge a fallen comrade, Ith, who was killed by the Danann nobles out of jealousy for the land of Ireland. After Ith praises Ireland for its plentiful harvest, fish, honey, wheat, and moderate climate, he seeks to return home and is ambushed by the Danann lords.[27] They react to Ith's compliments as though the land is a woman and Ith an unwelcome bridegroom coming to steal her away in the dead of night. Although the Danann race wields powerful magic, the threat of abduction is very real to the Danann men, perhaps even more so for Mac Greine, Mac Cuill, and Mac Cecht, whose wives are

---

24. MacAllister, *Lebor Gabala Erren*, verse 64.
25. Keating, *The History of Ireland*, section 12, 223.
26. Ibid., section 12, 225.
27. Cross and Slover, *Ancient Irish Tales*.

the very soil of the land. The Danann lords' hasty reaction and decisive strike against Ith hints at the character of Eriu and her sisters. As the land itself, it is possible that Eriu, Banba, and Fotla care little for the actual group that rules Ireland, as long as the land is well cared for. After all, Eriu has already had sex and birthed a child with a Formorian. Perhaps the land wishes to be honored for the power that she is, not for the power she can bring.

After hearing of Ith's unwelcome treatment in Ireland, the Sons of Mil gather their forces and sail to Ireland. The Danann princes use magic and druidry to hide the island from the Milesans, but after circling the island three times, the invaders find purchase at the harbor of Inber Scene. They walk out to explore the land and enact their revenge. Three days after landing, they meet Banba with her retinue, who states that the land is named after her and she asks that the invaders give the island her name. Her visit is followed by Fotla, who also claims the name-right of the land, praying that the Milesans allow her name to remain on the island. Neither sister tries to stop the invaders through words or deeds. Indeed, the daughters of Ernmas appear to accept the appearance of the Sons of Mil as appropriate and expected. Instead of pushing the men back into the sea, they request boons and favors.

The reasoning for this acceptance is explained when the Milesans finally meet Eriu, in the very center of Ireland, at Usneche. Eriu welcomes the invaders with grandeur and nobility, stating, "Welcome, welcome to you. It is long since your coming is prophesied. Yours will be the island forever."[28] Obviously, Eriu, Banba, and Fotla have divined the fate of their land and seen that the Dananns would not rule the island forever. Gracefully, as branches swaying in the wind, the sovereign queens of the land accept the change of rulership and honor the line of new kings. Yet, Eriu demands her own respect as well, exacting an equal, give-and-take relationship with the Milesans. When one of the men scoffs at Eriu's words, boasting about his own gods and demeaning her power, Eriu states that the power of his gods means nothing in the claiming of Ireland. She suggests that only through her will the land be taken. Then she insists that the land be named after her. The chief bard of the Milesans, Amergin, undoubtedly noting her power and sovereignty, agrees, stating, "It will be its chief name forever."[29]

---

28. Ibid.
29. Ibid.

After countless magic spells cast by the Danann princes and a honey-tongued plea to the land (that verges on wooing) by Amergin, the Milesans troop onto the island and, amid much bloodshed, rout the Dananns. During the final battle, the queens Eriu, Banba, and Fotla and their kings Cethor, Sethor, and Tethor, die. The essence of the land is returned to the soil, winds, and waters from which it sprang. The power of sovereignty returns to the living land under the feet of the Milesans. But Eriu can never truly die, for as long as the land thrives, the goddess lives.

She arises, once again, to grant sovereignty, in the eleventh-century manuscript *Baile in Scail*. In this, she is known as Flaith Erenn, the bearer of the cup of sovereignty and power. Many years after the struggle between the Dananns and the Milesans, a descendent of the Sons of Mil, Conn, is greeted by the sovereign goddess. After stepping upon the Stone of Destiny (or Lia Fail) and hearing its screams, Conn's druids tell him that he and his children will be kings of Ireland. After this proclamation, a mist forms around Conn and his advisers and he is spirited away to an unearthly house. There, they meet a mysterious horseman, the god Lugh, and a young female cupbearer, Eriu. The men eat and drink of the bounty of Ireland and are made most welcome. At the end of the feast, Lugh tells Eriu to give the cup to Conn. She does, naming every ruler of Ireland until Judgment Day. Then she and Lugh melt into the shadows, the fog lifts, and the house disappears. However, the cup of sovereignty remains with Conn.

Like the cup, Eriu stays with each of us who has been touched by the beauty and majesty of the land of Ireland. The land is alive, a deep spirit that roots each of us into the very heart and soul of Ireland and the goddess Eriu. Eriu *is* Ireland. She cannot be separated from its birds and beasts, its air and rain, from its mist and shining sun. Through the invasions of seven peoples, through the use of plowshares and the building of highways, she remains with her solid presence. She is the very essence of Ireland and praises deserve to be sung in her name. Hail Eriu, mother of Bres! Hail Eriu, queen of Cethor! Hail Eriu, lover of Amergin! Hail Eriu, cupbearer of Lugh! Hail Eriu, essence of the land![30]

---

30. Much of the story of Eriu first appeared in *Goddess Afoot!*, 146–152. For more information and intimate workings with Eriu, Irish Goddess of the Land, including a guided meditation and ritual, please see chapter 8 of *Goddess Afoot!*

Pathway to Eriu

My daughter brought home a charming children's book the other day after visiting the library with her grandparents. It is told in the form of an Irish folktale and is entitled *One Potato, Two Potato*, written by Cynthia DeFelice. Similar in format to many folktales around the world, DeFelice adds a typically Irish element to the story by making her main characters spectacularly poor. Mr. and Mrs. O'Grady share one potato between them every day and are so skinny that they can comfortably sit on one chair. Yet, these Irish peasants are not bitter about their lot in life, but rather count themselves lucky to have each other, one blanket with holes, a tattered coat that they share in the winter, and one potato a day.

As you can imagine, their lives change when they find a large pot (which looks suspiciously like a cauldron) buried deep in their garden, deep in the Earth of Ireland herself. This cauldron reproduces anything that is thrown into it. So one potato becomes two and two potatoes become four. Well, you get the idea. And so did the O'Gradys, who proceed to throw just about everything they owned into the pot, becoming miraculously, magically abundant! The story evolves into some silliness until the O'Grady's realize that they have manifested everything they could possibly need. They then thank the pot and re-bury it for someone else to find.

One Potato, Two Potato is a wonderful book to aid you in connecting with the power of the land of Ireland and manifesting earthly abundance. The wanton silliness is fun and enjoyable, while the details are reminiscent of Irish folktales of old. (The *Fear Ghorta*, as re-told in the story "Famine" by Michael Scott,[31] immediately came to mind when I began reading it.) Read this book out in the sun on a summer day. Share it with others during a drafty winter night. Give it as a gift. But, above all, remember its message: the land provides for us, and she deserves our respect, our thanks, and our love.

RITUAL FOR THE ENVIRONMENT:
LOVE FOR A TREE, LOVE FOR ALL

Suggested Ritual Days

March 14: International Day of Action for Rivers, as founded by the International Rivers Network

---

31. Scott, *Irish Folk and Fairy Tales Omnibus*, vol. III, chapter 6, 131–138.

April 22: Earth Day, as celebrated in the United States

Last Friday in April: National Arbor Day, as founded by the Arbor Day Foundation in the United States

May 16: Love a Tree Day

Fourth Sunday in May: Love Tree Day, as founded by Michelle Skye

June 5: World Environment Day, as founded by the United Nations

Summer Solstice: World Whale Day, as founded by Reed Behrens

July 12: National Tree Day (*Día del Árbol*), as celebrated in Mexico

Any Thursday or Friday

Items needed

an outside tree of your choice

a flexible tape measure

a large length of ribbon in your choice of color

a bowl of water

a small rose quartz

A week or two before your ritual, take some time to explore your environment. Walk in a local park, swing at a local playground, investigate your yard and the street on which you live. While connecting to your environment, be always on the lookout for a tree that calls to you. (Preferably one that is in the public domain or belongs to you or someone you know. It is never a good idea to plunk yourself down on someone else's lawn and start fiddling with their tree!) When you find your tree, measure the width of the tree using your tape measure. This measurement will help you to determine how much ribbon you will need for your ritual. I usually add a foot (12 inches) to the measurement, to ensure there is enough ribbon to make a bow. Now that you've got your measurement, go to your local fabric store and buy your ribbon. It doesn't matter how thick or thin it is, just so it is long enough to tie around the trunk of your tree. I do not recommend using wire-edged ribbon as it is usually stiffer in texture and will be more difficult to use. However, if you fall in love with a wire-edged ribbon, go for it!

On the day of your ritual, gather your items and go to your tree. (If your tree is far away from your house, pack a water bottle with your water and pour it into the bowl once you get to your destination.) Sit under your tree and relax. Take deep, cleansing breaths. Try to connect to the essence of your tree. Feel her bark under your fingers.

See what insects live among her roots. Notice the feathery patterns of her leaves and the shadows they cast on the ground. Pay attention to the colors of your tree and her scents and smells. How does the wind brush through her branches? How does it sound? Do not rush this section of the ritual, as you are allowing yourself to come in communion with your tree while calming and centering your mind.

Once you feel relaxed and completely connected with your tree, place the rose quartz in the bowl of water. Place the ribbon in the bowl of water and begin to think about all the love you have in your life—all the people who care about you and call you friend, daughter, sister, or mother. You are loved. Now consider the animals that you care for and/or see every day—the dogs that wag their tails in welcome, the squirrels that chatter above your head, the birds that sing sweet melodies to you. You are loved. Now begin to think about the Earth all around you—the oceans teeming with life, the land providing food and shelter, the wind bringing sweet scents and seeds. You are loved. Could any one person feel more love than you feel right now? You are surrounded by love, sweet and pure, innocent and giving.

And now, with your mindset of gratitude and love, consider the issues that hold most importance to you, the situations that seem too big for you to change—the plight of the polar bears, the children in Asia forced into prostitution, the families in the Sudan ripped apart by civil war, the clear-cutting of forests, the mysterious disappearance of the honey bees. Think about whatever cause or issue feels most important to you and send love through the roots of your tree to that situation. Tie the ribbon around your tree, surrounding it with your love and the love of the rose quartz crystal. Your love will be felt by the tree and will travel down its long roots, into the mysterious watery aqueducts deep in the Earth's belly. There, the love will flourish, moving to the place and time and people most in need of it.

After tying your ribbon and spending a moment sending love to your tree, take the bowl of water and sprinkle it around your tree, giving back to the wondrous life that is serving as a conduit for your powerful message of love for the Earth. Then, tuck the rose quartz among the roots of your tree, taking care to simply follow the flow of the root structure; you should not gouge or tear into your tree.

Your ritual is now finished! You can replenish your love tree throughout the year, at various times that have meaning to you (birthdays, holidays, or other special days are wonderful times to give the gift of love). If enough of us perform this simple act, we can begin to change our environment and the world, one tree at a time, one person at a time, one issue at a time. Love is the great unifier. Our world has forgotten about the power of love. It is time for us to remind them.

CHAPTER FOUR
Goddess Mantras for Love

LOVE: BINDING THE WORLD TOGETHER

Love is the great connector, bringing separate and unique individuals together to forge bonds that go beyond thought or care or worry. Love is a mystery. Intangible, unquantifiable, it is not of this mundane world. It cannot be touched or tasted, and like cotton candy or snowflakes, it melts away when you try to hold it too tightly. If untended or ignored, love simply disappears, leaving a stain on our psyche but keeping our favorite pair of jeans clean. We can see evidence of love: couples holding hands, smiling, and winking. But if you were to describe the form and shape of love, you would be hard pressed to do so. It is invisible to the naked eye. You might do better in pinpointing the sounds of love. The sighs and moans and sloppy kisses that make up romantic movies and teenage imaginations. But are those really love or simply its manifestations? Can we define love by what we, as humans, do? Is not love greater than us? Is not love transcendent in its possibilities and endless avenues of exploration and adventure? Is not love our own best selves realized and projected back to us through the eyes and breath and beliefs of another?

The Other is imperative in a discussion of love. Certainly, one wants self-love, in a reasonable, restrained, non-narcissistic way. No one wants to be so self-involved and so in love with themselves that they refuse to involve others in their tiny sphere of influence in this world. The woman with the red bandana on the bus, the toddler with the bright froggie toy, the lumberjack with flannel shirt, and the receptionist with stiletto heels— all would pass us by without another look if we solely focused on self-love. Looking inward, to our own selves and our own ideals, we would close ourselves off to the experience all around us. Safe in our little controlled universe, we would nurture our love of self and possibly never open up enough to love others. Our heart would remain our own.

The heart is the muscle associated with love. But what is the purpose of the human heart? It is a giant muscle that pumps our blood through our body in order to circulate oxygen to the cells of our tissues and organs. The oxygen feeds the cells, allowing them to stay alive, and they in turn work to keep us alive. The heart, when looked at biologically, is nothing more than an eighteen-wheeler delivering necessary supplies throughout the country of our body. It is a distribution center. Why then, do we equate love with this most vitally important organ in our body? Could it be that love is as necessary to the human condition as the heart is to the health and well-being of the body?

The heart has been used as a symbol in drawings and carvings since the Neolithic era. No direct evidence has been found to fully comprehend what the heart stood for in those ancient times, yet it is significant that such a symbol was in use and would have been recognized by early humans. In ancient Greece, from around 600–400 BCE, the heart was associated with the lyre, an instrument of Aphrodite's son Eros, the god of new-found relationships and sexual desire. When the Romans adopted Eros into their own pantheon, they named him Cupid (the Latin word for desire or lust) and changed his symbol from the simple heart to a heart pierced with an arrow. (The arrow, as a symbol, traditionally indicates energy, flow, and penetration.[1]) Today, this is the symbol we most associate with falling in love. Love has entered our heart and we are forever changed.

One of love's most abiding qualities is its ability to alter our thoughts and feelings on a grand scale. We may love a partner for years and then break up with him or her, erasing the person from our lives. We no longer eat dinner together, no longer wash his or her clothes or hear his or her whiny voice. We throw away all the gifts and burn all evidence of the relationship. It is over. We are through! But the experience of being in love with another is never erased. It lingers in the dark shadows of the mind, in the recesses of the heart, dormant but still there, waiting for just the right time to re-emerge. Once our heart opens to another, we are linked. We are joined. Even if you never see the other again, you have been changed by the experience and, thus, you and your ex are still a part of each other. You are not the person you were before the relationship. You must forge ahead, learning from each new encounter and reveling in the ambiguity and uncertainty of love. Embrace each relationship's lustful life, and believe in the best of humanity.

---

1. Symbols.com, "Symbol 20:18, the Heart Symbol."

Love is the great human connector, bringing together individual organisms. At its best, love allows you to become greater than you ever imaged, giving you strength and will to accomplish magnificent feats. At its worst, love can be pitilessly cruel and callous, forcing you to gather your inner wisdom and believe in the power of the self. Either way, love is a generator, a mover of emotions and feelings. It creates action, giving birth to the new and unexplained. Love shifts our world, for better or worse, and never leaves us quite the same again. The human experience is about growth and connection. Love gives us both. Is it any wonder, then, that we so yearn for love?

ENERGY RETURN

The consequences of actively seeking love on a magical or spiritual level are many. It is important to speak and act with care and with conscious thought as you request romantic love to enter your life. One slip of the tongue, one hasty action can mar your pure intent and create chaos in your life. Once the gods and goddesses of love are raised, the situation usually runs its course, for good or ill, until the energy settles once again.

It is important to be specific when you are thinking about the love you would like to bring into your life. What kind of love do you want? Do you want a bed-partner only? A companion who will have the same hobbies? A long-term relationship? Truly define your individual needs and wants. Don't be afraid to describe your ideal love physically, if that's important to you. If age, money, or location is a factor, let the universe know. Make a list of your ideal love's qualities and characteristics. Tell the universe your dreams; if you don't, you never know who's going to show up on your doorstep.

At the same time, it is not a good idea to name an actual person in your romantic request. This limits the wonderful possibilities that the universe might have in store for you. If you haven't yet met a person, you won't that know he or she exists and is the perfect match for you. Such a request forces the universe to focus only on one individual, leaving out all the possibly perfect strangers you have never encountered. Also, and most importantly, naming a person in a love spell or mantra takes away their free will. Their opportunities become as limited as your own. You take away their right to choose their own reality, binding them to *your* intention and *your* ideals. This restricts their life and does not allow them to grow as needed. Restriction is never good way to begin a relationship (unless you're into bondage and, well, that's a whole other book!).

Love is one of the most sought-after human experiences. With care and thought, you can supplement your mundane search with some spiritual love aid. Don't be afraid to request the help and guidance of the Great Goddess. She wants you to be happy! Just be sure to be ethical and conscious in all your love requests and before long you'll have received one of the greatest gifts from the Goddess—a heart-to-heart connection with another.

VENUS
Roman Goddess of All Things Love-ly

MANTRA

Light my fire.
Stoke my desire.
Venus!
Send my love to me.

Venus, even more than her Greek counterpart Aphrodite, embodies the vision of earthly love. In astrology, the planet named after her represents relationships and connection, indicating an interest in the affairs of men and women. (Incidentally, Venus is the only planet in our solar system named after a goddess! All the rest are named for Roman gods.) Modern marketing companies slap her name on products ranging from razors to swimsuits (even a feminine "enhancement" lotion) in an effort to project an air of seduction, beauty, and allure. In 1986, the British all-girl pop band Bananarama rocketed to international success with their hit song "Venus," which was actually a remake of the Dutch rock band Shocking Blue's number-one hit from 1970. Bananarama replaced the haunting vocals and deep-rooted, grounded guitar stylings of the 1970s with kitchy MTV costumes and a bouncy, synthesized backbeat. But it all worked, as they sang their hearts out to the goddess Venus, just as Frankie Avalon had done more than twenty-five years earlier. His song, also called "Venus," reached the number one spot on Billboard's Hot 100 in March 1959. A completely different song than the Shocking Blue/Bananarama number, Avalon entreated the goddess to send him a girl to love, with an innocence that epitomized the gently yearning, sweetly charming love songs of the 1950s.

In Republican and Imperial Rome, as now in the modern era, Venus presented various faces of love. In all of them, she was a very accessible and willing goddess. A goddess for the masses, so to speak, and why shouldn't she be? Everyone desires and deserves love. Even today, she is not usually the subject of scholarly study; rather, she is most generally found in love-addled rantings and thick-voiced poetry. I think Venus prefers it this way: raw, impassioned, unpredictable emotion. The ancient Romans worked very hard to put a civilized and controlled veneer on this unpredictable goddess, and in some ways, they succeeded. But, in others, her nature flies outward, wrapping you in winsome arms and gossamer scarves.

Several temples to Venus were constructed in Rome, none more telling than the Temple of Venus and Roma and the Temple of Venus Genetrix. The Temple of Venus and Roma was built by the Emperor Hadrian and inaugurated in 135 BCE. The temple was not completed until 141 BCE, having been started twenty years previously in 121 BCE. This temple was the largest temple to Venus in ancient Rome and was located to the far east of the Forum Romanum near the Colosseum. It is not by accident that Hadrian linked the goddess of the city of Rome to the goddess of love and beauty. Venus bestowed on Rome an ancient lineage and old power. As the mother of the mythological founder of Rome—the handsome, wise, and ferocious Aeneas of Troy's ill-fated fame—Venus linked Rome to ancient stories, thus giving them a lineage that belied their pastoral upbringings. In short, Venus brought the Romans respectability in a Mediterranean world run by philosophizing Greeks and war-mongering Carthaginians.

No family better understood Venus' ability to bestow integrity than the Gens Julia, or the family Julius, whose illustrious members include Julius Caesar and the Emperor Augustine. Julius Caesar created the Temple to Venus Genetrix in 46 BCE, nearly one hundred years before Hadrian crafted the Temple to Venus and Roma. As Venus Genetrix, Venus took on the attributes of loving mother and domestic caregiver. She was seen as the mother of Rome, and the Julian family established their authority to rule by claiming direct descent from Aeneas, Venus' son. In fact, Caesar even established a cult of Venus Genetrix, which focused on her powers in the realms of marriage, motherhood, and domestic life. Eventually, she began to be seen as an all-encompassing goddess, including power over nature as well as her typical role in bestowing love and beauty.

It is not surprising that Caesar assigned a nature element to the goddess Venus Genetrix, as Venus originally was seen as a goddess of gardens, vineyards, and agricultural fertility, as well as human fertility. The patron goddess of Pompeii was Venus Pompeiana, and she was often preserved in small shrines in the gardens of Pompeii. Although it is unknown if she was honored religiously, the Romans thought it best to give her a cursory nod of acknowledgement in relation to their garden pursuits. A vase, found amid the ruins of Pompeii, sums up the Roman attitude toward Venus' connection to agricultural fertility. It states: "Allow me pure wine: then may Venus who guards the garden love you."[2]

It is possible that "the garden" in the Pompeian phrase could have more than one meaning. After all, despite her agricultural beginnings and her political uses, Venus is, first and foremost, a goddess of love, including all sexual and non-sexual aspects of the word. Love is a bodily experience. It makes the heart pound and the breath quicken. It resonates with images of interlocked limbs and stolen kisses. Love, by its very nature, brings us out of our heads and into our bodies, into the present moment. It is as much about fertility as it is about sensation. It is an emotion in motion, following the quick-silvered passion of the moment. Love reminds us to feel with every inch of our bodies and express those feelings in words or actions or deeds.

So is it any wonder that Venus is often a mercurial goddess—one moment pleased and smiling, the next damned and defiant? Here is a goddess who had numerous extra-marital affairs with gods and humans alike. She was even caught *in flagrante delicto* with Mars, the god of War. Her husband, the smithy god Vulcan, had suspected the love affair and constructed a net to hold the two lovers, despite their otherworldly qualities. When they did "come together," Vulcan sprung the trap, catching the lovers in the midst of lovemaking. They could not move or disengage themselves. Vulcan then called in some of the other gods to shame his philandering wife. But it's difficult to shame someone who is simply following their true nature. Venus went on to have other affairs, namely with the humans Adonis and Anchises, the father of Aeneas.

Venus' affair with Adonis is fraught with tears, kisses, and feigned death. She is madly in love with him and uses every conceivable method to convince him to love her. However, Adonis is but a child in many versions of the story and so can only think of manly pursuits. The hunt and the chase call to him; love holds no allure. Throughout the encounter, Venus visibly and vocally expresses her emotions. Often holding Adonis

---

2. Johnson, "Venus in Pompeian Gardens."

down against the ground, using guile and guilt to wring kindness from his hard heart, Venus is not shy to utilize every one of her many attributes, which stem, most noticeably, from the five senses. In William Shakespeare's epyllion "Venus and Adonis," Venus waxes lyrical for four stanzas about the beauty of Adonis as expressed by the five senses. She praises his voice as "ear's deep-sweet music," his smell as "breath perfumed that breedeth love by smelling," and his taste as a "banquet."[3] She says, "Though neither eyes nor ears, to hear nor see, / Yet should I be in love by touching thee."[4] And throughout the whole poem she waxes lyrical on Adonis' beauty, even stating that he is "Thrice-fairer than myself,"[5] which is quite a compliment coming from the goddess of beauty and love.

Venus' power of attraction stems directly from the senses of the body, which bring the human race back to Earth, back to the present, and away from the philosophical mind, which is prone to meanderings on heaven and the future and the future of heaven and the heavenly future and . . . well . . . you get the idea. Venus is about connection. Now. Here. In this world and in this reality. Shakespeare associates her with all elements while in the throes of love. "'O, where am I?' quoth she, 'in Earth or heaven, / Or in the ocean drench'd, or in the fire?'"[6] And, indeed, Venus encompasses all of the elements that make up our existence. She was born from the foam-flecked sea, burns with the fire of passion, is temperamental as the changeable wind, and gives us the fertility of the soil. Venus is herself a four-in-one spirit, bound together by the variegated qualities of love, by the four elements of our Earth, and by the complexities of our lives. Venus is a complex goddess and I have merely scratched the surface of her truth with this brief introduction to her greatness and power. Still, she is intimately accessible in her greatness. If you would bring love into your life, with all its scope and breadth, Venus is waiting for you to open yourself to her passionate guidance.

Pathway to Venus

For me, nothing is so evocative of Venus as a love poem. Whether ripped from the shattered remnants of love or shining with its eternal promise of hope, love poems transcend

---

3. Shakespeare, "Venus and Adonis," stanzas 71–74.
4. Ibid., stanza 72.
5. Ibid., stanza 2.
6. Ibid., stanza 82.

the mind to focus on the soft, squishy nether regions of the heart and soul. Raucous and racy, sweet and saucy, or pious and passionate, love poetry speaks to our elemental natures and reminds us that there is more to living beside bills and work and—oh, why bother with that now when there is nectar to nibble upon and a caressing gaze to meet? I could go on and on but, really, Venus would say, "Forget about the explanations! Just jump into it, Girl!" And she'd be right. So get yourself some sumptuous food (strawberries dipped in chocolate are nice), pick up a good book of love poetry or love stories (style and substance completely up to you), grab your significant other (or go it alone, it doesn't really matter), and INDULGE! Because that is what makes life worth living!

CAELIA
British Faerie Queen of Eternal Love

MANTRA

I am here
And there
And everywhere.
I am love.

Not everyone is going to agree that Caelia is a goddess. She most definitely is an English faerie queen and has been immortalized in two stunning works of art: *The Faerie Queen* by Edmund Spenser (1590) and *Tom a Lincoln* by Richard Johnson (1599). In recent times, Caelia has been drawn and designed by faerie artists as diverse and talented as Jessica Galbreth, Selena Fenech, and Paulina Stuckey Cassidy.[7] In the FaerieCraft Spiritual Tradition, founded by English couple Alicen and Neil Geddes-Ward, Caelia is a faerie queen to be remembered and honored. They utilize the faerie queens of legend in much the same way other religions worship and pay homage to the various forms of the masculine and feminine Divine.[8] A faerie queen, in my opinion, is just one more representation of the Divine Feminine in the world around us.

---

7. The websites for these artists are: Jessica Galbreth: http://www.enchanted-art.com; Selena Fenech: http://www.selinafenech.com; and Paulina Stuckey Cassidy: http://www.paulina.ws.
8. Geddes-Ward and Geddes-Ward, *Faeriecraft*, chapter 5, 101.

It is no surprise that faeries were so prominent during the time of Shakespeare and during our own period in history. Shakespeare wrote most of his works between the years of 1590 and 1613. This is a time when literary works involving faeries flourished. From Shakespeare's *A Midsummer Night's Dream* (1595/1596) to Edmund Spenser's *A Faerie Queen* to lesser known writings such as *Nimphidia* (1627) by Michael Drayton and *Entertainment at Althorpe* (1603) by Ben Jonson, faeries were *de rigueur* in polite society. All of these faerie-centric works were created within twenty (or so) years of the beginning of a new century—a period of time of great change, evolution, and inward seeking.

Despite the fact that centuries are arbitrary markers of time created by our own human minds, they still hold power for us, precisely *because* we believe in the symbolic ideals and attitudes and the timely constructs they represent. So, while our logical minds scoff at the idea that December 31, 1999, is any different from January 1, 2000, our intuitive, creative, illogical minds are reaching to grasp significance and meaning from the event. In the liminal spaces between centuries, as created by mortal minds, spiritual pursuits creep in and seek to expand. Sometimes these spiritual ideas take the form of faeries, as we saw in Shakespeare's time and which we are experiencing now in our own shifting time from the twentieth to the twenty-first century.[9]

Today, our society hungers to find meaning in our existence in this world. We are just now "waking up" to the perils of our planet and to our own power—as individuals, communities, and nations—to create the world of our dreams. And it is no surprise that Caelia has entered our consciousness again, reminding us of the responsibilities of loving others and the necessity of loving ourselves. Caelia, the faerie queen, embodies love in so many ways that it is hard not to listen to her stories without blushing, without seeing our own lives hidden in the triumphs and tragedies of the lovely faerie queen.

Caelia is best known as the lover of the Red Rose Knight, Tom a Lincoln, who was the bastard son of King Arthur. In *Tom a Lincoln*, the Red Rose Knight travels with his friend Lancelot and sundry other knights of Camelot to find the origins of his paternal parentage. (Obviously, he is unaware that he is Arthur's bastard son.) On the journey,

---

9. In the shift to the eighteenth century, we have the Salem witch trials as well as the publication of Charles Perrault's book of fairy tales, entitled *Tales of Times Past.* In the shift to the nineteenth century, one saw the rise of Spiritualism, in the form of séances, medium circles, and the Theosophical Society.

his boat is buffeted by strong winds and winds up on an isolated island. Grateful to be off the teeming water, the men beach their boats to stand on solid ground. However, they are met by two thousand women warriors, of which two are sent as messengers to the men. They request the men return to their boats and leave the island. The men plead their case, saying they will die if they have to go back onto the ocean waves, and then they ask the female messengers about the then-strange occurrence of an all-female army.

The messengers explain that many years ago in this land, known as Fairy Land, there was a king who lusted for land and constantly warred with his neighbors. Eventually, he had gone to war so many times that he emptied his kingdom of all men, no matter their age, for a final battle. The women, left all alone, bemoaned the fact that they were defenseless and without the company and comfort of their men. They sent a letter requesting the return of their men. The king answered that he would prefer to see the women and children held as captives and given as spoil to his enemies rather than give up his advantageous position, besieging the cities of his enemies.

As you can imagine, the women were incensed by this answer and they concocted their own plan. They killed all the male children that had not marched off to war. Then, when the men returned, festooned with glory, the women slew them in their beds that very night. Not a single male lived through the onslaught except the king, who was put into a boat and sent across the seas to seek his fortune. From that time forward, men were not welcome in Queen Caelia's Fairy Land. Yet Tom a Lincoln, true to form, has a golden tongue that can charm even the crustiest warrior-maid. He tells the warrior messengers that he and his men will surely die upon the water and they would rather thrust themselves into honorable battle against the female warriors than fight the treacherous sea. However, he hopes that the goodly queen will see the righteousness of his actions and will grant kindness unto him and his men. Queen Caelia does, but only after consulting with her warrior messengers.

When Caelia sees the Red Rose Knight for the first time, she is instantly won over by his courtly ways, courtesy, and nobility. And before too long (as is always the case in fairy tales), Caelia is won over by Tom, has opened her castle and rooms to him, and given a fairy maid to dance attendance for each English knight. She shows Tom her riches and jewels and tells him that all can be his, along with her body, if he will just marry her. Three times, Tom denies the advances of the queen, telling her that he must complete his quest before he can even think about marriage. Three times the love-sick queen is saddened by his reply, as she feels the meeting is fortuitous, an answer to her prayers so that her city can continue to thrive and grow with additional babies.

At this point in the story, Caelia is responding to outside influences of betrayal in a very human, un-goddesslike way. Her father, the king, damned the women of his city to torture, rape, and death at the hands of his enemy rather than come back home and be with them. He betrayed their trust, choosing to care about his dreams of conquest rather than take care of his relationship with family. Caelia and the women responded as spurned lovers, lashing out in anger to hurt their men. Rather than live together, knowing the men cared more about conquest than protecting their loved ones, the women cut the offending men out of their lives forever. I think we have all been in such a sad, angry place before. We shore up our defenses in order to protect ourselves from feeling such pain and betrayal again. When Caelia allows Tom and the knights access to her land, she is beginning the healing process of allowing love back into her life. Tom's refusal of marriage and kingship still does not dissuade Caelia because she is starting to feel the heady, wondrous effects of love after a long drought.

Caelia now has a choice. Does she return to her strong, fortified, loveless position behind the walls of her heart? Or does she break down those walls and choose to love selflessly, purely, with all her heart? Well, since this *is* a chapter on love, I think you probably know which choice Caelia made. That night, torn between her fear and her love, between her shame and her heart, "at last the heart was conqueror,"[10] and Caelia embraces the path before her, sneaking into the bedchamber of Tom a Lincoln. And Tom, never one to turn a lady out into a cold night, with "the nature and courage of a man,"[11] passes an extremely amorous evening with the queen of faerie. For the space of four months, the ladies of the faerie court entertain the knights of England, with the result that many of them are heavy with the Englishmen's seed when the men finally make plans for their departure. Queen Caelia is large of belly with Tom's child and asks him to stay until the child is born. But Tom cannot be dissuaded from his quest (at least, not any longer) and, having promised to return if he is able, he sails off to find the truth of his father.

Caelia gives birth to a son, known throughout the legends as the faerie knight. She waits and waits for Tom to return to her. But, alas, her story ends sadly, for she spies

10. Johnson, *Tom a Lincoln*, chapter 4.
11. Ibid.

Tom's ship in the distance as he returns home to England. His ship is caught in some strange, supernatural windstorm that will not allow him to make his way to the island. Caelia sees him sail by, without so much as a warning signal or flaring torch. After six weeks, Caelia knows, deep in her heart, that Tom will never return. Sad, despairing but not angry, she writes a letter to him in her own blood, rains kisses upon her infant son, and throws herself into the sea, from which she washes up dead next to Tom's ship. Her letter bemoans Tom's betrayal and his inability to keep his promise. Despite the pain he has caused her, Caelia still loves Tom and calls herself "thine own true lover,"[12] even unto the end. She could no sooner relinquish her love as she could remove her name. It is a part of her, just as Tom is a part of her, forever connected through their son, the faerie knight.

The ultimate lesson of Caelia, as shown in the literary work *Tom a Lincoln*, is that love lives beyond our mortal minds and bodies. It is a truth unto its own and should not be hidden from nor embraced without thoughtful consideration. Love involves more than the individual and, as such, should be treated with respect. Once given, love cannot ever be fully retrieved. It may change form and substance (betrayal, anger, fear, despair), but it is an absolute, a linking of spirits that stays throughout all time. It is wonderful and painful and difficult and easy and we as humans long for it, for the connection of beings and souls. It is the ultimate high and the ultimate low. It is, in truth, the only reason for our existence.

Pathway to Caelia

In Caelia's story, love is really about connection, a melding of spirit and energy to form a brilliant burning star of emotion. Love is the ultimate bond between two human beings (or between a human and a faerie, as in Tom and Caelia's case) and as such, it exists outside of the tangible here and now. There is nothing more *present* in time than love. At the same time, love cannot be captured with the hands, seen with the eyes, or heard with the ears. It is intangible and abstract on the material level, while being so very true and real on the emotional and spiritual level. It is a paradox. (How fun!)

To understand and fully get to know the nature of love, take some time to contemplate one of your relationships in which you feel love. This can be a current or past relationship with a lover, a friend, or a blood relative, such as a child or parent. Don't

---

12. Ibid.

overanalyze your thoughts and memories of the relationship, just focus on that one person. Take a sheet of plain, white paper and, using colored markers, paints, or crayons, begin to draw your relationship on the paper. Don't think about it! Just feel! Allow the colors to call out to you, to resonate in swirling dips and ridges, to vibrate in colorful starts and stops. Fill your paper as much or as little as you want. Take your time with the design, feeling your way around the edges so that it truly incorporates your idea of that particular love. Then, when you feel ready, turn the paper over (or attach another sheet) and write yourself a love poem or note about that relationship. Again, don't overthink it! Just allow the words to flow. They don't have to make sense, after all, because this is a love note *just for you.*

When you are finished, carefully fold the drawing and the love note and place them in your journal, scrapbook, Book of Shadows, or photo album. Your association with this relationship can never truly go away; it has become a part of your very self. This love, this relationship, this friendship has forged aspects of your core truth. Honor the you that lives inside that relationship and that survives away from it. For love is not love unless we are given room to breathe on our own, stand on our own, and be on our own, as well.

FREYJA
Norse Goddess of Passion and Sex

MANTRA

Enter my womb.
I am ripe for the plucking.

Freyja is the goddess that all women want to be and all men want to bed. She is completely comfortable in her own independence, her own ferociousness, her own sexual power. She does not need anyone but desires everyone, with a shamelessness that would make a stripper blush. Societal rules and regulations, mores, and morals do not apply to Freyja. She is her own lady, bringer of wealth, love, fertility, and death.

Freyja is a member of the Vanir, one of two pantheons that comprise Norse divinity. In general, the Vanir are closely connected to the Earth, to the fertility of the planet and the people and animals who live upon her. The Aesir, the other clan of deities, are similar to sky beings, working with universal and mythic forces that are almost too large for humans to comprehend. Most of the Norse gods and goddesses in the Poetic and Prose Eddas (medieval texts of Norse mythology) are members of the Aesir, but there are a few Vanir deities who hold extreme importance. Among these are Freyja, her twin brother Freyr, and their father Njordh, who live among the Aesir.

Freyja and Freyr are blood relations but they are also divine lovers. Freyja and Freyr unite to ensure the fertility of the Earth, as well as material wealth for all. Freyr is the fertile Earth to Freyja's energizing presence. He is the seed and she is the sun, warming the soil and coaxing the seed to be reborn. She is the raging fire to his calming earth, the spark that kindles his divinity. Freyja is the wild woman to Freyr's green man, the life force to his life vessel or container.

Freyja's powerful life spark is represented by two symbols, one modern, the other from the original sources of Scandinavian and Icelandic mythology. The simple, familiar heart was suggested by Edred Thorsson in *A Book of Troth*, as a sign of the blessings of Freyja, given to those who undertake her mysteries. The heart is a stylized impression of the female genitals and/or buttocks and indicates the life-giving power of female sexuality. The other symbol is Freyja's necklace Brisingamen, which she received from four dwarves after a night spent with each one of them. (And you can almost bet that they weren't playing canasta.)

In the Icelandic saga, *The Tale of Hogni and Hedinn*, Freyja happens upon four dwarves who are just completing a beautiful necklace. Desiring it above all else, she offers them gold and silver in exchange for the piece of jewelry. They tell her that they have gold and silver a-plenty but they'll sell her the necklace for four nights of her love. She agrees and after four nights, she leaves the dwarves adorned with her new necklace. The four dwarves are easily recognizable as the four dwarves who support the four directions in Norse mythology; although their names are different, the number indicates a strong correlation between them. As Freyja slept with each in turn, she gained knowledge of each direction and the corresponding four elements that craft our world: earth, air, fire, and water. This wisdom allowed her to embody the essence of life, taking it into herself and claiming it as her own. Freyja's vast life-giving and revitalizing power is undoubtedly the reason numerous giants try to steal her or coax her into marriage and the reason Loki (the Norse god of cunning and mischief) tries to steal her necklace for Odin. Freyja's power is stored in her necklace, as well as in her body.

Not satisfied with her brother Freyr and the four dwarves, Norse mythology is rife with stories of Freyja's sexual escapades. In the *Lokasenna* of The Poetic Edda, Loki, not invited to an Aesir party, decides to attend anyway and stir up some trouble. He insults each god and goddess in turn. Freyja stands up for Frigg, the wife of Odin, telling Loki that he is "mad" and pointing out that he has done "ugly, hateful deeds." Loki retaliates by pointing out some of Freyja's deeds, saying:

> Be silent, Freyja! for fully I know thee,
> Sinless thou art not thyself;
> Of the gods and elves who are gathered here,
> Each one as thy lover has lain.
> Be silent, Freyja! thou foulest witch,
> And steeped full sore in sin;
> In the arms of thy brother the bright gods caught thee
> When Freyja her wind set free.[13]

Obviously, in Loki's mind, the easiest way to insult Freyja is through her abundant sexuality.

Freyja's sexual exploits are known even among the Etin-folk or Giants. In *The Song of Hyndla* of The Poetic Edda, Freyja rides her lover Ottar (now disguised as a boar) to the home of the giantess Hyndla in order to learn some information about his family tree. (I do not doubt that her position on top of Ottar is perfectly crafted to evoke the act of sex.) Hyndla casually calls Ottar the lover of the goddess and then, after realizing she has been duped into relating information about Ottar's family, the giantess retaliates by demeaning the goddess. Comparing Freyja to Heithrun, the mead-giving nanny-goat of the gods, Hyndla says, " . . . in the night who runnest – your noble friend – / in her heat as Heithrun the he-goats among."[14] However, the giantess is not satisfied with this brief description of Freyja as a rutting she-goat. She continues, in even more graphic detail:

> Were you ever ready to lie with Oth:
> Under your apron still others have crept in the night,

---

13. Bellows, *The Poetic Edda*, 161–162, verses 30 and 32.
14. Auden and Taylor, *Norse Poems,* "The Lay of Hyndla," verse. 30.

Who runnest – as you noble friend –
In her heat as Heithrun the he-goats among.[15]

It is unclear who the giantess refers to by the name of "Oth." He may be another of Freyja's lovers or it may be another name for her husband, Od.

It is hard to imagine a Norse warrior comfortable with a philandering wife, but Od is represented in the Eddas as loving Freyja without end, and the feeling appears to be mutual. When Od leaves Freyja on long travels, Freyja cries tears of red gold and searches for him among the varying cultures on Earth. Little is known of Od other than his role as Freyja's husband. Od may have been a later addition to the Eddas, in an attempt to "purify" the goddess and tone down her promiscuity. Since Od has no exploits in the mythology (apart from the leaving of Freyja), he may actually be Odin in disguise. After all, Freyja and Odin share many of the same characteristics and interests, including a rather loose interpretation of wedding and marriage vows.[16]

Freyja is deep and rich and varied, like the very Earth itself. Indeed, she might be the daughter of the earth goddess Nerthus, who is often connected to Freyja's father, Njordh. As the possible daughter of earth and sea, as the possessor of elemental knowledge, and as the holder of Brisingamen (one of the items of power in Norse mythology), Freyja is far more than a sexy, pleasure-loving goddess. Don't get me wrong, she loves a good romp in the hay, but Freyja's energy encompasses the hidden power within the act of love. This hidden power is at the very heart of creation, one of the greatest forces on Earth. Freyja can help us ground in the present moment, in the pleasure all around us, while launching forward into our next endeavor and our next level of personal advancement. She is sensuality in all its many meanings—the taste of a tart strawberry, the sound of the moaning wind, the sight of our lover's smile. As we ground ourselves in the goodness of our current reality, she then pushes us to expand, to reach for the very apex of climax, and then to harness that energy for our own needs and desires. Love and sex for Freyja are just gateways to the Divine, to our own understanding of the possibilities all around us. Love as power . . . it's pretty heady stuff!

---

15. Ibid., verse 31.
16. Much of the story of Freyja first appeared in *Goddess Alive!*, 76–80. For more information and intimate workings with Freyja, Norse Goddess of Passion and Sex, including a guided meditation and ritual, please see chapter 5 of *Goddess Alive!*

Pathway to Freyja

The most well-known symbol of the goddess Freyja is her necklace Brisingamen. The medieval texts do not tell us what the necklace looked like, but it is known that the gem amber was highly respected in the Northlands, thought to possess mystical and Divine qualities. (It was also worth quite a bit of money.) Amber was used for specialized items such as beads and pendants for jewelry, gaming pieces, spindle-whorls, and finger rings. Due to amber's fiery appearance and Freyja's fiery energy, it is often associated with the goddess. Was Brisingamen made of amber or of gold or both? We cannot know.

Regardless, amber is the gem most associated with the goddess Freyja. It is usually thought to connect to either the second or sacral chakra or the third or solar plexus chakra. After much gemstone work, I feel as though amber resonates with the sacral chakra more than the solar plexus chakra; however, I encourage you to use your intuition and decide for yourself. My personal decision hinges on the fact that the sacral chakra seems to emulate many of the attitudes and ideals expressed by Freyja (who likes her some amber!). The sacral chakra houses our sexual appetites and inhibitions. It is dedicated to the expression of creativity, to the expansion of sexuality, and to the primal pull of the moon and the waves. It is a very feminine energy center that helps us nurture

Figure 3: Sacral Chakra

ourselves and others, celebrate our innate sexuality, access our deepest emotions, and receive the blessings and abundance of the universe.[17]

Besides being associated (in my eyes) with the sacral chakra, amber helps with all sorts of physical, mental, and spiritual ailments. Amber purifies the mind, body, and spirit when it is worn and cleanses any space when it is burned. It can sharpen the mind, assisting in making decisions and in retaining memory. It is a calming stone that can aid in balancing male and female energies. With this in mind, it is often used in the renewal and keeping of marriage vows. Amber helps us when dealing with abuse, negativity, or emotional blockages. It assists the body in letting go of the past and creating anew. Physically, it will strengthen the thyroid, inner ear, and neurological tissue.[18]

So, taking in all the wonderful qualities of amber and its connection to the sacral chakra, what better way to connect with Freyja than through a necklace of amber? Amber can be expensive but you can choose to craft your own amber "Brisingamen" with a few choice amber pieces, accented with jet or silver beads. (Jet is another stone found at the gravesites of ancient Norse peoples.) Or you can purchase an amber pendant and dedicate it to the goddess Freyja and all she represents. Since the heart is a symbol associated with Freyja, you might consider getting a heart-shaped pendant. Once you have made or purchased your "new Brisingamen," light some amber incense and run the necklace through the smoke. You can also dab some amber oil on the necklace or pendant. While you do this, think about Freyja and all the attributes of the sacral chakra and the gemstone amber. If you have some specific aspect of love you'd like to work on, state that out loud. If not, simply state your intention to connect with Freyja.

RITUAL FOR LOVE:
ALLOWING LOVE TO ENTER

Suggested Ritual Days

February 13–15: Lupercalia, a fertility festival, as celebrated in Ancient Rome

February 14: Valentine's Day, as celebrated in the United States

May 1: Global Love Day, as proclaimed by The Love Foundation, whose motto is "Love Begins With Me"

---

17. Simpson, *The Book of Chakra Healing*, 49.
18. Permutt, *The Crystal Healer*, 42; and Meplon, "Amber."

June 12: *Dia dos Namorados* (Day of the Enamored/Day of Boyfriends and Girlfriends), as celebrated in Brazil

September 20: *Dia del Amor y la Amistad* (Day of Love and Friendship), as celebrated in Colombia

Any Friday: Friday is "Freyja's day"

Items needed

heart-shaped, rose-scented floating candle
a lighter
heart-shaped pendant or token
bowl of water

This ritual gives you the ability to open up to love. Whether asking for that "special someone" to enter your life or wishing to reconnect with the idea and passion of love itself, this ritual seeks to send your desire for love into the universe, where it will be heard and made manifest. Think of this ritual as a re-dedication to the art of love. You are remembering the power of love to bring pleasure and satisfaction and depth into your life.

Once you have collected all of your items, choose a Friday when you feel relaxed, peaceful, and happy. If this is an impossibility due to your everyday stresses, do this ritual on the next Friday that you have available! You really need this time to connect with love! Now!

Gather your items in a place that is warm and relatively secluded. Outside, amid the trees or by a stream or on the beach would be perfect, but if the weather is inclement, perform the ritual in a room that is free of daily hustle-bustle. You could try your bedroom or meditation room. Take some deep cleansing breaths and focus only on your breath. Feel the breath moving into your body and then, as you exhale, out of your body. Concentrate only on the breath. If you find this difficult, you can try thinking "breathe in" on the inhale and "breathe out" on the exhale.

As you do this, you will find that your mind tries to wander away from the breathing. Gently nudge it back to the breath and away from everyday concerns, worries, and plans. This exercise is meant to bring you into the present and into your body, aligning the body with the mind. (This is known in some Buddhist practices as "mindful breathing." You can learn about mindfulness as a spiritual practice in the writings of Thich Nhat Hanh.)

Once you feel your mind and body shift and come together, place the candle in the bowl of water and light it. Continue breathing mindfully, taking in the aroma of the candle. With the breath in mind, begin to "take in" positive thoughts about love and breathe out negative concepts. You may, for instance, breathe in warmth and breathe out jealousy; breathe in laughter and breathe out anger. You can do this for as long as you want, individualizing the practice to coincide with your particular experience with love. You may actually breathe in and breathe out particular deeds that occurred during various loves in your life. You should take care, however, not to breathe in the essence of another individual. This ritual is for you and you alone. Be sure to breathe only experiences and sensations that were and are completely yours.

After breathing for some time, dip the heart-shaped pendant or token into the bowl of water. While holding on to the pendant or token, continue breathing with love in mind, breathing in the positive and breathing out the negative. When you feel ready, take the pendant or token out of the water and place it on your body—around your neck, in your shoe, around your wrist, or in your pocket. Know that the pendant is a physical reminder of your ability to connect to the idea of love and that by wearing it, you are a part of love itself. You radiate love.

You can repeat this ritual as often as you would like, recharging your pendant or token with the power of love. Often, you will be able to recall the benefits of love through the practice of mindful breathing, which can be done at any time and in any place.

CHAPTER FIVE

Goddess Mantras for Self-Love

SELF-LOVE: THE HEART OF TRUTH

If there is one issue, one vexing, niggling, worrisome item deep in our psyches that affects all other aspects of our lives, self-love would be it. Simple to understand in philosophical terms but so hard to implement in everyday life, self-love rules our thoughts, our emotions, our words and actions. Full of self-love, we stride forward to greet the world and all its myriad faults and foibles. We are ready to embrace life in all its messy grandeur. Without self-love, our foray into the world isn't quite so jocular. We are unsure, questioning, and anxious. We enter new situations with trepidation, waiting for the belly-punch, ready to duck and weave in an effort to avoid being pummeled. In fact, we expect the pummeling and sometimes even search it out. We begin to believe that we deserve the pummeling. After all, we've been pummeled before; it must be our lot in life. We shrug, accept, and trudge through like a stalwart soldier, but we're not having any fun.

By now you might be wondering how self-love can be the miracle cure to fix your life. (And you should be wondering, because if we could all love ourselves, we'd all be a heck of a lot happier and a lot less inclined to drag others down into the dark abyss with us.) Let's look at self-love rationally. Self-love indicates a love for the self, for the body that is right now sitting down on the sofa, the commuter train, or the outside lawn furniture and reading this book. That, by itself, is huge! You are taking time to do something special for yourself, an activity that means something to you. Reading this book! Bravo! You have taken one small step toward accessing and re-affirming your self-love.

Now imagine if you loved yourself enough to make yourself happy, all the time. You would make choices and base decisions according to your life preferences. Not on the interests of your mother or best friend. Not on old insults thrown at you by angry high school girls or boys. Not on your significant other's concepts of a good time. On *your* ideas, *your* inclination, *your* intuition. You would live life for yourself. Now some people might see this way of life as extremely self-centered but I would say that it is actually exactly the opposite. When you make decisions based on self-love, you free yourself from the baggage of jealousy, tension, and guilt. You give to others not because you are *forced to*, out of necessity, but because you *want to*, out of an overwhelming extension of grace.

Taking the example of a harried, stay-at-home mother, we can see the concept of self-love in action. Mother of twin toddler boys with a husband who works sixty hours a week, this woman, we'll call her Janet, spends her time watching *Sesame Street*, cleaning up toys and dirty clothes, doing laundry, playing Hi Ho! Cherry-O, refereeing arguments, smashing trucks into blocks, going grocery shopping, playing on the playground, and cooking, cooking, cooking. Her every activity revolves around her children and her home life. She is on auto-pilot, doing what needs to be done in order to provide security and comfort to her children and her significant other. And she is bored. Her adult interaction is limited to a few polite words at the check-out counter of the grocery or toy store. She is alone with her children for a large portion of the day.

After a few months or years (the threshold is different for everyone), Janet begins to feel resentful of her situation. She starts yelling at the twins on a regular basis. When her husband comes home, she is cranky and irritable. Communication ends. Their sex life suffers. Janet feels more and more alone. Her resentment grows until it becomes the only feeling inside her. Things look bleak. Now is the time for Janet to really take a long, hard look at herself and decide what is missing in her life. She needs to find out what will make her happy. She needs to honor herself and her interests just as she honors the interests and preferences of her family. (You know those pepperoni slices and arcade marathons aren't for her.) The first step in Janet's recovery is to decide what she can rationally implement in her life that will help her say, "Yes! Life rocks!" Perhaps Janet gets a part-time job at her favorite store. Maybe she signs up for yoga at a local gym that provides babysitting. It doesn't matter what Janet decides to do, as long as it is for herself. Within a few weeks, Janet's resentment fades. She once again enjoys spending time with her children. She is relaxed and happy when her significant other returns from work. She no longer feels forced into a role that is binding and restricting. Instead, she embraces it as only one aspect of her glorious, lovely self.

Now, what kind of changes could Janet make if she expanded her self-love even further? Perhaps she tackles a project she's been meaning to take on—a shed in the backyard, a new faucet in the kitchen, a fancy dinner of quail. And she succeeds. Her success further builds her love of self and she chooses to pursue her life-long dream of running a catering business or creating a you-can-fix-it school for women and girls. Maybe she develops a brand-new approach to education, based upon hands-on techniques that work for her. And this system evolves into a local alternative school that gets press coverage and, eventually, lands on the desk of the state education director who finds the courage to implement it in several schools. Could Janet, in truth, craft a revolutionary method of education? Absolutely. Could she have done it without self-love? Absolutely not!

Without self-love, we refuse to see the beauty and wonder of our innate selves. We give up on ourselves, blocking our truths, gifts, and skills. We feel we have little to offer to the world. In fact, we believe the truth we are telling ourselves: we are not worthy. In order to change our lives, to truly enjoy life, we need to stop the self-deprecating mantras that repeat over and over inside our heads. And we need to act. You can carry a rose quartz and state positive affirmations until your face is blue, but if you don't act on your newfound self-love, you really haven't found anything. Action and movement are at the core of self-love.

Self-love begins in the womb. Children emerge from the womb completely comfortable with themselves. Babies look in the mirror and, recognizing themselves for the first time, gurgle and smile with glee. I imagine them thinking, "How cool! That's me!" But over time, the influence of others strips away our initial love of self. We don't have the right bodies, sneakers, hair styles, clothes. We look different, think different, talk different, worship different. And, so, we change ourselves in order to "fit in" and blend with the crowd. How ridiculous!

Self-love stems from recognizing that you are perfect just the way you are and that you have unique gifts that only you can offer to the world. As adults, we need to slough off all the old influences that taught us to think badly of ourselves. We need to return to the beautiful innocence of youth, when we were so excited and awed by the image of ourselves in the mirror. We can talk and lecture about self-love, but the truth is that it will not change our lives for the better until we take steps to implement it. Only through action can we see the positive effect of one small change in our lives. Like Janet, our mythical harried housewife, her choice to leave the house and do something for herself, no matter how small, led to a huge shift in attitude. These attitude adjustments then created space for achievement and confidence. She was no longer focusing her attention on the negative—what she didn't have: choosing instead to work with the positive—what she could have. This subtle change in outlook affected her family life, but also extended her reach into the outside world. Suddenly Janet was creating her own opportunities, *because she believed she could do it*. She always had the ability; she just needed to believe in herself. She just needed to love herself. If we all truly expressed self-love on a daily basis, we could affect positive change on a huge scale. And we'd all feel good while doing it.

ENERGY RETURN

The one down-side to bolstering self-love is becoming enmeshed in the trap of egoism. When accessing your love of self for the first time in years, it can become easy to adopt a my-way-or-the-highway attitude. You begin to pay attention to your own needs, sometimes at the expense of others. The essence of self-love is the spreading of love to others, not the winnowing away of their possibilities to make room for the blossoming of your own. Self-love is not selfish love. In fact, it is the very opposite. As your dreams come to fruition, you work to help others achieve self-love and success. You are so comfortable within your own self that you want to perpetuate this wonderful feeling by helping others achieve it.

If you find that you are ripping and tearing others down so you can attain your life vision, take a moment to assess the situation. You may find that you haven't *really* found self-love yet. You may be combating old influences that you haven't fully released. At this point, stop outward movement to manifest self-love and instead revert to inward movement. Instead of working to achieve a goal or dream in your life, focus on yourself only. In other words, what small thing can you change in your life to make you happier? Maybe it's getting TiVo so you won't miss your favorite shows or perhaps it's switching to an organic diet. Maybe you decide you'll indulge in your favorite tea once a day or in meditation once a week. These activities have no purpose other than to make you happy. A shocking statement, I know, but the truth, nonetheless. This is where your rediscovery of self-love should begin—with the self. Leave the goals and desires and dreams alone for the moment and focus on the wonderful, engaging, beautiful being that is you.

VENUS OF WILLENDORF
Paleolithic Goddess of Self-Celebration

MANTRA

I am here.
See me.

The Venus of Willendorf statuette was found by archeologist Josef Szombathyin in 1908 in Willendorf, Austria, approximately 30 feet above the Danube River. Unearthed with several other finds from the site, at about 4½ inches tall, she is probably the most recognizable female figure from the Upper Paleolithic period. The Upper Paleolithic period is the third and last subdivision of the Paleolithic or Old Stone Age and spans about 39,000 years, from 50,000 BP to 11,000 BP. (bp indicates "Before Present," taking the present at 1950 when radio carbon dating began.) Such huge swaths of time are hard to comprehend. After all, the United States as a country has been in existence for less than 250 years, a mere drop in the bucket when compared to the Upper Paleolithic. Due to the length of time, the vastness of the planet Earth, and the differing climates around the planet, it is difficult to make generalizations about this time period and the people who lived during it. Therefore, it is important to see the Venus of Willendorf as a specific example of art, possibly sacred art, created in a specific place for a specific purpose.

The Venus of Willendorf was found in Austria but may have been made someplace else. She is crafted from fine porous oolitic limestone, a form of limestone that is usually formed in warm, shallow seas. It is not found in the region around Willendorf and thus it has been surmised that the Venus figurine was carved someplace else and transported to Austria. This is not surprising since at the time the Venus figurine was carved, around 22,000 BP, the northern reaches of Europe were gripped in a huge glacial mass that extended down to present-day Germany and Poland.

Although Austria was not entrenched in ice, the region was experiencing cold temperatures and a steppe-tundra vegetation. In a steppe-tundra climate zone, vegetation grows at 50 percent of what is seen in modern-day tundra environments. Only found during the Upper Paleolithic period, the region would have been characterized by sparse low-lying vegetation, few shrubs and trees, and soil with a low organic content. In this environment, there would be few opportunities for a rock to be formed in a low, shallow sea. However, Morocco experienced a warm, rainy, temperate climate, called the Mousterian Pluvial, from 50,000 BP to 30,000 BP. Since limestone caves and deposits have been found in Morocco, a country that is but a short leap away from Spain and Europe, there is a possibility that the oolitic limestone came from there. As recently as 2007, small, oval, Nassarius Mollusk shells were found at a limestone cave at Taforalt in Eastern Morocco.[1] Probably used for ornamentation as beads, they are especially important for the Venus of Willendorf because they were colored with red ochre, a pigment also found in trace amounts on her statuette.

The Venus of Willendorf figurine is most noted for its corpulence. Let's face it, she's fat. She has large, pendulous breasts, a wide, flat bottom, a rotund stomach, and thick thighs. The main portion of her bulk is focused on the torso, as her legs taper into small stumps and her arms are thin and spidery in appearance. Because of her thin arms, some modern goddess-lovers have labeled her as pregnant rather than fat. This concept, I feel, has more to do with our own current cultural mindset than the actuality of the statue. The Venus of Willendorf is round and—when compared with Neolithic pregnant, Earth Mother goddess figurines—has different aspects of her body emphasized. Her hands rest on her breasts, not on her stomach, as pregnant statues often show. Her breasts and buttocks are exaggerated, whereas the pregnant statues display only exaggerated stomachs. As noted archeologist Marija Gimbutas explains, "Even the famous 'Venuses' of Willendorf and Lespugue are probably not pregnant. Their breasts and buttocks are the focus of attention, not their bellies."[2]

If the Venus of Willendorf is not pregnant, then her association with fertility becomes tenuous. The Earth Mother goddess figurines, with their oversized stomachs, represent the Earth and its ability to grow seeds into food to eat. They are the soil that is nurtured by the rain and gives forth a bounty. Before the Neolithic era, there was no farming among early man. Instead, during the Paleolithic period, the time when the Venus of Willendorf was created, humans hunted and gathered their food. They did not plant seeds and harvest crops. Therefore, a fertile Earth Mother goddess would be of little use to the men and women of an Upper Paleolithic hunter-gatherer society. They

---

1. Oxford, "Discovery of Oldest Human Decorations."
2. Gimbutas, *The Language of the Goddess*, 141.

would have no reason to honor the Earth as bountiful because, in a steppe-tundra environment and a hunter-gatherer society, she would give them little nourishment.

So, if the Venus of Willendorf is not a fertility goddess connected to the Earth and agriculture, what is she and what was her purpose? One theory suggests that she was a wealthy woman who paid to have her likeness preserved on a piece of stone.[3] Although possible, I find this theory to be improbable due to the number of Venus figurines with large breasts and buttocks that were crafted around the same time as the Venus of Willendorf. Found in the Czech Republic, France, and Italy, they display very similar body shapes yet were found across Europe. Could one artist have trudged through the cold, by himself, to visit these disparate but same-shaped rich people and craft the figurines? Possible, but it is highly improbable that they were the creation of one individual with a fat patroness. Another theory concerning the Venus of Willendorf indicates that she may have been linked to menstrual cycles, due to the tracings of red ochre on her statue and the prominent display of her vulva.[4] Since the Venus of Laussel, a limestone carved drawing, painted with red ochre and possessing a similar body shape, is also sometimes seen in connection with the menstrual cycle, it is a tantalizing theory. However, I wonder how important a woman's menstrual cycle would have been to a Paleolithic spiritual artisan in the middle of a glacial period.

One of the most difficult aspects of studying pre-history is that people left lots of items and carvings, but no instructions on how to interpret them. We are left with fascinating deposits of tools and baskets and weapons but no instruction manuals. It is up to us to determine their function and importance, based on knowledge and conjecture. We can never *really* know what the lives of our Paleolithic brethren were like. We can only make educated guesses. With that in mind, let's take a moment to try to rationalize the priorities of our Paleolithic ancestors.

Living in a glacial period, life would have been cold. Although they probably possessed fire, they didn't have the tools or the skills to create warm, toasty, insulated houses. Our ancestors would have spent a lot of time outside, in chilly weather, without the comfort of returning to a warm home. According to the Quaternary Environments Network, the average temperature in August would have been 42 degrees Fahrenheit,

---

3. Witcombe, "Venus of Willendorf."
4. Ibid.

dipping down to 13 degrees Fahrenheit in February.[5] Chilly. I think we can pretty convincingly state that warmth would have been one of their priorities, even if they were accustomed to the frigid weather. After all, frostbite is frostbite. The second and perhaps the most important priority for our Paleolithic ancestors would have been food. Living in a steppe-tundra is not an easy existence. Generally categorized as arid, sparse, and mostly treeless, the most common form of vegetation was in the Artemisia family.[6] These hardy plants produce volatile oils and grow well in dry or semi-dry areas. The most common herbs in the Artemisia family are wormwood, mugwort, sagebrush, and tarragon. Bitter in taste, these plants would have been edible, if not especially tasty, for Paleolithic humans. Luckily, our ancestors would have supplemented these herbs with fresh meat, typically bison, horse, and mammoth.

If our assumptions are correct and ancient Paleolithic man concentrated a majority of his energy on keeping warm and well-fed, it only stands to reason that a well-dispersed female goddess figurine would have something to do with these priorities. And the Venus of Willendorf is fat. Abundantly fat. Luxuriously fat. When viewed through the mindset and life priorities of our Paleolithic ancestors, she is the epitome of all their wants and desires. She obviously gets enough to eat and, thanks to that occurrence, is well insulated from the cold of the steppe-tundra. Bonus! It's a win-win situation. Also, her large breasts and large thighs and large buttocks are reminiscent of a staple food in Paleolithic times—the mammoth. The mammoth was the largest mammal in Europe at that time and it has numerous evolutionary features to protect it from the cold. Its skin is surrounded by a layer of blubber and secretes an oily fat in order to coat the hair and seal in warmth. The teeth of the mammoth were "composed of a set of compressed enamel plates that are held together with cementum" in order to withstand the wear and tear of eating coarse vegetation, like grass.[7] These teeth layers look surprisingly like the hair-do or cap resting on the top of the Venus of Willendorf's head. Could she be connected to the mammoths, due to their importance as food and warmth to early man? We will probably never know but it is fun to speculate.

In any event, whether a goddess of the mammoths or of the hunt or of the realization of all early human's desires, the Venus of Willendorf is a wonderful, abundant god-

---

5. Adams and Faure, "Europe east to 40 degrees E (the Urals), and including Asia Minor."
6. Ibid.
7. Illinois State Museum, "Mammoths."

dess. Obese, covered in body fat, the Venus of Willendorf is unashamed by her appearance. After all, she is the symbol for all her people's wishes and desires. It is she they call on to make their lives better. The Venus of Willendorf looks the way she does because she is the carrier of all Paleolithic people's hopes and dreams. Only a truly large woman would be able to give so much back to her community. Only a very large woman would be able to provide heat and food for all.

A larger-than-life goddess, the Venus of Willendorf connects us to our ancient past and reminds us that we can achieve all our wishes. Imagine the surprise of our Paleolithic ancestors upon entering a grocery store or feeling the intrinsic warmth of an electrically heated home. We live their dreams every day; we no longer have the daily and hourly worries of warmth and food. Perhaps it's time for us to show gratitude for these wonderful realities in our lives. Perhaps it's time to thank and honor the Venus of Willendorf, who heeded her children's cries. Perhaps it's time to put away our dismay over our own bodies, our shame over not fitting a culturally specific model of beauty. The Venus of Willendorf is beautiful exactly as she is created, just as each one of us is beautiful exactly as we are.

Pathway to Venus of Willendorf

Venus of Willendorf luxuriates in her existence, serving as a reminder to her people of a better life, free of worries. For many of us in the modern era, we labor under different but no less debilitating worries than our Paleolithic ancestors. But, like them, we can find solace in the ample arms of the Venus of Willendorf.

On our quest for self-love, one of the first things we need to remove is our shame—shame over our bodies, shame over our past choices, shame over past actions. Sometimes our shame stems from ourselves and sometimes it stems from the words and actions of other people. No matter where it begins, the feeling of shame can end with each one of us. We do not need to carry around that excess baggage, those stories that are no longer our true selves and our true visions. People try to tell us who we are all the time but you—and only you—can know your true self and live your authentic life.

So, in beginning the process of removing shame (and yes, this may take awhile), we will make a True You Mirror. First, assemble the following items, which can usually be found at your local craft store: a mirror with a wooden frame around it; four small pictures of the Venus of Willendorf; school glue or decoupage glue; magazines, pictures, and stickers; scissors; and any other crafty items such as glitter, ribbon, or googly eyes.

Once you've gathered your items, glue the Venus of Willendorf pictures on each of the four corners of your mirror. These will remind you that beauty is always in the eye of the beholder. Hold yourself as beautiful. After gluing the goddess images, look through her eyes at the magazines and cut out pictures of things that appear beautiful to you. Be sure to include things that remind you of your own accomplishments and achievements. Don't be afraid to find old pictures of yourself as a child, as well as current pictures of you and your family and friends. Lay out all these pictures, along with the decorative items, on your mirror and glue them into place. This is your individual mirror of accomplishment and beauty. Look what you have done! Look what you can do! Look at who you are! You are bountiful and wondrous!

Every day look into your wonderful True You Mirror and smile at yourself. Glance at the Venus of Willendorf in each of the corners and know that beauty exists inside, as well as outside. You are a gorgeous individual, rife with an infinite number of possibilities. Tell yourself that all those shameful thoughts are old stories, no longer helping you become your most vibrant self. Refuse to believe in those old stories. Refuse to even hear them. Replace them with new stories, written by yourself, with the aid of the Venus of Willendorf and your True You Mirror.

HINA
Hawaiian Goddess of Self-Liberation

MANTRA

Rainbow Woman,
Running deep,
Follow your feet to the moon.

Hina is a Polynesian goddess, which means that her stories can be found on many of the islands of the South Seas. Legends of Hina abound on Tahiti, Hawaii, and New Zealand, as well as on lesser known Polynesian islands such as Mangaia, Tuamotu, Samoa, the Hervey Islands, Tonga, and the Paumotan Islands.[8] Each Hina story lends itself to the

---

8. Westervelt, *Legends of Maui*, chapter 15, "Hina, The Woman in the Moon."

culture from which it originates, leading to a multifaceted goddess. Hina is connected to corals and spiny creatures found therein, the making of tapa (traditional cloth created from tree bark), the moon, the sunrise and sunset, chanting, hula, surfing, fishing and fishermen, seaweed, and on and on. The list is practically endless. There is even an aspect of Hina that is seen as a mermaid! Indeed, each of these facets of Hina is differentiated from the others through the adjectives attached to her name. So Hina of the corals is *Hina 'opu hala ko' a* (literally, Hina stomach passing coral) and Hina of the fishermen is *Hina puku i' a* (Hina gathering seafood).[9] These differentiated Hinas are often said to be sisters or daughters of the goddess simply named Hina. However, these "*sisters and daughters* are often to be understood as manifestations of the same deity in several forms, each of which has its own distinct place in myth and ceremon[y]."[10]

Due to the breadth of information on the goddess Hina, I have opted to focus on her well-known Hawaiian stories. In Hawaii, Hina is the grandchild of Kai-uli and Kai-kea (Dark Sea and Light Sea) and seems to have been born from herself (or, at least, a Hina with a different adjective) and her younger brother, Ku-kea-pua.[11] Her most important lineage stems *from* her, as she is the mother of the Hawaiian demi-god Maui, who is a trickster and hero in the mythology. There is no one man to whom she is connected romantically. Akalana is sometimes said to be Maui's father, as is the god Kanaloa.[12] A completely separate and unique story ties Hina to the warrior and storyteller Ai-kanaka.[13] (Remember, these are simply the Hawaiian men and gods to whom she is connected; numerous other Polynesian myths have Hina as wife and lover to other mystical creatures and men.) Hina, as a goddess, appears to be complete unto herself, having no solid tie to any one divine male entity. In a quest for self-love, this is important, for Hina listens to her own needs and chooses her companions as she wishes. There is a sense of freedom and a measure of self-care built into the very core of the Hina myths. She is as flexible and fluid as the tides of the ocean or the phases of the moon.

Indeed, one of Hina's symbols is the moon, and the moon plays an important role in her most well-known story, "The Woman in the Moon." In this story, Hina has already

---

9. Springs, "Hawaiian Goddess Hina."
10. Beckwith, *Hawaiian Mythology*, 223.
11. Westervelt, *Legends of Maui*, chapter 15.
12. Ibid., chapter 1.
13. Thompson, *Hawaiian Myths of Earth, Sea, and Sky*, 76.

birthed Maui and is married to a man known as Aikanaka, a fierce warrior but not a particularly helpful husband. When he is away, Hina spends her days taking care of herself, with daily visits from her son Maui to lighten the workload, And the work is considerable! She must gather water in her calabash (or gourd), start and tend the cook fire, pound poi, make tapa, and (on important days) tend the fire of the earth oven or imu. She is busy, but Hina does not despair because she enjoys island living and is heartened by her son.

When Hina's husband returns, however, he brings with him a dark cloud and fretful personality. Always complaining, Aikanaka wants to direct his wife's work without ever pitching in to help. He spends his days telling stories while Hina must mend his clothes, get him water, and prepare his meals. He never helps with gathering water or firewood and is always cross. Finally, the day arrives when Hina is thoroughly sick of her home situation and can endure no longer. Aikanaka tells Hina that he wants shrimp for dinner and orders her to use his nets to catch some. When she reaches the water's edge, Hina sees a lovely rainbow forming before her. In that instant, she decides to leave behind her life on Earth and she begins to climb the rainbow.

Being a goddess, Hina has no difficulty walking up the rainbow, but as she nears the sun, the heat and intensity become too great for her to bear. (The sun in Hawaiian mythology is often depicted as being greater than the gods who walk the Earth, such as Maui and Hina.) Hina falls down to the Earth and lies on the ground, completely exhausted, covered in blisters and boils and burning with fever. She stays there for the rest of the day, unable to move, unable to do anything but rest and recover. At moonrise, Hina feels her strength returning, and picking up the shrimp nets, starts for home. On her way, she meets Aikanaka on his way back from filling the calabash at the spring. He is angry because he had to go fill his own calabash and he is complaining about the slothful nature of his wife. Without a word of excuse to her husband, Hina grabs the calabash and drains its entire contents. With a roar of rage, Aikanaka raises his hand to strike Hina. As she steps back to avoid the blow, Hina sees a moon rainbow forming. And, suddenly, she knows what she has to do.

Still without speaking, Hina steps around her husband and retrieves her favorite calabash and tapa board and beater from their cave. Then, with sure and steady steps, she approaches the moon rainbow and begins to walk up it. Enraged, Aikanaka lunges for Hina but the rainbow will not support his weight. Still, he is able to grab her ankle in an effort to hold her to him. Hina, however, kicks out and escapes, badly twisting her ankle. (Some versions say her leg was broken.) Limping, the goddess travels up into the sky where she lives forevermore among the stars and the moon and the clouds. On full moon nights, if you look up at the moon over Hawaii, you can just make out her form on the moon, with her calabash, tapa board, and beater resting right next to her.

This story of Hina has obvious overtones of domestic abuse, awful living conditions, and disrespectful individuals who do not honor a person's Goddess-given worth. It would be easy to slap Hina into the category of disenfranchised women and be done with her. However, Hina is a varied goddess, a goddess of action who works to help herself and her people. Movement is a key factor in understanding Hina's personality. She does not sit by and allow things to happen; she works to create her own reality in a life that she aspires to and will enjoy. Words are another key factor to understanding Hina. She often uses her voice to craft her ideal life and to change her situation. Another version of the story "The Woman in the Moon" tells of Hina chanting incantations after her ankle is twisted (or broken), in order to be accepted by the night and the stars and the moon. Naturally, she is made welcome and aided by these powers of nature, eventually creating her home on the moon.

A further story that illustrates Hina's affinity for words and action is entitled "The Monster Mo-o," or "Hina and the Wailuku River." In this story, Hina lives by herself behind Rainbow Falls, beside the River Wailuku on the Big Island of Hawaii, near Hilo. You can actually visit the location of this story if you walk along the Wailuku River in Hawaii. Here we see Hina living behind the rainbow mist of the falls (again with the rainbow!) and creating tapa, content in her life. Her son Maui lives nearby but is often off on adventures. Such is the case when this story begins. Above the Rainbow Falls, farther up the river, lives a large lizard-like dragon named Kuna, who is attracted to Hina. In the story, Hina spurns his advances until finally his love turns to hatred and he begins to pester her and seek to hurt her. He throws dirt, logs, and stones into the river so they must pass by Hina's home and either harm her or block up the river and flood her home. Hina remains unscathed until one night, Kuna throws a massive boulder into the river's gorge below Hina's home. The water has no place to go and begins to rise, eventually flooding the home of the goddess.

At this point in the story, Hina does one of two things. In one version, Hina uses her voice and calls for her son, Maui. "Again and again her voice went out from the cave. It pierced through the storms and clouds which attended Kuna's attack upon her. It swept along the side of the great mountain. It crossed the channel between the islands of Hawaii and Maui."[14] Hina's voice becomes larger than life, traveling across oceans and many miles to reach the ears of her son. It is only through the opening of her mouth, through the use of her voice, that Hina is saved. She utilizes her power of speech to call for help and save herself. Due to Hina's ability to trust her voice and the power contained therein, Maui does hear her. He arrives at her home, smashes the rock that is creating the flood, chases the dragon, and, eventually destroys it. (Not bad for a day's work!)

The second version of the story describes Hina taking charge of the situation by acting to save herself. After printing designs on a piece of tapa cloth and bringing it to her cave to dry, Hina discovers the flood waters in her home. Grabbing a tapa cloth that she uses as a sleeping cover, Hina rushes outside, only to be confronted by the terrible lizard-dragon. She tries to run but slips along the muddy banks of the river. Kuna inches closer to her. There seems to be no place to escape! Just then, the goddess looks down and notices the tapa cloth she is carrying. Tying a stone around one end of the cloth, she throws it to the other side of the river, causing it to stretch with her goddess power. Then, as the mist and the damp causes the colors to run and form a beautiful cloth rainbow, Hina swings across the river and into the topmost branches of a large tree. She escapes Kuna! Maui, having been warned of the danger at home by a little cloud that serves him, returns to Rainbow Falls and, as in the other story, smashes the rock, chases the dragon, and destroys it.

Stories of Hina, goddess of Hawaii and Polynesia, explode with action and energy. Like the islands of the South Seas, she is an active, assertive goddess. At the same time, she holds great love for her family, her lovers, and her people on Earth. Stories tell of her offering herself (her actual body that can never be destroyed) to provide food for her people. Her enjoyment of her son is obvious, as the two stories related here indicate. After all, he visits her every day and lives right next door. Both of them feel a deep commitment and love for each other. (How many people can say they visit their relatives every day?) Hina also displays great passion and care for her lovers in the other Polynesian stories.

Hina is really as diverse as the rainbow that plays such an important role in her legends and in her cultural environment. Like the rainbow, Hina is about balance—individuality and connection, freedom and commitment, softness and strength, action and

---

14. Westervelt, *Legends of Maui*, chapter 13, "Hina and the Wailuku River."

words. Unable to be categorized or pigeonholed, Hina is all women, everywhere, creator of herself, first woman, defined in her own right. The Hawaiian word for woman is *wahine*, derived from Hina's name. Acknowledging and accepting Hina's power is to realize our own innate rainbow power and ability, if only we make the choice to use our voices and take action, to take action and feel love, to feel love first for ourselves and then for those around us. The life of our dreams hangs before us, just over the rainbow. It is time to walk forward and claim it.

Pathway to Hina

There's nothing like visiting the cultural roots of a particular goddess to understand and welcome her entrance in your life. The very environment of Hawaii explains the relationship of Hina to the land and to us, her people who live upon the land. Without the foliage, the surrounding ocean waves, the humidity, the daily sun and rains of the islands of Hawaii, it is more difficult to grasp the diversity and complexity of this wonderful Polynesian goddess. So, I recommend travelling to Hawaii! Unfortunately, not everyone can drop everything and travel over to Hawaii to experience Hina's wonderful energy and the beautiful Hawaiian Islands. So, we'll have to do the next best thing: bring the Hawaiian Islands to us.

We won't create a Hawaii with the tacky plastic leis and paper tiki decorations found at your local party store, but with a traditional activity of the islands—hula. That's right, hula dancing! And don't tell me you can't do it, because you can! On the mainland, hula is often associated with Middle Eastern dance or bellydance. While both dance styles place an emphasis on the hips, hula is less sensuous and flowing than Middle Eastern dance. Bellydancing is often depicted as sexy, with sweeping circular hip motions, torso undulations, and soft, floating arms. Hula, on the other hand, often sways the hips from side to side and has surprising elements that "pop" the dancer out of fluid motion. In short, like the goddess Hina, hula balances soft and sharp, graceful and strong dance movements. It celebrates the many sides of womanhood.

You can probably find a hula dance school (or halau hula) near you, as they are located in just about every state.[15] However, I personally like the many hula dance videos available, mostly because they are filmed on location in Hawaii and showcase the lovely Hawaiian landscape and weather. There are several on the market, so you have quite a

---

15. Try http://www.mele.com/resources/hula.html for a comprehensive listing.

variety from which to choose. I have had good luck with the "Island Girl" series, hosted by the lovely Kili. These are only thirty minutes in length; the steps are fairly easy to follow and lead you to performing a hula dance at the completion of the workout. There are even child-friendly hula videos (such as "Be a Hula Girl") that will allow you to incorporate your new Hawaiian obsession into your family life.

And don't be surprised if it does turn into an obsession! There is something about Hawaii that is beautiful and raw and brilliant and pure. You can check out the molten lava of an active volcano, explore rainforests, visit comet craters, relax on black sand beaches, dive into turbulent ocean surf, and gaze up at the stars on a lonely, isolated beach. It's a mystical land and it is the home of the goddess Hina.

If you absolutely feel that hula is not for you, you can still experience the wonders of Hawaii with a different form of exercise. There are many videos that are filmed on location in Hawaii. Usually, these are yoga- or pilates-based but, if you look around and do your research, I'm sure you'll be able to find a kickboxing or aerobics workout featuring Hawaii. I have tried and enjoyed Sara Ivanhoe's twenty-minute yoga series, which was filmed on location in Hawaii. You can start there or delve into your own favorite exercise style.

Not into exercise? No problem. Explore another side of Hawaii with the romantic coming-of-age film *Blue Crush*. While not Oscar-worthy film-making, it is a movie that captures the essence of modern day Hawaii and the surf culture prevalent there. My jaw dropped when I saw this movie in the theaters. Having just come home from Hawaii (Oahu and the Big Island), I was surprised at the movie's authenticity. (My husband said the exact same thing to me as soon as the movie was over, so you know it wasn't just a freaky coincidence.) Also, check out the surfing documentaries *Stepping into Liquid* and *Billabong Odyssey*. Although filmed around the world, they have amazing footage of big waves off the coast of Oahu and Maui. Let the images of the waves and sun wash over you, just as the self-love of Hina washes over us all.

CESSAIR
Irish Goddess of Self-Esteem

MANTRA

Flying free,
I'm happy to be me!

Cessair (KAH-seer) is a goddess of manifestation and action, which doesn't, on the surface, seem to have much to do with the concept of self-love. However, when looking at her story, it is obvious that she has a great amount of self-esteem and self-love, which frees her from the shackles of other people's pre-supposed ideas about her. She is truly, wondrously, boundlessly herself and, as such, is able to move beyond traditional cultural roles, even beyond the gates of her homeland, in search for something better. Her story is so astonishing that it could have been accomplished only through belief and love of the self. Her growth and progress begins within. Once love of self is achieved, Cessair is able to truly grow into a goddess, free and liberated.

Cessair's story begins in the East, several years before the biblical flood that changed the world. Cessair is the daughter of Bith and the granddaughter of Noe or Noah, who built the ark according to Yahweh's commands in order to preserve life after the flood waters receded. Unfortunately for Cessair and Bith, they were not allowed aboard Noah's ark. In the text, as collected in *The Book of Leinster* (a collection of poems and narratives compiled by an anonymous scholar around 1160 CE), Noah gives no reason for excluding his son and granddaughter. But he does give them an idea of how to live through the flood. "Rise, said he [and go] to the western edge of the world; perchance the Flood may not reach it."[16] The Lebor Gabala Erenn, a section within The Book of Leinster, states that Cessair took her grandfather's advice and led three ships to Ireland, but only one survived. The other two wrecked on the rocky shores of Erin.[17]

In the account of Ireland's founding as told by Geoffrey Keating in his book *The History of Ireland*, completed around 1634, Noah still gives no reasoning for excluding his family from the ark, and now he offers no viable alternative either. In short, he

---

16. Best, Bergin, and O'Brien, "Lebor Gabala Erenn," verse 27.
17. Ibid., verse 28.

leaves Bith and Cessair to the fate of the waves. Bith, Fintan (a mystical poet, known as the "White Ancient" who lives for thousands of years after the flood), and Cessair take counsel together and Cessair tells them that if they listen to her, she will save them. The men agree and Cessair tells of her plan to turn away from Noah's God by creating an idol and worshipping another deity. Bith and Fintan perform this task and the idol tells them to build a ship and "put to sea"[18] but, unfortunately, this other God[19] does not know the exact timing of the flood, so the Cessairans spend the next seven years and three months living on the ship before reaching Ireland.

Both accounts agree that fifty women and three men survive the voyage from the East and land on Ireland's shores, at Dun na mbarc (or Dun na mRarc) which is now known as Donemark, on Bantry Bay in County Cork. Keating goes on to elaborate their settling at Bun Suaimhne, at the junction of the Suir, Nore, and Barrow rivers.[20] These three rivers exist in Ireland today, in the southeast section of the country, covering massive distances and draining sections of five counties. They enter the sea near Waterford City and Hook Head. Together, they are known as the Three Sisters.

As the Lebor Gabala Erenn and *The History of Ireland* relate the arrival of Cessair and her people from the East, it is important to note the many feminine attributes in the story. First, the people are led by a woman, a woman who is shut out of the religion of the patriarchal God of the Israelites and destined to die. Unlike the quiet and reserved women who worshipped Yahweh in the East, Cessair does not merely accept her fate and agree to drown in an ocean of regretful tears. Instead she wrests the situation from the hands of two very capable men, and casting about for inspiration, suggests a plausible if unorthodox plan—leaving the religion of Yahweh for another deity. To the men of Yahweh, creating and eventually turning to an idol for help was in direct violation of God's edicts, as written in biblical commandments three, four, and five. The Bible is full of admonishments against idol-worship, which proves that such worship still existed. (Otherwise, the writers of the Bible would have forbidden something else!) Numerous ancient idols have been found throughout the Middle East, and one of the most prominent kinds have been ascribed to the goddess Asherah, named Ashtaroth in the Bible.

---

18. Keating, *History of Ireland*, 143.
19. Keating uses the pronoun *he*.
20. Keating, *History of Ireland*, 145.

Asherah was the "Great Mother Goddess" of the Caananites. Small house shrines were often dedicated to her, and communities would celebrate her fertility by erecting large phallic poles or trees. The sacred groves and hill shrines were called "aserah," after her, and it is these locations that were condemned by many of the biblical prophets.[21] Like all mothers, the "Great Mother Goddess" Asherah had diverse interests and skills and her people called on her for a variety of needs. As a mother of seventy children, she was honored for her fertility. Yet, as a deity of a seafaring people, she was also turned to for good travel and calm seas. One of her many titles is "Lady Asherah of the Sea" and her full title, as found in the ancient Syrian city of Ugarit, is Rabat Athiratu Yami, meaning "Great Lady She Who Treads on the Sea." In Phoenicia and Carthage, under the name of Tanith, she is often shown with dolphins or fish.[22] As a mother goddess known to the Israelites, connected to idols and shrines and well-known for her association with the sea, it is not inconceivable to suggest that the idol Cessair crafted was a representation of the goddess Asherah.

No matter what idol was crafted, a strong feminine energy surges through the story of Cessair and her people. Not only are they led by a strong, independent woman, but their company consists mainly of women and they land at a place known as The Three Sisters. The number 3 is often seen as an especially sacred number to the Irish Celts, who divided their world into "sea, land, and sky," and whose deities, such as Brigid and Morrigan, are presented in a triple nature. In fact, the rivers known as The Three Sisters could be aspects of the goddesses of the very land of Ireland—Eriu, Banba, and Fotla— who were, indeed, sisters in the mythology. All of the female aspects of the story relate back to the inescapable fact that without Cessair, there would have been no story to tell. Cessair is the heart of the tale of the First Invasion of Ireland. She spearheads the voyage, taking on roles and learning skills that are antithetical to her culture and her former self. The voyage of Cessair from the East to the West is as much a story about personal growth as it is a story of survival. And, when you think of it, survival and growth are intrinsically entwined. As humans, we grow in order to survive in order to live. Cessair just did it in a splashier way!

After Cessair's people settled themselves at Bun Suaimhne, the difficult task of creating a community began. Fintan, Bith, and a resourceful pilot named Ladra were the only

---

21. Jordan, "Aserah," *Encyclopedia of Gods*, 27.
22. Lilinah, Qadash Kinahnu, "Asherah."

men in Cessair's company and "for peace and for reason,"[23] the women broke up into three household groups, containing one man and either seventeen or sixteen women. The extra woman (perhaps Cessair herself, as she is a member of his household) was given to Fintan, presumably because he was neither "war-like,"[24] like Bith, nor "bold,"[25] like Ladra. Unfortunately for the Cessairians, they arrived on Ireland's shores only forty days before the Flood swept from the East, engulfing the West, including Ireland. All the members of Cessair's party die, except for the resourceful and magical Fintan, who lives for thousands of years more in various shapes and forms. Ladra is the first man to be buried in Ireland and Ard Ladrand is named after him. Sliab Betha is named for Cessair's father, Bith, who died in the mountains, trying to climb higher than the encroaching sea. Cessair, on the other hand, fled to a nook, called Cul Cessrach, where she and her fifty maidens died. Her burial site is often said to be to one of the cairns on Knockmaa Hill in Connacht.

Despite the unfortunate conclusion of Cessair's attempt to escape the flood, her story resonates with power and passion. In order to save her life and the lives of her loved ones, Cessair risks everything. She ignores the edicts of her grandfather's God and creates an idol. She wrests the position of leader from her father and an accomplished magician, in a society where men held authority over women. She leads her people across the globe on what probably felt like an endless search for safe land, leaving her own country and her own customs behind. In the face of adversity, Cessair reshapes her sense of self. She becomes greater than she ever thought possible. Cessair teaches us that only by giving up what we think is necessary can we expand our horizons and grow toward the wisdom and mystery of the Great Goddess. In the end, Cessair, surrounded by her fifty maidens, is welcomed into the loving embrace of the Goddess as a complete woman, fully aware of her innate abilities, skills, and characteristics. She has found her true self.[26]

---

23. Best, Bergin, and O'Brien, "Lebor Gabala Erren," verse 29.
24. Ibid., verse 36.
25. Ibid., verse 29.
26. Much of the story of Cessair first appeared in *Goddess Afoot!*, 128–133. For more information and intimate workings with Cessair, Irish Goddess of Self-Esteem, including a guided meditation and ritual, please see chapter 7 of *Goddess Afoot!*

Pathway to Cessair

Like Cessair, it is time for you to build your boat of self-love and sail it westward, toward wisdom and truth and feeling, toward adventure and risk, toward your wholesome, true self. Don't delay! It's time to step into your destiny! The only things you'll need for this project are one pound of modeling clay in your color of choice, a pin or toothpick, and a flat surface to work on. You might consider using sturdy cardboard to protect the flat surface if you are using your prized dining room table or the newly refurbished wood floors. The cardboard will also serve as a base for your boat of self-love and allow you to carry it to your location of choice. Make sure that you use modeling clay, not air-drying clay—you want your boat to stay fresh throughout its lifetime. Also, you might want to create numerous boats of self-love through the years. Using modeling clay will allow you to recycle the same clay over and over again. (Gotta save that environment!)

Begin by pinpointing some aspects of your life that could use a dose of self-love. Perhaps you are chronically tense and could use a regular massage. Maybe you rarely watch your favorite television programs, opting to give the kids or your significant other their choice of shows. Maybe your self-esteem is shot and you feel worthless. Maybe you don't even respect yourself, never mind your work, and feel you have no skills or abilities. We all have self-doubts and days where our self-confidence flags. Don't beat yourself up when you start assessing your life. Now that you're looking at the situation constructively and objectively, you can do something about it.

After finding four or five life aspects that could use some self-love, think about them one at a time and finish this phrase: *I deserve* _____. At the end of the exercise, you will have four or five *I deserve* phrases, each one corresponding to a particular part of your life that needs self-love. For example, if you are considering your feelings of worthlessness, you might finish your *I deserve* phrase with the words "to go back to school to learn new skills" or "to go to a therapist to find out the root cause of my self-worth issues." Allow yourself some liberty during this part of the activity and write down what first comes to mind. Trust that you know yourself best.

With your four or five *I deserve* phrases in hand, it is time for you to build your boat of self-love. Concentrate on the first thing you feel you deserve, take a hunk of clay (¼ pound works well) and shape it into a long, tubular line. Between 5 and 12 inches long is a good size. It will look like a long, round snake or worm. With your toothpick or pin, write your first *I deserve* phrase on the tubular clay, then mold it into the shape of a boat. (The shape is roughly an oval with points on the skinny ends.) This is the first layer, the bottom rung, of your self-love boat. You will be building your boat up, log-cabin style, by creating round, tubular lines for each *I deserve* phrase and placing them on top of each other. By the time you are finished, you should have a boat with four or five layers, all inscribed with a phrase that serves as a goal for you. These goals are gifts of self-love that you are offering to yourself without prejudice or judgment. Now it is time for you to work toward bringing these gifts into your life, using your self-love boat as a physical reminder of your commitment to yourself. Once you have received the gifts inscribed within your self-love boat, you can dismantle her and store the modeling clay, or craft another self-love boat. The possibilities are endless!

Optional: If you would like to insert a touch of whimsy to your self-love journey while adding energy and positive vibrations, consider performing this additional activity. After your self-love boat is created, anoint each tier of your vessel with oil (any oil, even olive oil from your kitchen, will work). As you touch your finger to each layer, state the *I deserve* phrase out loud, rubbing the oil onto the clay. Just a small amount of oil will be fine. Once all layers are anointed, carry your self-love boat to your computer and go to the homepage for YouTube (www.youtube.com). Now comes the silly part. Search You Tube for the theme song of the television program, *The Love Boat,* the popular hour-long show that ran on ABC from 1977 to 1986. Once you've found it (and there are many versions to choose from), hold your self-love boat between your hands, click the play button on the YouTube video, and sing along to the crooning of Jack Jones. This is truly a step back in time and a way to remind yourself that life is fun and you *do* deserve each and every one of those things on your personal self-love boat. After all, love, especially self-love, is "exciting and new" and one of "life's sweetest rewards." You deserve it! Happy sailing, captain!

RITUAL FOR SELF-LOVE:
AWAKENING YOUR RAINBOW BODY

Suggested Ritual Days

February 14: Valentine's Day

Your birthday: your personal day of power and love, when your mother brought you into the world

May 1: Global Love Day, as proclaimed by The Love Foundation, whose motto is "Love
Begins With Me"

Items needed

lavender essential oil

cleansing or purifying room spray, such as sage or the "Water" elemental vibrational essence myst from Garden of One[27]

CD of your favorite relaxing music

chart or diagram of the chakras

scarf or bandana to cover your eyes

two pieces of rose quartz

Begin by finding a day when you are completely alone. Relax and enjoy doing your favorite activities. Reading, gardening, painting your toenails, skeet shooting . . . it doesn't
matter what you do, as long as you enjoy it. Before the day is too far gone, give yourself the luxury of taking a bath. Pour a teaspoon of lavender oil in your bathwater and
relax in the warm, soothing water. Imagine all your anxieties and worries melting away
into the water and running down the drain. When you are finished with your bath, you
should be calm and focused, able to concentrate on yourself and your needs.

Go into your bedroom and gather all of the other items needed for the ritual. Place
them on your bed, being sure to spray the cleansing room spray all over your room and
on the sheets and coverlets of your bed. The scent should be noticeable but not over-
powering. (It is always best to do a "test spray" a few days before you plan to complete
the ritual. Nothing breaks your concentration like an sneezing attack!) After spraying
your room, turn on your relaxation music, sit (or lie) on your bed, and look at your
chakra chart or diagram. Take some time to *really* notice the colors and attributes of
each chakra. Chakras are energetic centers of the body that help to balance the body,
physically, emotionally, and mentally. When they are open and functioning well, they
spin in a clockwise direction. When they are blocked, they spin backward or not at all.
In Eastern philosophies, any problems we experience can be traced back to our chakras
and their movement (or lack thereof). As you study the chart, notice that the chakras

---

27. You can find Garden of One products on-line at www.gardenofone.com. There are numerous books on the market that include chakra illustrations. For a less expensive alternative,
you can purchase Chart #5 Rainbow Chakra Centers from InnerLightResources.com.

form a rainbow up the body. Try to locate where each chakra would be placed on your own body. Get to know your body in relation to the Eastern concept of the chakras.

When you feel like you know the color pattern and general location of each chakra, put aside the chart and cover your eyes with your bandana or scarf. It is time to go on a guided meditation. You may want to record this meditation for yourself or have a friend or family member read it aloud. It can be done from memory, but people often prefer to hear the guided meditation as they are performing it.

Take a deep breath. In through the nose and out through the mouth. Take another deep breath, filling your stomach, your diaphragm, and, finally, your lungs. Hold this breath for five seconds . . . 1-2-3-4-5 . . . and exhale, allowing the breath to exit your lungs first, then your diaphragm, and finally your stomach. One more deep breath and as you breathe in, feel the energy of the graceful rainbow, guiding and supporting your fingers, your toes, your legs and shoulders, even the top of your head. Hold the breath for seven seconds . . . 1-2-3-4-5-6-7. As you exhale, feel all tension leave your fingers, your toes, your legs and shoulders, even the top of your head. Continue breathing deeply, in through the nose, out through the mouth. Feel the warm sun, the gentle mist, warming and condensing on the exposed parts of your body. Your head. Your face. Your hands. The air is charged with the cleansing power of rain, the soothing touch of the sun. Both are necessary to create a rainbow—water and fire, light and shade. You feel the soothing rays of the sun massaging your weary muscles, re-moving any tension, any stress, any worry. You sigh and the massage moves inward to your soul and your spirit. You breathe deeply and have never felt so relaxed, so secure, so calm.

You are walking along a shoreline on a warm, tropical island. The sand is soft under your feet and the waves lap gently against your toes. The island is small and covered in co-conut and palm trees. They are thick on the island and crowd the tiny beach on which you walk. Although the trees and forest vegetation huddle very close to you, you are not afraid, for they seem like old friends, welcoming you home. Take a moment to acknowledge their presence. Turn away from the sea and face the forest. Pay your respects in whatever way feels right to you. If you feel drawn to a specific plant, tree, or animal, approach it and speak to it. Listen to see if it has a special message for you concerning your quest for self-love.

After honoring the spirits of this island land, you turn, once again, back to the sea and behold a wondrous sight. A glorious rainbow arches full and bright directly in front of your eyes. It is only a hand's breadth away; you can feel its powerful energy tingling all up and down your body. You reach out a hand (pause) and feel a warmth you have only known once in your life. It is like the comfort of a soft, cuddly blanket or the security of your moth-er's womb. You still your movements for a moment and slow your breathing to listen. Do you hear it? The soft, rhythmic thump-bump, thump-bump of your heart? (pause) And there, right below the sound of your own heartbeat, a deeper tone, rich and all-pervasive. It is difficult to distinguish from the eddying waves and the soughing wind and the gentle beat of your own life blood. (pause) But there it is, part of and yet separate from all of those things. Thump-bump. Thump-bump. The heartbeat of the Great Mother—your mother, my mother, all mothers everywhere, gifting life to their little ones.

You bathe in the sound of the heartbeat of the Great Mother, breathing slowly in and out, in and out. As you relax even more, you feel a gentle pushing at your back. It is the wind playing, urging you forward, closer to the rainbow. You obey and find yourself at the foot of a pulsing, brilliant arch of light. Take a moment now to see the colors of the rainbow in all their splendor. Red. Orange. Yellow. Green. Blue. Indigo. Violet. These colors present themselves to you in their most pure form. They are completely, totally their color. Which color are you most attracted to right now? (pause) Remember this information—it will help you in accessing and re-activating your love of self.

When you feel ready, take a step onto the rainbow. This will be the first of seven steps that will take you to the very height of the rainbow. Each step resonates with a different color and thus with a different chakra in your body. The first step is for the color red. Feel the deep, rich, grounding presence of the color red in your body, especially around your base chakra, near your tailbone. It swirls around you and through you, vibrant and full. Lush and intense, you are red and red is you.

Take another step and feel the rush of orange engulf you. Warm and juicy, yet refresh-ing, orange tantalizes you with its tangy scent and saucy texture. It is a luscious orange, a pearlescent peach scarf trailing over your body, a deep, warm carnelian stone in the palm of your hand. Alive and vibrant, orange enters through the very pores of your skin and centers around your lower belly or sacral chakra. Perhaps it forms a flower inside your belly, un-folding to welcome the world.

A third step brings you face to face with the brilliance of yellow. Warm, shining with energy, the color yellow surrounds you, lighting your arms, your face, your legs. Your entire body is drenched in enlivening yellow, fully alive and invigorated. The color settles around your third chakra, at the top of your rib cage, in the middle of your breastbone, and you feel it warming your body, radiating outward in ever-widening circles of warmth.

You take a deep breath and step into green. Cool, moist, refreshing green. Deep green like the densest forest glade, and spring green like the sweetest dappled meadow. The color green swirls around you, smelling of promise and fulfillment, of possibilities not yet realized. You breath it in and feel it settle in your heart chakra, right near your physical heart. There, the color pulses with each heartbeat, growing more and more brilliant with each passing second.

You step again, and enter the freedom and grace of the color blue. Light, ethereal, fresh and clean, blue billows around you in playful eddies and spirals. Clouds of sky blue brush your face and linger in your hair and eyelashes. They tickle your skin. You have a compulsion to laugh and sing, to dance and jump. You open your mouth to breathe it in and the blue plunges into you, resting comfortably in your throat chakra, nestled at the bottom of your throat.

With a skip and a hop, you leave blue and enter the depth of indigo. Soft and velvety, indigo lingers around you, cloaking you in wisdom and understanding. Thick and heavy, the cloak does not weigh you down. Rather it opens you up to the reality of all-that-is. You look at the cloak and see millions of tiny stars twinkling back at you. Indigo is more than meets the eye. You rest in the shade of the lovely color of indigo and feel it enter your body, settling in your forehead, at your third eye chakra.

With deliberation and wisdom, you take the last step, the seventh step, into the color violet. The violet light envelops you, more bright, more luminous then anything you have ever imaged. The color is less a color than a shocking radiance. It is white and pure with tinges of violet along the edges, as if the violet was greater than its color on Earth. It takes your breath away, and, for the moment, your reason disintegrates. You are bathed in pure light. The violet-tinged color rises above your head to settle in your crown chakra.

You are now a being of light, a vision of color. Rising above the seven steps of color, you stand in your own power, feeling the energy of the colors red, orange, yellow, green, blue, indigo, and violet flow through you. (pause) Make note of how you are feeling. This feeling of balance, power, serenity, joy, and grace can be yours all the time. This is your true self, shining and free. This is who you are—beautiful, loving energy. Hug yourself right now, as you stand bathed in color at the top of the rainbow. Love yourself. You deserve love, for you are a wondrous creation of the Great Mother. Allow yourself the time to bask in your greatness and remember your love of self. (pause)

When you feel ready, begin the seven steps back to the beach on the little island covered in coconut and palm trees. At each step, you briefly re-live the colors but you do not lose any of your own colorful brilliance. This is yours. This is who you are! The universal rainbow has enough color for every single being on the planet, so there is no need to give anything back. Step down through brilliant violet. Down through soothing indigo. Down through playful blue. One more step down leads you to luscious green. Down through warming yellow. Down through vibrant orange. Down through the depth of red.

You take one more step and you are once again on the sandy beach. The sun is setting and the trade winds ruffle the palm fronds of the trees nearby. You breathe deeply as the rainbow slowly fades away before you, disappearing from view. (pause) It is gone for right now but it is always available to you. All you need to do is ask for its presence and it will appear, refreshing your innate color power centers, reminding you of your wondrous self. With a smile, you walk back down the beach, heading home.

Now, take a deep breath. In through the nose and out through the mouth. Take another deep breath, filling your stomach, your diaphragm, and, finally, your lungs. Hold this breath for five seconds . . . 1-2-3-4-5 . . . and exhale, allowing the breath to exit your lungs first, then your diaphragm, and finally your stomach. Breathe deeply once more and as you breathe in, feel the energy and the wonder of the world around you in your fingers, your toes, your legs and shoulders, even the top of your head. As you exhale, wiggle your fingers and your toes. Shake your legs and move your shoulders up and down. Take another deep breath and, as you exhale, move your head from side to side. Feel the ground under your body, touching every nerve ending and muscle. Hear the rustlings of the world around you. Notice the movements outside. Continue breathing. Stretch your arms out above your head. You are returning to the present, to the here and now. Continue stretching. Continue breathing. When you are ready, open your eyes, blink and focus, and sit up.

CHAPTER SIX
Goddess Mantras for Forgiveness

FORGIVENESS: RELEASE THE PAST

Forgiveness is one of those topics that no one wants to *really* discuss. We like to couch it in terms of divinity and holiness and sanctity. In the Western world, we are inundated with the concept of Divine forgiveness from an early age. After all, didn't God (a.k.a. Yahweh) give his only son to remove our sins? If that is not the ultimate act of sacrifice and forgiveness, then I don't know what is. Throughout time, saints have worked to emulate the Holy Father's example, enduring unspeakable tortures and still forgiving their transgressors. Even in the modern worship of the Divine Feminine, the Goddess forgives us our petty offenses, seeing them as a small issue (a run, a discarded remnant) in the ever-expanding fabric of the cosmos. Forgiveness, as we have been taught, is something bigger and greater than humanity. It is sacred.

Bull-poop. That's right. You heard me. Bull-poop! Forgiveness is one of the earthiest of actions there is. We do it every day, in the face of large and small catastrophes. Your daughter smacks you a little too hard as she's playing ninja-fighting girl? You forgive her. No questions asked, and often, without even the need for an apology. You happen to be on the tail end of a car crash? Ugh! You despair over the paperwork, but the other driver—you barely give him a second thought. He obviously didn't mean to do it, so you forgive him and move on with the tediousness of the insurance company. The woman who cuts you off in traffic? The harried registry worker who gives you wrong advice? The friend who spills ketchup on your new white suit? Forgiven, forgiven, and forgiven. Why? Because we all realize that we make mistakes. We're not perfect; we're human. There's a world of difference between the two.

So, if forgiveness is such a human action, why don't we talk about it? In a way, it's our ego's fault. Even though, deep down, we know we're flawed, we still want to believe that we're perfect. We don't make mistakes. We have a *plaaaaan*. We know what we're doing and where we're going and everything is going along "according to plan." If we discussed forgiveness, we'd have to admit that sometimes we make mistakes and hurt people, and sometimes the people in our lives make mistakes and hurt us. Mistakes are not part of the plan. Ever.

But, why not? Why are we so wedded to the plan? What makes the plan great enough that we ignore a fundamental aspect of being human? The plan represents our goals, our aspirations, and our ideals. It is the great cumulation of a life of hard work and drive. The spouse, the kids, the house, the picket fence, even the dog are testaments to our worth on this planet. Look what we have accomplished. Look what we leave behind. Are we not worthy? Are we not wonderful?

Of course we are worthy and wonderful, but the plan is not what make us so! The items gathered in following the plan are not aspects of ourselves. The plan is fantastic if it truly makes us happy. However, it also shackles us to a thought process that takes us outside of ourselves. The perfect plan represents what we wish to project to the world. Our success, our happiness, our worth is codified into tangible, materialistic items. But the essence of humanity lies not in the things we possess, but rather in the emotional core at the very center of ourselves. In order to understand forgiveness and welcome it in our lives, we have to relinquish the outward-thinking construct of "the plan" and rely on the inward-thinking concept of ourselves.

Now, I'm not advocating giving up all your goals and dreams and wandering around the Earth living at the mercy of others. What I am suggesting is a release of the stagnant, suffocating energy you have built up in trying to keep up with the Joneses. Every single person on this planet is an individual, unique and wondrous unto himself or herself. So why are we constantly striving to be as good as Joey or Suzie or Gigi or John? Why can we not strive to be as good as ourselves? We can, if only we allow ourselves the luxury of loving our place in the world, right here and right now. Once we begin to release the trappings of the material world, we realize that forgiveness is hard because we want to hang on to the past, just as we want to hang on to our stuff. It is difficult to alter the mindset from outward justification to inward reflection.

And forgiveness is, perhaps, the ultimate release. When a person causes you or someone you love harm, you have two options. You can either: a) hold on to the hurt feelings, keeping them alive until they begin to affect your judgment and choices, or b) release the hurt feelings and live your life according to your inner judgment and wisdom. It's not a difficult decision when stated so boldly. Most people would automatically choose option b, allowing their own individuality and thoughts to steer their life. However, with forgiveness comes hurt, sorrow, and grief—deep emotions that are not easy to assimilate. The Buddhists believe that all of the world's sorrow comes from an inability to accept that the world is transitive, always moving and shifting, being destroyed and created in the blink of an eye. We feel those dark emotions because we long for a past that is no longer available to us. The way is shut. However, around us lies the glorious pathway of the present, if we but choose to open our eyes and see it.

Forgiveness is not easy. We have to accept that someone hurt us or that we hurt someone else. We have to acknowledge that our lives, our very selves, are not perfect, and that we meandered far from "the plan." Everything is not going according to our perfect little plan, and that's okay, because the plan rarely affords us the inner satisfaction for which we long. Yet release of the plan, release of the hurt (whether felt toward another or toward ourselves) is possible. We must acknowledge that we made a mistake and that our lives are not perfect. Once that is done, forgiveness is just a moment away.

ENERGY RETURN

The one pit-fall connected to forgiveness revolves around a sense of self-worth, for forgiveness should not confused with what I like to term the *doormat mentality*. Many people hold on to past grudges because they don't want the other person to be relieved of his/her guilt. This, of course, does nothing beneficial for the affronted party, serving only to perpetuate the emotions of sorrow, guilt, and betrayal. They work to re-live the hurt on a daily basis so they do not fall into the same situation again. They cannot forgive because they are afraid the same thing will happen.

Others forgive easily. They learn to live with transgressions, small and large, not allowing them to linger any period of time in their psyche. They stay in situations that may not be healthy for them, because they are also afraid. They are afraid of change, of standing on their own, of movement beyond the "known" course. These people have a doormat mentality. They experience situations that cause them pain again and again, forgiving again and again. Instead of listening to their inner wisdom, they have removed their voices and hunkered down to withstand the never-ending storm. They have become doormats in their own lives, allowing everyone else to walk all over them.

Forgiveness is not about becoming a shrinking violet or a doormat. We should learn from every experience in life. We need to take stock of what makes us happy and unhappy and then do something with that knowledge. After all, we only come this way once in this incarnation! But, while we need to assess our lives, we do not need to harbor the old hurts and wounds. We can learn from those past actions and, then move on, releasing the pain on airy breezes. Forgiveness is not about chaining yourself to the tried and true. Quite the opposite! It's about release. Release of the hurt, release of the sadness, release of the actions and situations that brought about the pain. Release of the past. Forgiveness is about moving away from the doormat mentality into a glorious world that only you can imagine.

TLAZOLTEOTL
Aztec Eater of Filth

MANTRA
Through voice
And blood,
The chains are released
And forgiven.

It probably seems strange to include a goddess from the blood-loving pantheon of the Aztec Empire in a discussion of forgiveness. Warriors, flayers of skin, destroyers of towns, sacrificers of humans, the Aztecs have a violent and cruel reputation. Perhaps the violence of the Aztecs necessitated a goddess of forgiveness. The strong emotions stoked and unleashed in war could not have been easily subdued in everyday life. What's an energetic, young Aztec warrior to do when his blood boils or he thirsts for illicit love? Some, perhaps, took out their aggression and lust on the field of games. Others, undoubtedly, indulged in a different sort of game with the local prostitutes or the winsome wife next door. (Now, before casting judgment on the Aztecs, consider this statistic that I came across just the other day: In modern America, it is estimated that 22 percent of married men and 14–16 percent of married women will have an affair sometime during their relationship. And that's without the aphrodisiac of a shorter life span and blood sacrifices at the local temple.)

Tlazolteotl is a complex goddess with many forms and functions. In modern times, we tend to equate her with the role of "Mother Goddess." She is, indeed, connected to fertility, midwifery, and healing.[1] She is the mother of the corn god, Cinteotl, and the love goddess, Xochiquetzal. Deeply connected to the welfare of her people through the nourishing aspects of food and love (her son and daughter), Tlazolteotl is one of a group of fertility deities classified as the Teteoionnan.[2] One of the most popular birthing statues accessible to modern women is an image of her as a small statue with an enlarged head, grimacing. Her shoulders and neck appear strained. She is squatting down with her knees bent, as a baby appears between her legs.

As Tlazolteotl is associated with fertility and birthing, it comes as no surprise that she is also thought to be a goddess of love and of the moon. In one of her many incarnations, Tlazolteotl is known as Ixcuina, a love and moon goddess with four aspects. These aspects are sisters and were born in the following order: Tiacapan, Teico, Tlaco, and Xocutzin.[3] It is common for Aztec gods and goddesses to be divided into four aspects, and it is equally common for four aspects to be unified into one god. The differentiation often occurs when one specific deity is seen as resting in each of the four sacred trees at the corners of the universe at the same time. The multiplication of divinity indicates the pervasiveness of the particular deity. In effect, this god or goddess is everywhere; there is nowhere you can go to hide from his/her view. Such is the case with Tlazolteotl.[4]

Although revered as a mother goddess and a fertility goddess, Tlazolteotl's main role in the Aztec pantheon was that of enticer and seducer. She was known to be the "sexy little voice" inside one's head, suggesting all the morally wrong but physically pleasurable acts possible in the world. This darker, alluring aspect of her personality fits with her overall interest in love, fertility, and sex. She understands the baser elements of human sexual interaction, while still encouraging and aiding the positive facets of sex and love. Tlazolteotl embodies lusty, illicit sex and fertile, giving love. In Aztec society, sex out of wedlock was not permitted but happened just the same. Thus, Tlazalteotl became a necessary goddess: a scapegoat who instigated the illegal behavior and an absolver who forgave the penitent individual.

Yet, oftentimes what is necessary is not always well-liked. Tlazalteotl, when in her role as temptress and forgiver, was not a welcome goddess, since her pathway was difficult and

---

1. Ann and Imel, *Goddesses in World Mythology*, 36.
2. Jordan, *Encyclopedia of Gods*, 264.
3. Took, "Tlazolteotl."
4. Carrasco, "Uttered from the Heart," i1 1.

uncomfortable. She forced the transgressor to sublimate to her will (as expressed through her priests) and to give up or remove the ego. Only in this altered, humble state, could she accept the confessed sins and remove them from the individual forever. Indeed, once the sins were confessed, it was as if they had never been committed. This ability to remove guilt and sin and grant absolution (but only once in a lifetime) is the reason why her name means "filth goddess" or "eater of filth." She removes the filth (the sins), making the individual pure and clean. But, remember, Tlazolteotl also urges people to commit such sins in the first place! She needs this filth, these sins to sustain the balance of dark and light, good and evil found in all human intimate relationships, over which she rules. We all have the ability to harm as well as heal, and Tlazolteotl embodies this truth. She is as much a part of human nature as breathing. This balance between dark and light can be seen in her elaborate confession and absolution ritual. It purified the individual, freeing him or her from punishment under Aztec law, but the ritual also involved painful physical and mental punishment that, undoubtedly, lasted until the end of days.

The ritual began when the penitent requested forgiveness of his sins from the priest of Tlazolteotl. The priest would consult his books and calendars and designate a time and date that would hold the most meaning for the energy of the rite. When this day arrived, the priest would arrive at the penitent's house and conduct the ritual there. The Aztecs believed that adultery and illicit sex could create disease for all the members of the family, living and dead. Adultery caused the liver to secret a toxic essence that could send sickness on all members of the household, including children and even innocent bystanders. Thus, the ritual took place in the sinner's household. Once there, the adulterer would disrobe and, completely naked, recount all his sexual misdeeds in the order in which they occurred. This was often likened to a song or a journey along the path of the sinner's life. The telling was rather formal in structure, even though there were no specific words or phrases that needed to be used. "For the Aztecs, the confession, which was the cleaning of one's heart, had to address the amount of phlegm and soil that has covered the heart. It was thought that too much weight of guilt on the heart would drive a person crazy."[5]

Following the confession, which was recorded in a book (the deeds shrouded by the glyphs and symbols), the confessor was given a penance from the priest, which corresponded in severity to the confessed sins. The man or woman was expected to fast

---

5. Ibid.

in order to remove the sin of eating food from the Earth, which was thought of as the death of one thing in order to sustain the life of another. In fact, many of the Aztec sacrificial offerings, including the blood offerings, were done in atonement of living at the expense of some other beings on Earth. Therefore, fasting was the surest way of instigating purity of body and mind, which was the ultimate goal of the confession to the priest of Tlazolteotl. After fasting, the penitent would then be instructed as to the shape and manner of further self-sacrifice. This could involve dancing, singing, or the making of images and it almost always included a sacrifice of blood. Often the sinner was instructed to use straw or reed to pierce his tongue, that which spoke the sins, and to pierce his penis, that which performed the sins. The piercings could be anywhere between 400 and 800 pricks. After the blood-letting, the sinner was led to the temple of Tlazolteotl and told to humbly pray to the goddess for an entire night, in nothing but a piece of paper painted with obsidian points, the emblem of the goddess. On the following day, the sins were no more, having been eaten by the goddess Tlazolteotl.[6]

Leave it to the Aztecs to turn confession into an all-day, blood-letting event! But, seriously, the goddess Tlazolteotl understands guilt and sin and their effects on the sinner and other people in the sinner's life. Through the elaborate confession, the sins are destroyed. The sinner is completely brand-new, purified of all immoral past actions. The raw cotton spindle often depicted on Tlazolteotl's headdress symbolizes the new life of the former sinner. He or she needs no longer hold on to negative actions from the past. Those are forever erased from the heart, mind, body, and soul. Cleansed and pure, the sinner has become as innocent as the newborn babe.

Such is the power of Tlazolteotl. She gives us the freedom of removing the sins of ourselves and of others that affect us. Instead of living with the guilt, shame, rage, and pain, Tlazolteotl suggests we let it go. She wants us to unburden our hearts so we can live in equilibrium with the world around us. She invites us to call on her, to unburden our souls by using our mouths, and allow her to eat our filth. It is not easy to admit one's mistakes, to accept the pain we have caused others or that others have caused us. But it is possible. Release of the sins from our souls and destruction of them at the hands of Tlazolteotl is feasible. This strong Aztec goddess promises self-sovereignty, if only we can give up that which we have always kept buried.

---

6. Ibid.

Pathway to Tlazolteotl

Despite Tlazolteotl's rather dark personality, getting to know her doesn't have to be as painful as, say, sticking a straw or reed through your tongue! It can actually be quite sweet and enjoyable, as well as purifying. It may sound strange to talk about enjoying the company of the "eater of filth," but there is an immense and immediate feeling of freedom upon unburdening yourself to her. You have released your worries to a higher power. The Divine mother of the cosmos, she who sits in all four sacred trees, has taken away your transgressions, as well as the pain and hurt you feel from other people's sins upon you. You are reborn.

Working with Tlazolteotl is neither quick nor easy, but it is worth the effort! If you choose to unburden yourself to this ancient Aztec goddess, you will need to set aside three weeks of time to devote yourself to the process. Don't worry! You won't need to spend every minute of those three weeks thinking about your issues. However, it would be fruitless to begin this pathway in the midst of the hectic holiday season or when your life is in upheaval. You're going to need some down-time to integrate all the wisdom and knowledge you'll be receiving. Pick a time when you have at least two or three free evenings each week.

For the first week, gather some raw organic cacao beans for a frothy, spicy, Aztec drink. Grind up the beans using a cutting board and rolling pin. You can also use a mortar and pestle, if you have one. Make sure the beans have already been roasted so you don't have to worry about their hard, outer shells. I like cacao beans used in "raw" cooking because they haven't been over-heated and still retain their beneficial enzymes. Add the finely ground cacao to cold water, adding "chili water" (or water that has had chili peppers boiled in it), vanilla beans or pods, and honey. Place this mixture on the stove and let it boil while stirring constantly. When it starts to get bubbly or frothy, remove the pan from the heat and let it cool slightly. Repeat the boiling, stirring, and cooling process three more times. When finished, you will have a drink that is similar to the Aztec chocolate drink—rich, bitter, frothy, and thick. The Aztecs drank their chocolate cold, so place the mixture in several coffee or tea mugs and wait for it to cool. Once it has cooled, choose the fullest mug and, going outside at sunset, speak aloud your sins or the sins of those who have hurt you. Allow yourself the time to feel the weight of these events. When you are ready, pour the cup of chocolate on the ground in offering to Tlazolteotl. You have taken the first step in unburdening yourself of these actions.

Feel free to consume and/or share any remaining Aztec chocolate with your friends and loved ones.

Now that you have lowered your defenses and shown your vulnerability to Tlazolteotl, the time has come for a ritual cleansing. It is time to sweat! Some sources state that Tlazolteotl was connected to steam baths, so what better way to cleanse yourself than an afternoon at the sauna? Although this sounds like a monumental task, finding a sauna is actually not that difficult. Many gyms and health clubs offer sauna facilities. If you already belong to one, ask at the front desk or membership office. If not, check out the health clubs in your area. You can go on a private tour. If they have a sauna, ask for a complimentary week-long membership. It'll only cost you the gas of driving there! When in the sauna, focus on driving out any impurities. This is your time to remove the effects of the past, sweating it out through your very pores. Take as much time as you need but don't overdo it. Saunas can be powerful experiences, especially if you're not used to the heat. Take it easy and remember to drink lots of water!

Once you've admitted your pain and removed it through sweat and steam, the time has come to get back to enjoying life! For the third week of your experience with Tlazolteotl, pick a time when you can be alone and watch the movie *Chocolat*, which stars Johnny Depp (ooh la la) and the beautiful Juliette Binoche. This movie has a dual character and purpose. On the one hand, it is a sweet love story, a story about finding love of self, love of place, and love with another. On the other hand, it is very much about the concept of sin and our perception of justice and goodness in the world and in ourselves. In the movie, the chocolate (for which the movie is named) serves to remind the people of a small French village that life is more than fear and drudgery and denial. Indulgence in life, symbolized by the chocolate, allows the people to actively participate in forgiveness—forgiveness of self and forgiveness of others—so they can release the past and move forward toward the future. And did I mention it's got Johnny Depp?

MARY MAGDALENE
Christian Sacred Prostitute

MANTRA

My cleansing tears
Bring joy and peace.

There's something about Mary Magdalene that connects to our stomachs, our pelvises, our wombs. If she's not birthing the rumored child of Jesus Christ, then she is an adulterous woman or a prostitute from the town Magdala, which was known for its "loose women" in Biblical times. But the funny thing about Mary Magdalene is that if you read the Bible, there is no mention of her as a sexual object. She is a messenger, a teacher, an apt listener, a pious follower, and a penitent woman. Her sexuality is conspicuously absent. Yet, sex has become synonymous with Mary Magdalene, thanks in large part to a very influential pope from the sixth century.

In 591 CE, Pope Gregory I began a series of sermons about Mary Magdalene. In these, he put forth the idea that three women in the Bible (one named Mary Magdalene, one named Mary of Bethany, and one unnamed adulteress) were, in fact, the same woman. Under the guidance and interpretation of Pope Gregory the Great (as he came to be known), Mary Magdalene became the epitome of the sinful, repentant woman, who was saved when she met Jesus Christ. Her lessons, her Divine connection, her spirituality diminished and was forgotten, drowned out by Gregory's sordid explanation of her life in the Bible. Indeed, Gregory took a powerful female spiritual leader and reduced her to a sexualized, earthly trollop who was reformed due to her encounter with a pure, heavenly man.

To Gregory, writing during the sixth century, this interpretation of Mary Magdalene made perfect sense. In the Middle Ages, women were relegated to sexually submissive roles in an effort to remove their power and thus their threat to established male-dominated religious sects. Women gave birth, which automatically connected them to sex. Sex, thanks to the story of Adam and Eve, was linked to temptation. Temptation was put forth in the world by the devil and (I'm sure you know where this going) leads to sin. So, women, due to the very nature of their bodies and the human need to reproduce, were products of the devil and sin. This scenario was very convenient for the celibate male clerics who were able (in theory) to give up sex in order to eschew the devil and gain closer access to God the Father and his son, Jesus Christ. If women were intrinsically unable to connect with spirit on a higher level because of their bodies, then the men would not need to compete with them for religious influence (and money). Mary Magdalene became the symbol in the church of the sinful, sexual woman saved through the auspices of pure, male-dominated, asexual spirituality.[7]

Yet in modern times, the passion and sexuality of Mary Magdalene have come into focus and scrutiny once again. Could she have been the wife and lover of Jesus Christ? Did she bear a child of Christ's lineage here on Earth? In truth, we may never know. This newest foray into the complex character of Mary Magdalene is intrinsically linked to the concepts of femininity put forth by Pope Gregory the Great. Without Gregory's emphasis on Mary Magdalene's sexual nature, she might have served a purpose in the Catholic Church similar to that of Mary, the Holy Mother. She might have been stripped of her earthy womanliness for a pure, clean (possibly even asexual) persona. So, even if we dislike Gregory's interpretation of Mary Magdalene, we cannot truly separate ourselves (or Mary Magdalene) from it. Pope Gregory's influence continues to this day, having shaped and molded the goddess Mary Magdalene into the Divine presence we acknowledge today.

Mary Magdalene first bursts into the Bible in Luke 8:2 as a repentant follower of Jesus. Using her full name, "Mary who was called Magdalene,"[8] she is said to have been exorcised of seven demons. This is the only mention of Mary's demons throughout the whole Bible. After this, as "Mary Magdalene" she is shown as one of Jesus' staunchest followers. She travels with him to Jerusalem from Galilee at the time of his death. She watches over him, from a distance, throughout his ordeal and is even said to "minister to Him."[9] In all of the four traditional Gospels—those attributed to Matthew, Mark, Luke, and John—Mary Magdalene, along with other female followers of Christ, is first given the news of Jesus' resurrection. This important news, indeed the very cornerstone of the Christian faith, is entrusted to women, who must safeguard the information and disseminate it to the male apostles. At this time, the male apostles are sitting snugly in their room in Jerusalem, fearing for their lives. The female followers of Jesus, on the

---

7. Carroll, "Who Was Mary Magdalene?"
8. New American Standard Bible. www.biblegateway.com
9. Ibid., Mark 15:39.

other hand, are busy honoring their sacrificed teacher with unguents and spices for his body.

Not only is the resurrection proclaimed to women, including Mary Magdalene, but, in John 20, the first person to glimpse the Divine essence of Jesus is Mary Magdalene. Not Peter. Not Paul. Not Thomas and his doubtful ways. But Mary Magdalene. As she stands, crying, outside the empty tomb of Jesus, two angels arrive and ask her why she is crying. She answers, "They have taken my lord away . . . and I don't know where they have put him."[10] Suddenly a man appears before Mary Magdalene. It is Jesus but she does not recognize him until he says her name. At which point, she turns to him and calls out, "Teacher." Jesus responds with the dictate, "Do not hold on to me, for I have not yet returned to my Father. Go instead to my brothers and tell them, 'I am returning to my Father and your Father, to my God and your God.'"[11]

After reading and understanding the role Mary Magdalene plays in bearing the "good news" (Jesus' resurrection) to the world, is it any wonder that an entire spiritual tract, in truth an actual Gospel, was attributed to her? In 1896, a section of the Gospel of Mary Magdalene, copied into a fifth-century manuscript, was brought to Berlin from Cairo by Carl Reinhardt. Additional fragments of the gospel, written in Greek, have surfaced in the twentieth century. These finds total approximately eight papyrus sheets, indicating that a lot of the Gospel has perhaps been lost or destroyed over time.[12]

The Gospel of Mary Magdalene is not like the traditional gospels found in Bibles around the world. Many of the philosophies and tenets shy away from well-known Christian teachings. The Gospel begins at Chapter Four, since Chapters One through Three are lost. It appears, in Chapter Four, that Christ has descended to Earth once again to give teachings to his beloved disciples. In these teachings, he says that, "All nature, all formations, all creatures exist in and with one another,"[13] indicating an energetic connection between all beings, living and non-living, on the Earth. Jesus continues with the assertion that there is no such thing as "sin" on Earth. Rather, the sin is within

---

10. Holy Bible, New International Version, John 20:13. www.biblegateway.com

11. Ibid., John 20:16–17.

12. King, "The Gospel of Mary of Magdala," excerpted from *The Gospel of Mary of Magdala: Jesus and the First Woman Apostle*.

13. The Gnostic Society Library, "The Gospel According to Mary Magdalene," Mary Magdalene 4:22.

our actions and only by learning and understanding spirituality in daily life can we come to understand spirituality in the Divine sense, both in relation to deities and to our inner selves. If we accept the spirituality of ourselves, and thus the spirituality of all around us, then we will have learned the lesson of "Good," and will have attained a higher nature, where there will be no sickness or death. Before he departs, Jesus suggests looking to the various forms of nature whenever one is distraught or downtrodden in the teaching and understanding of these ideas.

After Jesus leaves, the disciples are upset and fearful. They ask Mary Magdalene to share some wisdom of Christ, taught exclusively to her. This is, of course, significant because it shows Mary Magdalene as an equal of the male apostles and as a special confidant of Jesus Christ. She calms their fears by proclaiming the greatness of Jesus Christ. Through her simple faith and love, Mary Magdalene "turned their [the apostles'] hearts to the *Good*,"[14] which is the term Jesus uses when describing the path to personal and Divine spirituality.

After praising Christ, Mary begins with an account of a time when she talked to Christ about a vision she received. He praises her for persevering in allowing the vision to unfold, and then five pages go missing in the manuscript. When the Gospel picks up again, we are in the midst of an incredibly detailed philosophical discussion about the soul and its ascension. Many of the aspects of the original teachings of Christ, from the first section of the Gospel of Mary Magdalene, reappear here in the description of the ascension of the soul. Matter and the "All" are dissolved, both on Earth and in heaven. The soul is "released from a world . . . and from the fetter of oblivion which is transient."[15] In short, the soul moves beyond the limited concept of matter into a place and time greater than our understanding of the material world, into a communion with pure spirituality.

Mary's lessons are met with disdain, confusion, and hostility by the disciples. Andrew says he doesn't believe the Savior would ever have taught such strange ideas. Peter openly challenges Mary's relationship with Jesus, questioning whether He would have taught such concepts to a woman and not to His male apostles. Mary begins to cry and Levi steps forward to give support to Mary and her teachings. He advocates accepting Mary Magdalene

---

14. Ibid., Mary Magdalene 5:4.
15. Ibid., Mary Magdalene 8:17–24.

as a spiritual equal, as the one Jesus "loved . . . more than us."[16] Levi suggests that they lay aside their egos and go forth to spread the teachings of Jesus Christ. With Levi's calm influence, the apostles choose to follow his advice and preach the word of Jesus Christ. Thus, the Gospel of Mary Magdalene ends.

Mary Magdalene's lessons have forever been met with confusion and disdain. After all, she is a woman in a decidedly male environment. The Church rejected her Gospel centuries ago and she has been relegated to the role of woman-as-sinner, saved through the purity of Christ. But Mary Magdalene refuses to be pigeonholed into any rote stereotype. She is neither sinner, nor wife, nor spiritual leader, but all of these things together. In truth, she exactly encapsulates the teachings of her Gospel, going beyond the matter of here and now, the nature of life on Earth, to an understanding of all things as one in Divine spiritual union. But we, in our small minds, find it difficult to comprehend this greatness, and so she forgives us our confusion.

Through her tears at Jesus' tomb and her tears at the apostles' rejection, she cleanses and remakes anew. In both instances, the power of the Divine—of calmness and peace and clarity—shines through, turning aside pain and negativity. Is that not what forgiveness does? Forgiveness strips away the emotions that no longer serve us so we can sally forth into a blinding future of promise, untainted by the past. This is Mary Magdalene's gift to us. Whether we approach her as harlot, sacred grail, sinner, or saint, she welcomes us, wiping away our fears and transgressions with her tears, giving hope and joy with her acceptance.

Pathway to Mary Magdalene

The tears of Mary Magdalene seem to be a portal into her Divine nature and into her relationship with us. In her stories, she is not afraid to release her emotions through her tears. This is a lesson for all of us as we work to accept forgiveness of self and offer forgiveness to others. Tears are a wonderful release. They often clear away unnecessary thoughts and feelings, leaving us in a space of freedom and clarity. We should not be afraid to cry.

---

16. Ibid., Mary Magdalene 9:9. This phrase has often been used to show that Mary Magdalene was thought of as more than a student or apostle of Christ's. Many read this and believe it backs up their assertion that Mary Magdalene was Jesus' wife and lover, bearer of his child.

So, with that in mind, go ahead—cry! But it's not that easy, is it? We spend all of our lives reining in our emotions so as not to "embarrass" ourselves or others with our demonstrative displays. It begins in elementary school when we are ridiculed for "being a baby." And it just continues from there, until we simply can't express our darkest, deepest, most painful emotions. We suck it up, suck them in, and simply accept a sucky life. But we don't need to. We have the right to a life full of complete, whole emotions. Sadness is just as important as happiness or passion or joy. Anger plays a part in our emotions too, and you may find that you have to expel a lot of anger before you can access your grief and your tears.

Sometimes it is easier to cry when we have outside stimuli. If you are having difficulty activating your deepest emotions, try putting on a sad movie. Maybe even one with Mary Magdalene in it; *The Passion of the Christ* is a supremely shocking film in its violence and brutality and should not be watched by children of any age. (There's a reason it is rated R.) Yet, all that violence lends itself to a truly sorrowful ending when Christ is crucified. You could also rent *Jesus Christ Superstar*, a rock opera by Andrew Lloyd Webber. The most well-known song, "I don't know how to love him," is sung by the Mary Magdalene character and always brings me to tears.

If you don't like movies with non-stop blood or non-stop singing, I recommend *Bridge to Terabithia* as a wonderful vehicle to access your emotions. Centered on the friendship between a pre-teen boy and girl, the visuals are stunning, the story is moving, and the kids are just so darn cute. I cannot make it through this movie without crying at least two times. I cry even more when I watch *Titanic*.

Locate a movie, CD, or box of old photos. Wrap yourself in a warm, soft blanket. Place a box of super-soft tissues next to you, and give yourself permission to cry. It's okay. No one's looking. It's just you and your movie and your tissues and the healing power of Mary Magdalene.

ARIANRHOD
Welsh Sovereign Lady

MANTRA

I forgive myself.

Arianrhod is a goddess who is not easily understood. She is connected to the night sky and the luminous moon. Her light is diffused through multiple layers of time and karma and experience. In Welsh tradition, she oversees the Whirlpool of Creation, knowing all that occurs in the past, present, and future. It is to her castle in the sky, Caer Sidi, that the spirits fly upon their death. Arianrhod is beauteous maiden in the myths of *The Mabinogion*, serene and wise Moon Mother in the night sky, and tender, all-knowing crone of all wisdom and all time. Complex? You bet.

What does Arianrhod have to do with forgiveness? Arianrhod is a goddess who makes mistakes. She lies, disavows her children, abandons them, and actually curses one of her sons. In short, Arianrhod is not in the running for Mother of the Year. However, she never makes excuses for her behavior. She never even apologizes for it because she is acting in accordance to her own true calling, her sovereign self. Arianrhod is simply not interested in relinquishing her power and her current life for the children. For many of us, this action feels intrinsically wrong. We look at her actions and shudder. We think to ourselves, "What *kind* of mother would do *that*?!" In the end, maybe we should be asking ourselves, "What kind of woman *wouldn't*?"

An ancestral goddess of the ancient Celts, Arianrhod is the daughter of the mother goddess Don. Her father, like her consort Nwyvre, is little discussed in relation to her mythos. Some sources list her father as Beli, the Celtic god of light and healing,[17] but she is always referred to as her mother's child, possibly harking back to a time of "mother-rule" in the distant past. Her brother is usually listed as Gwydion, a god of magic and trickery. However, Gwydion has two brothers—Amaethon, god of agriculture; and Govannon, god of smithcraft—who do not appear to be directly related to Arianrhod. This confusing family tree leads to the possibility that Don may have exercised her right to

---

17. Jordan, *Encyclopedia of Gods*, 24.

pick her lovers freely in a time when a queen chose and dismissed her consorts as she wished, without the constraint of marriage.

If so, this "queen-right" explains the convoluted and conflicting passages relating to Arianrhod in the Welsh book of mythology *The Mabinogion*. Arianrhod appears to have followed her mother's example, as she lives by herself, without a husband, at Caer Sidi or Caer Arianrhod. She takes her mates as she wishes and is even said to have slept with mermen on the beach near her castle.[18] However, when her brother Gwydion calls her to the court of their uncle, Math ap Mathonwy (Don's brother and a powerful magician), her brother claims that she is a virgin. When Math asks her if she is a maiden, Arianrhod replies, "I know not but that I am."[19] Math tests her virginity (and the truthfulness of her word) by asking Arianrhod to step over his bent magic wand. (The shape of the wand is important to note because, in the text, Math actually takes the time to bend his wand, perhaps giving it more potency or a more phallic semblance.)

Without fear or hesitation, Arianrhod steps over the wand, and promptly delivers one baby boy, Dylan Eil Ton, Sea Son of Wave,[20] who immediately crawls to the sea and is not heard of again until his uncle (half-uncle?) Govannon kills him by accident. As Arianrhod heads to the door, another bundle of joy drops from her, unnoticed by everyone except Gwydion, who grabs the small child and wraps it in a silk sheet. The appearance of these two children seems to contradict Arianrhod's original claim that she is a virgin! In modern society, we, like Math, view virginity as a purely physical, sexual condition. However, if you accept the premise that a matriarchal culture existed at one time in the British Isles, then Arianrhod was not lying by calling herself a maiden. She saw virginity as a state of mind, rather than as merely a lack of sexual contact. She believed herself to be a free woman, complete unto herself, without ties or obligations to any man. She was simply confusing (perhaps deliberately) her uncle's question and answering it on her own terms instead of his.

Years later, Gwydion arrives at Arianrhod's court with the boy he had wrapped in the silk sheet. She asks him who the child is and he tells her, "This boy is a son of thine." Arianrhod replies, "Alas, man! What came over thee to put me to shame, and keep it as long

---

18. Monaghan, *The New Book of Goddesses & Heroines.*
19. Jones and Jones, *Mabinogion*, 54.
20. Ibid., 54.

as this?"[21] It seems startling that a mother would welcome her child in such a fashion, claiming that he "shamed" her and condemning Gwydion for taking care of him for so long. (She does not even treat her son as a person but, rather, a thing, by calling him "it.") However, the answer to her puzzling behavior may stem from her immediate response to birthing her children at Math's court all those years before. If Arianrhod purposefully mistakes Math's question about her virginity, answering on her terms of emotional and spiritual freedom rather than sexual purity, she chooses to hide her beliefs instead of stating them and confronting her uncle's culturally limited ideas. She doesn't argue with his questioning. She outwardly conforms, concealing her true nature. The birth of her sons gave her the ideal opportunity to discuss her beliefs with her uncle, her brother, and all the men of the court. Yet, she flees. Instead of gaining power from the birth of her sons and taking pride in her innate creative ability, she disavows them and runs away.

Arianrhod returns to her home, Caer Sidi, where her woman-centered, female-empowered ideas are understood and welcomed. Instead of reveling in her power as a woman at Math's court, she slinks away to her home. She does not declare her right to have children with whomever she wishes. She does not proclaim her equality with the men of Math's court. Instead, she succumbs to their ideas about her, to the socially accepted views of womanhood. Arianrhod allows the men to alter her perceptions about herself. For a brief moment, she agrees with them about her "unnatural" sexual liberation, about her inability to rule a kingdom, about her need to be protected by a male. It is this moment of weakness that shames Arianrhod. The boy is simply a reminder and Gwydion, having suggested Math send for Arianrhod all those years before, is the originator of the situation that caused her betrayal of herself. Gwydion's arrival at her court forces Arianrhod to recall her cowardly behavior; therefore, she lashes out at the young boy with a curse to never have a name unless she gives it to him.

The next day, Gwydion, in his trickster aspect, dupes Arianrhod into giving her son a name, Lleu Llaw Gyffes (fair, deft hand),[22] when he disguises the boy and himself as shoemakers, crafting shoes made of gold. After Gwydion reveals their true shapes to Arianrhod, she announces that her brother may have won this round but she will win the next. She exclaims, "I will swear on this boy a destiny that he shall never bear arms

---

21. Ibid., 55.
22. Ibid., 56.

till I myself equip him therewith."[23] This curse seems less an angry statement against Lleu and more a proclamation against Gwydion. It is as if the two siblings are fighting over who is more powerful and the boy is merely a pawn in their game.

Years pass and Lleu is trained in the martial skills of riding a horse and wielding a sword. When he is ready, Gwydion again disguises himself and the boy, this time as traveling bards, and they are welcomed into Caer Arianrhod to entertain the court. After singing songs and telling tales all evening long, Gwydion once again tricks his sister into breaking her own curse. The next morning, he creates the illusion of an invasion force surrounding Caer Arianrhod and convinces Arianrhod that every able-bodied man should come to arms. She agrees and even straps the armor on her son, at the prompting of Gwydion. Once she has done this, her curse is broken and Gwydion makes the false fleet disappear. Astonished, Arianrhod admonishes her brother by stating that many of her men might have been harmed because of his deceit. He is unrepentant, and so, in a pique against her brother, Arianrhod lays the final curse on her son. She proclaims, "And I will swear a destiny on him, that he shall never have a wife of the race that is now on this Earth."[24] This curse is foiled by Gwydion and Math. Working together, they create a wife for Lleu out of flowers, the goddess Bloudewedd.

In *The Mabinogion*, Arianrhod does not meet Lleu again in mortal form. Once Gwydion has received the curses and their subsequent releases from his sister, he leaves her alone. Lleu, following his uncle's lead, does not contact her either. In short, Arianrhod is left to her own life, which is exactly as she wanted it. Yet, it is not hard to conceptualize a time when Arianrhod might have regretted her actions in relation to her son and that fateful day at Math's court. Maybe not in outward appearance or in word or deed, but sometime, in the darkness of night, Arianrhod might have grieved, bemoaning a path that led her to her current place in life. The ancient and medieval myths do not mention any such outpouring of emotion, but it is conceivable.

It is this aspect of the goddess that understands the actions of which we may not be proud. Perhaps we yelled too often or gave our child up for adoption or had an abortion or succumbed to an addiction. Too often we beat up on ourselves for past actions. We live with that shame and guilt, allowing them to stifle our current connections and relationships. Arianrhod can help us forgive ourselves our mistakes, no matter how heinous. Arianrhod's

---

23. Ibid., 56.
24. Ibid., 57.

choices are difficult to understand. However, Arianrhod is no less a woman for her choices, no less warm, no less caring. Finding peace within herself, she has the ability to give so much more to the world because she followed her own path. By staying true to herself, Arianrhod is able to be a better person, free of bitterness and disappointment, free of second guesses and misunderstandings. She is able to move forward with her life as the best person she can be right here and right now. This is her gift to us. Accept it and live in the light of the present moment, free from the guilt and shame of the past. You deserve it.[25]

Pathway to Arianrhod

Since Arianrhod helps us to free ourselves of the real and imagined wrongs we have committed, it is necessary to truly face ourselves. This is not always easy, but in the end, what other choice do we have? It is time to look yourself in the mirror and accept the truth—the good and the bad, the beautiful and the ugly.

Anoint a white taper candle with oil. Start from the bottom of the candle and work the oil upward, toward the wick. While you are anointing the candle, focus on your intention to release your guilt and shame up to the goddess Arianrhod, giving it to her keeping in the Whirlpool of Creation where it will be transmuted into positive, life-affirming energy.

For the three nights of the full moon, go into your bathroom with your candle and turn off all the lights. By the soft, muted candlelight, gaze at your reflection. Take some time to think about your positive attributes and say three out loud. Think about three things from which you feel you need forgiveness. State the first forgivable action and then say the phrase, "I forgive you." Next, say the second forgivable action and then the third, making sure to say the forgiveness phrase in between and at the end. End the healing session with three more positive attributes of yourself. Graciously thank Arianrhod and snuff out the candle.

Don't be surprised if you have strange dreams, an urge to do something unusual, or an emotional response to this activity. You may find yourself crying a lot or feeling the need to send cards. You might want to burrow under the blankets at three in the afternoon or sit and watch silly teenage movies. This is all a completely normal reaction to Arianrhod's pathway. After all, you are purging yourself of energy that has been blocked

---

25. Much of the story of Arianrhod first appeared in *Goddess Afoot!*, 24–28. For more information and intimate workings with Arianrhod, Welsh Sovereign Lady, including a guided meditation and ritual, please see chapter 2 of *Goddess Afoot!*

and stifled for a while. Give yourself some time to heal. Follow your intuition and try not to close yourself off to the experience of self-forgiveness.

RITUAL FOR FORGIVENESS:
CREATING A MANDALA OF YOU

Suggested Ritual Days

Jewish month of Elul: usually begins in mid- to late August, lasting until Yom Kippur

Muslim month of Ramadan: the holy month begins when the first crescent of the new moon of the ninth month of the Islamic calendar is sighted (see a current calendar for exact dates)

June: Forgiveness week, seems to vary according to organization and year, but is always held in June

First Sunday in August: International Forgiveness Day, as proclaimed by the Better World Project and the Worldwide Forgiveness Alliance

August 27: Global Day of Forgiveness, as proclaimed by the Christian Embassy of Christ's Ambassadors

Last Saturday in October: National Day of Forgiveness in the United States, as proclaimed by the Center of Unconditional Love

Items needed

a 7x7-inch square of flat cardboard or wood

a pencil

colored sand

an extremely small funnel (often included in the purchase of colored sand)

incense in the scent of hyacinth, crocus, or violet

relaxing music

Begin by setting aside an entire day for this ritual. It may take you less time but there's nothing worse than feeling the guidance of spirit and having to stop because the mundane world intrudes. Protect yourself from this frustrating situation and devote the whole day to yourself. (I know this is going to be a challenge!) If you are extremely lucky and have wonderful babysitters or a very understanding significant other, try to schedule something fun and relaxing right after your forgiveness ritual. You may feel slightly tired and edgy after confronting your inner demons all day.

Once you have a space all to yourself, set up your 7x7-inch square of cardboard or wood on a level surface. This can be your dining room table, a counter, or the floor. Pick a place that is easy for you to use because you will be leaning over it for most of the day. Your ritual will consist of creating a unique sand mandala, individual to you. Sand mandalas are sacred rituals in Tibetan Buddhism, often taking many monks several days to complete. They are usually very intricate and involve several complementary colors of differing hues. For instance, it is common to see the colors blue, red, yellow, and green expressed in a dark, medium, and light hue—a primary, secondary, and tertiary color scheme.

The monks begin the creation of the sand mandala with an opening ceremony that includes mantras, drums, and flutes. Then, they begin to sketch out the design on a square surface, taking the time to pray during the creative process. Colored sands are then layered onto the mandala sketch using a very specific tool, called a *chakpur*. Two chakpurs are used at one time, to symbolize the union of compassion and wisdom. Once the mandala is complete, the monks perform a closing ceremony and then dismantle the design, sweeping it into a river or stream to symbolize the impermanence of all things. Sometimes they sweep all the sands together, forming a kaleidoscopic pile. They then give out handfuls of it to bystanders and observers. In both instances, the sands are meant to send healing energies throughout the world.[26]

It is important to focus on those you want to forgive (including yourself) during the creation of your mandala, so I would suggest staying away from the traditional Tibetan Buddhist mandalas, as they are very intricate and difficult to create. Focus on a symbol that means something to you personally. This can be anything at all—an object from nature, a spiritual symbol, or a free-form image that comes to you as you begin the creative process. Whatever you decide, don't second guess yourself! This will only cause you to focus on the negative when you are trying to rise to a higher level of understanding. Allow yourself the luxury of fluidity in order to simply "be" in the present.

You should follow the same steps as the Tibetan monks in the creation of your mandala. First, chant or pray to open your ritual. Second, sketch out your design on the cardboard or wood, using your pencil. Third, create a multi-hued, layered mandala with the colored sand. (This is best accomplished by pouring small amounts of sand into the

---

26. The Tibetan Monks of Deprung Gomang Monastery, "Sand Mandala, Sacred Art."

funnel and directing it to the appropriate place on your cardboard or wood.) Fourth, chant or pray to close your ritual. Fifth, dismantle your mandala by either pouring the sand into a river or stream, or dispersing it on the wind.

Throughout the process, you should be cognizant of the fluidity of life and the change and transformation that occurs every minute of the day. Forgiveness can be a wonderful experience of release. No longer do we have to hang on to the negative energies and the awful occurrences in our lives. We can let them go. Just as the colored sand washes down the river or flies away on the wind, our past transgressions, former wounds, and traumas can be given over to the spirit of the Divine. We can embrace the truth of impermanence and relish every moment in life right here, right now. Namaste.

CHAPTER SEVEN

Goddess Mantras for Healing

HEALING: REMEMBERING WHOLENESS

Look around you at the people on the street, in your office, at the gym, and around town, and you will find sickness. Dis-ease of mind, body, and spirit, wrapped up in a nice, neat Gucci and Prada package. The world loves to remind us of our lack—lack of pigment in our hair, lack of joy, lack of energy, lack of connection to the spirit realm, lack of sleep. And, as the world is wont to do, we are given excuses for our lack and products to make it go away. We will be able to sleep, laugh, talk to the dead, look younger, and our lives will be better if only we buy one more product. If only we fix one more problem. If only we remove one more issue. But the hard reality of the situation is that no product, no quick fix will bring us to health of mind, body, and spirit. For the truth of the matter is that we already are healthy, just the way we are. We have simply forgotten that fact.

If you were to continue walking down that street, full of people who have been told that they are dis-eased, you might see signs of their conditions. You might see a woman with lines around her eyes, a college student shrugging his shoulders, an elderly man wringing his hands, a runner limping ever so slightly. And if you were an especially friendly person, you might greet these people with a smile, a nod, a wave, or a soft hello. If you were suddenly transported back to twelfth-century England or happened to be strolling through your local Renaissance Faire, you might call out "Hail and well met" to your fellow man and woman, a common phrase of the time period. But "Hail and well met" is much more than a simple greeting. It is a healing invocation, if there ever was one.

In our modern world, we generally infuse the word *hail* with two meanings. As a noun or verb, it indicates large chunks of ice falling from the sky. As an interjection, *hail* gives honor to an individual, celebrating and touting their power. The Catholic Hail Mary prayer is another illustration of the use of the word to greet, acknowledge, and honor forces in this world and the Otherworld that are bigger than our small selves. Yet the Middle English *hail* is a derivative of the Old Norse *heill*, meaning "healthy," and the Old High German *heil*, meaning "unhurt and healthy." These two words from our Nordic ancestors also formed the beginnings of the Old English word *hāl* and the Middle English word *hool*, both of which evolved into the modern English word *whole*.[1] So, in our no-so-distant past, the words *whole* and *hail* meant pretty much the same thing—free from injury, in no need of healing.

The words *hail* and *whole* mean more than just good health as we view it through Western medicine. Being whole is as much about good cholesterol and low blood pressure as it is about enjoying every moment of being alive. Wholeness occurs when we are in sync with all the forces of energy around us. We are part of them and they are part of us. Being in the moment, we begin to realize that wholeness and healthiness is as much a state of mind as it is a bodily experience.

The English poet A. E. Housman illustrates the concept of multi-level healing in his poem "XII – An Epitaph."

> Stay, if you list, O passer by the way;
> Yet night approaches; better not to stay.
> > I never sigh, nor flush, nor knit the brow,
> > Nor grieve to think how ill God made me, now.
> > Here, with one balm for many fevers found,
> > Whole of an ancient evil, I sleep sound.[2]

The poem describes the chance meeting between two individuals with opposing views of the world. The first character speaks the first two lines. He is hospitable, but not overly so. He grudgingly offers room and board to a stranger but suggests that he move on due to the coming of night. His subtle anxiety concerning the darkness exhibits a certain amount of dis-ease, an inability to commit fully and wholly to the world around him and within him.

The second character in the poem, a wanderer, speaks the last four lines. In his lines, we see a man content with himself and his lot in life. He doesn't complain about the

---

1. *Merriam-Webster Dictionary.*
2. Housman, *Additional Poems* (1939).

past or worry about the future. He doesn't curse or weep over the life he has crafted for himself, with the help of spiritual guidance. Instead, he relaxes into the moment, falling asleep despite the difficulties of his life on the road. As he states, he is "whole of an ancient evil," an evil which could be thought of as the separation of man from his surroundings. After all, the poem implies that the wanderer goes to sleep under the stars. With this action, he is more in touch with his natural surroundings, with his wholeness, than the first character. If being whole is about enjoying every moment, then it is intimately connected to other living organisms, both plant and animal. One cannot be fully alive, healthy, and whole if the connection to the physical world is lost. When humans began to remove themselves from the landscape around them, when the land began to take on useful dimensions rather than spiritual ones, we lost our intrinsic wholeness. No longer tied to the natural undulations of the world around us, we began to experience, and even search out, dis-ease.

As children, we recognize the importance of the world around us. We splash in puddles and stomp in the mud. We search for worms and pluck beautiful flowers. And we are happy . . . most of the time. As we grow up, the world of houses and computers and schools and offices begins to impose itself on our life. One by one, the threads of connection between the natural world and our own selves become frayed and eventually severed, until we are left with only ourselves, outside of time and place. We are unable to be in the moment because we are uncertain exactly what that moment is or was or is evolving into. We flounder in a vacant sea, adrift without a tether to link us to the world. And, so we become anxious and worried (or worrisome) and this leads us to dis-ease and doctors and medications and cures to solve all our ills. But, really, we need to remember the roots of the word *healthy*. Hail and Whole. Whole and Hail. Wholeness of mind, body, and spirit is not an illusion or a pipe-dream. It can be accomplished if you but put aside the lessons of adulthood, and remember.[3]

_____

3. This section on healing and wholeness is not meant as a judgment against Western medicinal advice. There are many times when it is necessary to treat serious medical issues with medication, surgery, and a doctor's care. The essay "Healing: Remembering Wholeness" is meant to explore the topic of health from a spiritual perspective, opening minds to alternative ways of viewing the world, life, and the notion of health. It should not be considered medical advice.

ENERGY RETURN

As with all active magic or prayer, searching for healing can involve some difficulties and issues. The most intrinsic and difficult issue to accept is that some people truly believe they can't be healed. No matter what energy treatments they receive, no matter how many doctors' offices they visit, they don't seem to get any better. Or, if one health problem disappears, another one materializes right away. You may have friends who seem to fall into this category or you yourself may have this problem. The first thing to realize is that everyone can be healed, but it's not as simple as getting a medication or meditating every day. Dis-ease comes from our environment. Our connection to the world as children, teenagers, and adults affects our health. Personal relationships from the past, as well as the present, play a part in dis-ease. Any kind of unseen airborne material, such as mold, asbestos, and smoke, affects our health for many years after we've left the contaminated space. Abuse of any kind can physically materialize in our body time and time again, especially if we have not reconciled the situation physically, mentally, and emotionally.

If you or someone you know seems to be caught in the loop of dis-ease, take some time to honestly look over the environment of your life. What has it been like? Are there any common trends or themes? Do the same sorts of people keep showing up? Does the same situation occur time and time again? If so, these are signposts for you, pointing you toward the deeper reasoning for your dis-ease. You might even find that your dis-ease stems from an experience in the womb, a time when you were completely immersed in your environment, at one with everything around you. If you discover something unsettling or feel like you need help in finding the root cause of your dis-ease, go to a reputable therapist who specializes in hypnosis. Hypnosis will aid you in letting go of our structured, adult way of thinking, helping you to access memories that you may have consciously forgotten but stored away in your subconscious. Hypnotherapy, along with acupuncture, can supplement traditional Western medicine in your quest for wholeness, aligning you with the world and connecting you to life's every moment.

UZUME
Shinto Goddess of Laughter and Shadow

MANTRA

Create high.

Create low.

Create all,

From down Below.

Many doctors advocate the healing power of laughter. Have you ever see the movie *Patch Adams*, starring Robin Williams, where he dresses up like a clown to treat his patients? Or what about the Matthew Broderick flick *The Road to Wellville*, a truly funny, tender, wacky, and grossly overlooked movie about a Victorian-era wellness retreat center and the husband and wife who arrive to be "cured." I can still see all those tightly corseted and jacketed, well-bred Victorian ladies and gentlemen standing on the veranda chanting, "HA HA HA HA HA HA HA. HO HO HO HO HO HO HO," while I roll on my couch chortling to their simulated laughter.

And that's really what Uzume is all about—the bizarre, the silly, the absolutely ridiculous that, being so far removed from everyday reality, casts light on the truth of our current situation. Uzume is so disinterested in social norms and accepted standards of behavior that she shocks us out of our lethargy. Gasping, laughing, twittering behind closed doors, we arrive at the root of ourselves because we are no longer focusing on the rules and regulations of everyone else. In that once instant, when we are truly involved with the surprise and the awe of Uzume, our body and mind and spirit snaps together, re-connecting to form a whole, healthy being.

Uzume is the Japanese Shinto goddess of mirth, merriment, laughter, and healing. Her name means "Whirling" and she is alternatively called The Great Persuader, Heavenly Alarming Female, Heaven's Forthright Female[4] and the Terrible Female of Heaven. She is among the lesser Shinto gods, having only a few stories told about her in the *Kojiki* (*Record of Ancient Matters*, 712 CE) and the *Nohongi* (*Chronicles of Japan*, 720 CE),

---

4. Koleman, "Profile of a Goddess: Ama-No-Uzume."

yet she retains a strong presence in Japanese folklore rites and in Japanese society.[5] An annual Shinto ritual festival, called the Kagura, is dedicated to Uzume and a modern red-light district performance, the Todukashi—part art, part sex, and part myth—highlights her enduring power. Both of these mythic entertainments relate back to the first and most well-known myth about Uzume, the luring of the sun out of the Rock Cave of Heaven.

The sun in Japanese mythology is a female, the goddess Amaterasu, who brings light to the world and ensures the growth of the rice plants in the fields. Amaterasu has two brothers, Susanowa, the god of storms, and Tsuki-yomi, the god of the moon. Amaterasu and Susanowa are lovers and have children together; she is the illuminating force in the heavens, while he is the powerful, angry energy that protects his family and friends. One day, however, Susanowa turns his wrath upon Amaterasu out of jealousy for her central place in the world of humans. He defiles her sacred weaving room with a dead horse (an animal sacred to Amaterasu) and, in some versions, kills one of Amaterasu's attendants and even wounds the goddess herself. He destroys her crops by placing excrement on the newly sprouting seedlings.[6] In short, Susanowa destructively unleashes his frustration on the things that Amaterasu most loves.

Devastated by the betrayal of her love and fearing further injury, Amaterasu leaves the sky and retreats to the Heavenly Rock-Dwelling, where she seals herself in with a large stone door. The world dissolves into an endless night. The other gods become nervous and seek ways to draw Amaterasu out of her self-imposed prison. The wisest of the gods suggests a course of action that the eight hundred gods follow. They craft a rope of beautiful, shining jewels and use it to hang a mirror from the branches of the sacred Sakaki tree. One god gathers the birds that sing through the night, a.k.a. barnyard fowl or roosters. Another takes the shoulder of a stag and the bark of the cherry tree to perform divination. Still another recites poetry and liturgy to appease Amaterasu. But the sun goddess steadfastly remains tucked away in the rock cave, hiding her light from the world. [7]

---

5. Ziehr, "Ame-no-Uzume no Mikoto."

6. Goddess Gift, "Amaterasu, Goddess of the Sun; Uzume, Goddess of Mirth and Dance." Chamberlain, *The Kojiki*. Read before the Asiatic Society of Japan in 1882, reprinted 1919, Vol. 1, Section XVI. "The Door of the Heavenly Rock-Dwelling." Moss, "A Mirror for the Sun Goddess."

7. Chamberlain, *Kojiki,* vol. 1, section XVI.

Finally, the goddess Uzume arrives at the doorway of the Heavenly Rock-Dwelling. She is dressed as a shaman and carries a wooden platform or tub with her.[8] Climbing on top of the tub, Uzume begins to drum with her feet, creating a deep, rhythmic tone. As the drumming increases in tempo and her dancing becomes more and more frenzied, Uzume begins to perform a striptease. First she releases her breasts, baring them for all to see. Ecstatic, possessed, fully in the moment, Uzume reveals her nipples and pulls up her robes to showcase her gleaming genitals. She is laughing and hollering and singing and drumming and creating quite a cacophony of sound. The other gods are entranced by the mad dance and join with Uzume in laughing and singing. They cannot believe Uzume's actions!

Amaterasu hears the party-like atmosphere outside the rock-dwelling and is surprised that the gods can make merry without her. She asks them, "Methought that owing to my retirement the Plain of Heaven would be dark, and likewise the Central Land of Reed-Plains would all be dark: how then is it that the Heavenly-Alarming-Female makes merry, and that likewise the eight hundred myriad Deities all laugh?"[9] Uzume tells Amaterasu that they are laughing and celebrating because they have found another deity who is brighter and more illustrious than her. Curious, Amaterasu opens the cave door a crack and looks out. She does, indeed, see something bright and shining and opens the door wider and steps out. Immediately she is blinded, confronted by her own image in the mirror. The other gods close and bind the cave door so Amaterasu cannot slip back inside. With Uzume's help, Amaterasu remembers her true nature and decides that she would rather be the sun in the heavens than the sun in a cave.

Utilizing a mirror, a makeshift drum, and a sacred striptease, Uzume brings mirth and merriment to a dire situation. If Amaterasu had not left the Heavenly Rock-Dwelling, all the people, animals, and plants on Earth would have died. Of course, this archetypal myth is seen in numerous cultures (Demeter and Persephone spring to mind) but the inclusion of a cave and a bright, illuminating light are unique to the Uzume story. Uzume lures Amaterasu out of her cave not only with her sacred sensual dancing but by taunting her

---

8. Most modern interpretations claim that Uzume carried a tub with her, as indicated in the *Nihongi*. In the *Kojiki*, the Japanese character is written phonetically and relates to a "sounding-board." Either way, the item Uzume carried was meant to amplify sound and lift her up off the ground.

9. Chamberlain, *Kojiki*, Vol. 1, section XVI.

that some other deity is better than her. This, of course, is not true. When Amaterasu looks into the mirror, she is blinded by her own radiance. Hiding in the cave, overcome with grief and fear and past trauma, she had forgotten her own greatness. Only by looking at the truth of herself in the mirror was she able to remove the negative influence of the past on her emotional well-being. She let go of guilt, shame, and fear and left the past in the past, giving herself the freedom to live fully in the present. Amaterasu remembered her true self and reclaimed her goddesshood.

Uzume can do that for us as well, guiding us to an understanding and appreciation of the self. We are unique, fascinating, passionate, and pleasurable individuals. We do not need to embrace the difficulties of the past. Rather we can embrace the possibilities of each moment as it unfolds around us. In another myth about Uzume, from the *Nihongi*, she confronts a giant with a fearsome appearance as he is blocking the way for Amaterasu's son, Ninigi, to descend to Earth. Uzume appears to the creature, named Saruta-Hiko, and bares her breasts and genitals to him. He laughs and asks her why she is stripping for him. She replies that she wants to find out his reasoning for blocking the road that Ninigi wishes to travel. Saruta-Hiko states that he wishes to be a guide and attendant for the son of the sun goddess. In other words, he has no ill designs upon the boy. Uzume believes him, and Saruta-Hiko proves to be a valuable friend for Ninigi. However, without the courage of Uzume to confront and ascertain Saruta-Hiko's intentions, Ninigi might have missed out on a useful relationship with a powerful ally.[10]

In both myths, Uzume ferrets out the truth of an individual by revealing her own reality, symbolized by showing her breasts and genitals. The sacred striptease prevalent in both stories could indicate a stripping away of the norms of society and getting to the truth of a situation, of an individual. It takes courage to leave behind outmoded societal ideas that no longer serve you as an individual. It takes strength of self to leave behind the old stories that people have told you and to revel in your own magnificence. But this is at the heart of healing. If you believe in your innate worth, in your benefit to this planet, in the necessity of your life, then you are living a truly whole, actualized life. Uzume teaches Amaterasu this lesson within her first myth, as Amaterasu remembers her beautiful Divine state. In the second myth, Uzume learns this lesson once again by questioning Saruta-Hiko and realizing that he has kind plans for Ninigi.

---

10. Ziehr, "Ame-no-Uzume no Mikato."

Sexuality is a large part of understanding and internalizing wholeness in our lives and Uzume knows and lives this truth. Uzume has the courage to be bawdy and sexual in front of gods and demons alike. She is completely comfortable with her own body and its fertile, creative abilities. She embraces her life-giving energies as she metaphorically gives birth to Amaterasu and Saruta-Hiko. Without her, neither the goddess nor the demon would have been able to fulfill their life paths. Amaterasu would have stayed in her cave and Saruta-Hiko would have been either destroyed or ignored. Here, in her sexual state, Uzume is the creatrix. Through the acknowledgement and celebration of her sex organs, Uzume carries the inner spark of creation. And so do we.

We can honor our roles as creators by celebrating our juices and secretions and sex organs. With the act of sex, with our semen and our eggs, we create life. Life! We bring children into the world simply by the mingling of our organic, biologic selves. We are truly amazing individuals! All of us! But the time has come to continue our birthing abilities, expanding them to all aspects of our lives. Not only can we create babies, but we can create our own reality. We can manifest our perfect lives, if only we have the courage, if only we embrace our sexuality, if only we strip away the unnecessary. Uzume teaches us that wholeness is but one laugh, one dance, one bared breast away. Our healing resides within us if only we let go of anger and fear and let in humor, sexuality, and love. Are you ready to live a life of wholeness? Are you ready to choose to manifest your dreams? Uzume is here, waiting to help you.

Pathway to Uzume

Let's be honest—not much shocks the modern world anymore. We see live war coverage on the TV, explicit sexual scenes of every kinky fetish on video, and twenty-four-hour coverage of devastation and atrocities, both human and natural. Kangaroo with two heads? Been there. Man eating live, dung-covered cockroach? Done that. Bat boy abducted by aliens? Yesterday's news. We are jaded by the constant stream of information fed to us via internet, television, newspapers, and magazines. And it is time to turn it off. All of it. For how are we supposed to expose ourselves, emotionally and physically, with late-night TV blaring in the background?

Uzume teaches us that to get to a sense of healthy wholeness, we need to remove the old. Old baggage. Old ideas. Old stories. And, especially, old clothes. Get rid of them and revel in the completeness of you, as you are, in the moment. So here's what you need to do. Choose a day and cut yourself off from the information nation. Don't answer e-mail, watch TV, or read a newspaper or magazine article. Instead, pay attention to yourself and to your world, as you see it around you. Go for a walk. Press leaves or flowers. Peruse your closet and give away anything that you don't wear. Spend fifteen minutes patting your dog . . . in silence. Spend an hour coloring or making jewelry or painting or writing. In short, commit to yourself. Trust me, you're worth it!

In the evening, when the call of the television beckons, tap into the sexual nature of Uzume by reading a risqué novel or a sex manual. Play Kama Sutra sticker tag with your lover, using the *Kama Sutra Sticker Book*. Massage your significant other or go out for a professional massage. Re-connect to your body by eating chocolate-covered strawberries, lighting jasmine- or ylang-ylang-scented candles, and slathering cinnamon-vanilla lotion on your hands and feet. Buy yourself flowers (the sex organs of the plant) and enjoy their sweet smell. In short, turn off the mental manipulations of the mind and sink into the bubbly behavior of the body. When you do, the creation and birth of the true you will follow.

SULIS
British Goddess of Cures and Curses

MANTRA

Balance, balance is the key
To gain health of sun and sea.

The concept of duality becomes immediately apparent upon close investigation of the British goddess Sulis. The goddess' Roman heritage is as obvious as her British ancestry, as evidenced by her alternate name, Sulis Minerva. The Romans entered Britain in 43 BCE and stayed for almost 400 years. During this time, it was quite common for them to adopt traditional British heritage and re-mold it to fit the Roman mindset. Gods and goddesses were not immune to this particularly devastating Roman practice. In fact, since the Druids openly defied Rome and urged their fellow Britons into rebellion, the gods were some of the first British icons to be Romanized. Yet, it is rare to find hybrid versions of British goddesses—Sulis Minerva is a notable exception.

Sulis is intrinsically linked to the Roman town of Aquae Sulis, which boasted the only hot springs in all of Britain and was named after her. The hot springs have been considered sacred since the Neolithic times, but it was the Romans who constructed elaborate temples and baths around them. The main spring emits a quarter of a million gallons of 120-degree-Fahrenheit water each day. Forty-three different beneficial minerals have been found in its waters, including iron, magnesium, potassium, copper, and radium. During the Roman period, an elaborate system of lead pipes fed water to numerous bathing pools. The sick and injured would rest in these bathing pools, allowing the healing waters of Sulis to wash over them. Although the temples and baths crumbled after the Romans left, Aquae Sulis, now known as Bath, continued to be a popular spa and retreat center. Throughout the seventeenth and eighteenth centuries, it was quite common for royalty and nobility to travel to Bath to "take the cure," indulging in the warming, healing waters.[11]

Although the baths were an important part of the Roman construct at Aquae Sulis, equally important were the numerous religious sites. Altars, carved invocations, and offerings litter the Roman ruins at Bath, many of them naming Sulis or Sulis Minerva directly. In fact, thirteen stone inscriptions name the goddess Sulis and three mention Sulis Minerva.[12] Approximately 130 curse tablets with Sulis' name on them have also been found throughout the bath complex. The sheer numbers attest to the importance of Sulis as a goddess, even though her story has been lost.

Many of these inscriptions request the health, well-being, and/or safety of an individual since he has "willingly and deservedly fulfilled his vow."[13] As this phrase appears several times on inscriptions dedicated to Sulis, it is important to look at it closely. The expression indicates that Sulis works hand-in-hand with humanity. A reciprocal goddess, she grants wishes and goals based on the sincerity and gift of the supplicant. Should you request the aid of Sulis, you would need to offer to do something for her in advance. An interaction with the goddess would, therefore, involve two parts: first, asking for her help, stating what you will do to gain her well-wishes and second, after performing your stated activity, going back to the goddess and letting her know that you have fulfilled your vow and you'd be interested in her granting your desire. The

---

11. Gray, "Bath, England."
12. Evans, "Sulis."
13. www.Roman-Britain.org, "Aquae Sulis/Aquae Calidae . . ."

creators of these carvings vary from retired Roman soldiers to freedmen to citizens of Roman-occupied British tribes. In short, they span a wide variety of social standings, occupations, and even cultures. Rich or poor, working class or upper class, the carvings indicate that Sulis was a goddess for all people. She appealed to everyone, listening to all pleas without judgment or rancor, as long as you fulfilled your promises. Since Sulis was known for giving a gift in return for a gift, is it any wonder that archeologists have dredged up votive offerings in huge quantities in the baths and springs around Aquae Sulis?

Water goddesses have long been honored and praised through gifts thrown into their respective bodies of water. (The goddess Coventina, whose sacred area is near Hadrian's Wall, is yet another example of this style of goddess-worship in Britain.) These goddesses were often thought to be connected to the world beneath the ground, the Underworld, the originating place of the water that bears the goddess' name. Sulis is no exception, and her association with the Underworld uncovers a darker element to this healing goddess, that of leveler of curses and retribution.

The curse tablets dedicated to Sulis or Sulis Minerva all request that something heinous happen to the offending individual who stole a missing item. No item was too small, as evidenced by the curse tablet stating: "Docimedis has lost two gloves. He asks that the person who has stolen them should lose his mind and his eyes in the temple where she appoints."[14] Another tablet asks that the person who carried off Vilbia be turned into water. The most famous Bath curse tablet says: "To the most holy goddess Sulis. I curse him who has stolen my hooded cloak, whether man or woman, whether slave or free, that . . . the goddess Sulis inflict death upon . . . and not allow him sleep or children now and in the future, until he has brought my hooded cloak to the temple of her divinity."[15]

The curse tablets show Sulis to be a goddess of justice and fairness, of right action and judgment, qualities associated very strongly with the Roman goddess Minerva (a.k.a., the Greek goddess Athena). Yet, I think it would be wrong to assume that this darker aspect of Sulis relates only to her Roman identification. When approached for boons and favors, Sulis must be appeased before the wish is granted. Her offertory inscription stones indicate a goddess who demands reciprocal action and desire, who re-

14. Fairgrove, "What We Don't Know About the Ancient Celts."
15. Evans, "Sulis."

quires a gift from each and every supplicant. With this in mind, the curse stones make sense, for they are simply an extension of the goddess' personality and her traditional interaction with humanity. Sulis requires a give-and-take relationship with humanity. She offers aid and grants relief only if she is given a gift as well. It would be easy to categorize this behavior as selfish, but it is actually more self-reliant. Sulis takes care of her own needs in order that she can care of everyone else's needs. Her well does not run dry because she constantly replenishes it with the well-wishes and offerings of her supplicants. She does not believe in interceding with mankind until an individual's needs are great, as indicated by his or her offering.

As a self-assured goddess, Sulis is not depicted as the consort of any god. Most of the inscriptions and curse tablets simply utilize her name only. However, there is one altar stone that pairs Sulis with the god Anicetus. Anicetus is a little-known Romano-British God of medicine, "described on a dedicatory tablet as 'Sol Apollo Anicetus.'"[16] The Latin word *sol* means "sun" and Apollo is the god of light and inspiration, often depicted as driving the chariot of the sun across the sky. So, the god Anicetus reminded the Romans of their sun god Apollo, possibly linking him to the sun, or at the very least, the qualities usually represented by the sun. Interestingly enough, although Sulis is traditionally symbolized by water and hot springs, her name comes from the proto-Celtic word for "sun," from which the Old Irish *súil* (eye) is derived. Her temple also includes a pediment (a triangular carving of a scene) with a circular, sun-like figure in the center. This figure has been called the "head of Medusa" or "the gorgon head," but it looks more like a man than a woman. With wide eyes, a mustached mouth, and radiating hair, the figure appears to be in the throes of ecstatic divination or communion with the Divine. Could this sun-like figure be a depiction of Anicetus, or is it a priest serving at the temple of Sulis? Based on the archeological evidence, we cannot definitively say, but it is an intriguing notion to consider the connection between Sulis and Anicetus.

Sulis, as a healing goddess, focuses on maintaining balance in the body, mind, and spirit. Her entire personality and forms of worship indicate her comfort with all aspects of life, including those of a less-savory nature. Sulis was known through the Romano-British Empire for her curative capabilities, but she was also highly sought-after for retribution, as evidenced by the cursing tablets. Goddess of healing springs and quite possibly of the sun, Sulis linked the opposing elements of fire and water together. She may

---

16. Squire. *Celtic Myth and Legend*, chapter XVI, 275.

even have completed the universal cycle of balance, the pairing of man and woman, by working with a little-known god of medicine. Sulis balances many opposing forces in order to heal.

The focus of Sulis' healing is not about letting go or giving in or finding out. She doesn't ask you to delve into the darkness of your soul or expose yourself to truth. Rather, she requests that we experience life right here and right now. All of life. The good and the bad. The dark and the light. For it is only through acknowledgement of the All that we can attain true balance in ourselves, gaining health of mind, body, and spirit. At that moment, we are a perfect vessel. Sulis knew this truth and encourages us to realize it for ourselves and implement it in our lives.

Pathway to Sulis

We all know that balance is important to a fulfilling and happy life. Yet, most of us allow this truth to slip through our fingers on a daily basis. We run here and there, never stopping, never breathing, just doing what *needs* to be done. Groceries, laundry, carpool, work, work, work! It's enough to drive anyone batty. Is it any wonder that Americans are overweight and depressed? With short (if any) vacations, a time-sensitive culture driven by movement and speed, and little down-time, we live completely out of balance. Where's our siesta? Where's our five-week vacation?

Living in a culture so completely out of balance makes it especially difficult to find individual harmony and health. It's so easy to make those New Year's resolutions but so hard to find the time to follow through. We simply don't have the hours or the energy to do something good for ourselves. (Crazy!) So, when starting on the path to achieving balance, health, and well-being, it's important to start small. Tiny. Miniscule, in fact. Otherwise, our great intentions and grand ideas get shoved aside. They become too big for us to accomplish.

So, let's take a step on the pathway to balance and start with a simple exercise that can be done while watching TV commercials, waiting for the toaster to pop, or even photocopying papers at work, if you feel comfortable. See this exercise as a beginning that you can build on, one tiny block at a time. In essence, you are shifting your mind-set, as well as your activities, by choosing a life of balance, rather than a life of imbalance. Your mind needs time to acclimate to this new way of thinking and this truth is something we don't always consider when creating our resolutions. Slow and steady steps are the way to help your mind, your emotions, and your body attune to your goal of balance.

The exercise is simple. Stand on one leg and bring your other leg up so the thigh is perpendicular to the floor (knee bent). Bring your hands to your heart, palms together in "prayer position." Your elbows should be pushed out to either side of your body. Breathe deeply and focus on maintaining your balance. Switch to the other leg when you feel ready. As you become more comfortable with this position, rotate the ankle of your non-support leg in a circular motion. Be sure to rotate in both directions. Eventually, this will become easy for you and you can move your non-supporting foot to the inside of your supporting leg, either at the calf or thigh, pushing your knee out to the side. Once you have mastered this position, push your arms up over your head, keeping your palms together and your elbows straight. This last position is known as the Tree Position in Hatha Yoga. But remember, the goal is not to rush to attain the ability to do Tree Position. Take your time. Allow your mind to catch up to your body and your body to catch up to your mind. While you're balancing, think of Sulis and how she unites fire and water, retribution and healing, aggression and release. Before too long, balance will be an everyday part of your life.

AIRMID
Irish Goddess of Herbs and Plants

MANTRA
Patience.
Wait a bit.
Allow the healing (wisdom, knowledge) to surface.

Unlike many Celtic Irish Goddesses, Airmid (AIR-mit) is content to wait. She does not force her opinion upon others. She does not push to get things done. Airmid knows that life takes time, that growth and healing do not happen quickly. As a goddess of healing, especially herbal healing, her personality and mantra preaches patience. After all, even a goddess must bow to the temperamental mood swings of the gracious Earth Mother.

Airmid grew up in a family of healers. Her father, Dian Cecht, is the healing god of the Tuatha dé Danann, the mythical race of gods known as the Children of the Goddess Danu. One of six children born to Dian Cecht, Airmid and her brother Miach were gifted with their father's healing touch. Airmid's mother was the abundant Mother Goddess of the Tuatha dé Danann, Danu, which explains her connection to herbs and healing plant life.

As with many Irish legends, the story of Airmid begins in the midst of battle, when the king of Ireland, King Nuada, has lost his hand. Disfigured, King Nuada is no longer eligible to rule Ireland. (Celtic rulers had to be fit both mentally and physically, as the physical condition of the body indicated the health of less obvious features, such as the mind and the spirit.) Wishing that King Nuada could continue to serve as king, Dian Cecht, the healer of the Danann Lords, steps forward with a plan: he will heal Nuada and restore him to the Irish throne. Dian Cecht asks Creidne, the god of bronzecraft and intricate metalwork, to craft a hand made from silver. Through his magical healing skill, Dian Cecht brings the hand to life so that it moves and works like a natural hand. It is attached to Nuada's arm and he is made king once again.[17]

The glory of Dian Cecht shines brightly until his son Miach and daughter Airmid arrive at the gates of Tara. They offer an alternative healing cure for the king's hand and are invited in to voice their proposal. They claim that through herbs and incantations, they can heal the withered, wrinkled, dry stump that was cleaved off of Nuada's body. Once whole, this newly wrought hand could be reattached to Nuada's arm. Dian Cecht, furious at possibly being overshadowed by his children, demeans their plan in front of the whole Hall of Tara. However, Nuada gives them permission to work their craft.

Miach begins a long and arduous healing ritual, lasting nine days. At the end of that time, he presents a completely whole hand to the king, crafted through the magical nature of the body, the word, and Mother Nature. In the high hall of the king, Miach is met with a flurry of praise over his healing ability. But he also encounters the biting sting of a sword blade. Furious at being overshadowed by his son, Dian Cecht challenges Miach to heal several wounds on himself, inflicted by his own father! Three times Dian Cecht slices into the skull of his son and three times, Miach heals himself. On the fourth attack, Dian Cecht cuts right to the very center of the brain, actually removing it! Miach

---

17. Gray, *Second Battle of Mag Tuired*, verse 11.

cannot heal such a grievous wound and dies, at the foot of the king, by the hand of his father.[18]

Throughout Miach's magical healing and his ordeal with his father, Airmid disappears from the story. She does not aid her brother in reshaping King Nuada's hand. She does not help her brother when he is attacked by their father. Perhaps she withdraws out of respect for her father's feelings, or perhaps out of fear for her father's actions. Her delay may stem from her brother's arrogant attitude and healing techniques or from her quiet demeanor or unwillingness to take sides in a family dispute. Perhaps she loves her family so greatly that she cannot choose one family member over the other. Or perhaps Airmid does not have access yet to her own healing power, as it is hiding deep inside herself.

Whatever the reason, Airmid's healing magic blossoms only after the death of her brother, after it is too late to save his life. Angry at her father and distraught over her brother's death, Airmid spends an entire year[19] visiting his grave every day on the Hill of Tara, spending long hours at the site, ignoring her other responsibilities and duties. Airmid delves into a period of sickened grief, focusing entirely on her brother's death. Through this anguish and depression, she accesses a part of herself that she has never experienced before. The death of her brother forces Airmid to delve into the very depths of her soul, gaining her own wisdom and insight. She steps out of the shadow of her magical brother and controlling father and (in integrating the shadow) becomes powerful in her own right.

On the anniversary of her brother's death, Airmid notices several beautiful green shoots growing from the grave. Paying close attention, she realizes that they are various healing herbs, 365 healing herbs, to be precise—one for each joint and sinew of her brother's body. She leaves the grave and returns the next day, ready to learn the remedies of the herbs. On this day, a year and a day from Miach's death, Airmid gathers the herbs, laying them out on her apron or her cloak in a pattern that indicates their healing

---

18. Ibid., verse 34.

19. *The Second Battle of Mag Tuired* never states the length of time that Airmed visits her brother's grave. However, since 365 herbs grow from his burial site, one modern interpretation of the legend claims that she visited for the length of a year (365 days) and on each day a new herb appeared. Another modern interpretation states that she visited for the span of a year and on the following day (the 366th day), a blanket of herbs covered the burial mound of her brother. Neither theory can be verified by ancient lore.

properties. There is no mention in ancient sources of how Airmid gains the knowledge of the herbs. Some scholars have speculated that the way the herbs were growing on the earthen mound indicated their usefulness. Others believe that the herbs actually spoke to Airmid, telling her their healing powers. Perhaps her brother visited her in a dream or transferred all his considerable herbal knowledge to her in her sleep. Or perhaps Airmid already knew, intuitively, the properties of the herbs, and her brother's death brought this inner knowledge into her conscious mind. Miach's death catalyzed the birth of Airmid's healing power.

Unfortunately for Airmid, Dian Cecht follows his daughter to the gravesite and upon seeing her gaining the wisdom of the herbs, rushes out of hiding and roughly shakes her cloak. The herbs scatter and Airmid no longer knows, for certain, which herbs worked for which ailments. Despite Dian Cecht's behavior, Airmid does not lose the inner wisdom she has acquired during her solitary days of mourning. The knowledge of the herbs is hidden once again but waiting, always, for someone to dig a little deeper, to access their inner psyche and subconscious wisdom. Airmid, quiet and wise, daughter and sister, is the connective stream between us and the plant world. She is the forgotten knowledge that we all intuitively share. She guides the mothers and daughters and sisters who have been passing down information for centuries. Dian Cecht exclaims in *The Second Battle of Mag Tuired*, "Though Miach no longer lives, Airmid shall remain."[20]

In order to know the healing within the herbs—the intuitive knowledge of how to make ourselves whole—we cannot rely on the bright, obvious answers provided by Miach. (These were destroyed by his jealous father.) Instead, we must travel within the self in order to find the inner knowledge, just as Airmid gazed within to understand the meanings of the herbs.

Intimately connected to the growing cycles of the Earth, Airmid knows the beauty of life after death, the cyclical passing of one season into another, the blossoming and withering of the fragile plant world. Having experienced this cycle firsthand through her year-long vigil on her brother's grave mound, Airmid has found her reservoir of healing power in the gentle, unobtrusive knowledge of the herbs. Unlike her father and her brother, Airmid knows that healing comes from within each and every individual. We simply need to find the time to listen to ourselves, to our own intuitive wisdom.

---

20. Gray, *Second Battle of Mag Tuired,* verse 35.

Once we do, the answers will become obvious to us, just as the knowledge of the herbs became obvious to Airmid.[21]

Pathway to Airmid

Once again we see our ancient ancestors guiding us away from the hustle-bustle of the modern world and into a period of introspection, where we are confronted with ourselves, where we can access our own wisdom and make ourself well. In the case of Airmid, perhaps it is time for some tea, and in the tradition of the great Irish bards, poetry.

Go to your local grocery store or health food store and peruse the tea aisle. Take your time and really see each and every box of tea. Don't rush! Since we are working with the goddess Airmid, focus on the herbal teas but don't ignore any tugs or twinges of intuition if you feel called toward the black or green teas. Read the labels on the boxes and decide to concentrate on only one aspect of your health. You might choose peppermint tea for digestion or chamomile for relaxation. Whatever you decide, choose a box of tea that fits your needs, your pocketbook, your taste buds, and your personality. Your goal is to find a tea that you will look forward to drinking every day.

Sometime during your day, at least once a week, find a half-hour to simply sit and think and be. This might be after supper, after the kids have gone to bed, or before heading off for work in the morning. The time of day doesn't matter, as long as you can find some quiet time alone. Brew your tea and sweeten it with sugar or honey, if you wish. Don't leave your teabag too long in your hot water at first, as you might find that the tea is too strong for you. Play with the length of time that you allow the tea bag to steep until you have found your perfect cup of tea.

Sit down on your couch or at your dining or kitchen table. Don't read a magazine. Don't balance your checkbook. Don't make a list of things to do. Simply sit. Look out your window at the sky and the world around you. What do you see? Take in the different colors, the beautiful textures, the slow spinning of our beautiful Mother Earth. Drink your tea. Breathe deeply. Be in the moment. And, if you want to, pull out a poem and read it out loud, sharing it with the beauty of the world around you. There are numerous poems of value and worth, of beauty and depth, so choose one that moves

---

21. Much of the story of Airmid first appeared in *Goddess Afoot!*, 108–112. For more information and intimate workings with Airmid, Irish Goddess of Herbal Healing, including a guided meditation and ritual, please see chapter 6 of *Goddess Afoot!*

you. One of my favorite poems is in the form of a children's book, entitled *Where Have the Unicorns Gone*, by Jane Yolen. Simple, luminous, and poignant, the plight of the unicorns corresponds directly to the message of Airmid: Look within to the wisdom of your emotional center, ignoring the darkness and negativity all around you. You have the power to access that which is hidden.

RITUAL FOR HEALING:
THE RATTLE OF HEALTH

Suggested Ritual Days

April 7: World Health Day, as declared by Pan American Health Organization

September 30: World Heart Day, as declared by the World Heart Federation

October 1: National Child Health Day, as declared by the U.S. Department of Health and Human Services

October 10: World Mental Health Day, as declared by World Federation for Mental Health

December 1: World AIDS Day, as declared by the United Nations

There are many more health days sponsored around the world that deal with specific problems and issues. These are all listed on the National Health Observances Calendar, which can be found on-line or through the U.S. Department of Health and Human Services.

Items needed

your favorite meditation music
two candles and candle holders
rattle
a white sheet

Lay out your ritual items on a low table (like a coffee or end table), making sure there is a comfortable place to lie down nearby. You will need to be completely alone and uninterrupted for this ritual, so plan your time accordingly. It would not be a good idea to perform this ritual while the football game blares in the background, in between ferrying your children to their activities, or while waiting for your girlfriend to get off work. This is an intense ritual that demands space, time, and concentration.

Once your ritual space is set up and you have turned off the phones (including your cell phone), the TV, the radio, and the computer, put on your meditation music. If you don't have favorite meditation or relaxation music, be sure to listen all the way through a CD before you begin this ritual. There's nothing worse than being in the midst of ritual activity and having your music completely change tone and tempo. The first song is not always indicative of the entire album!

Listen to your music for a few minutes, relaxing, allowing all the stress and worry of the day to roll off your shoulders and drip from your fingertips. Tense and then relax each of your muscles in turn, releasing tension. When you feel calm, light your first candle. This candle represents the ailment you no longer wish to have in your body. This could be physical, such as arthritis, or mental, such as depression. Take some time to truly think about this ailment. How long have you had it? Where does it stem from? Why does it persist in lingering? Consider all the treatments you have undergone in order to rid yourself of this ailment. Have any of them worked? For how long? To what degree? What can the cures tell you about yourself and your ailment?

When you feel like you have explored all aspects of your ailment, turn to your other candle and light that one. This candle symbolizes your life without the ailment, you in full health. Think about what the end of your ailment would mean to you. What would you be able to do? How would life change for the better? Who would benefit besides yourself?

With these thoughts in your mind, pick up your rattle and begin to shake it over the area that best represents your ailment. (For instance, if you are working on depression, you might choose to shake the rattle over your heart or your mind. If you have arthritis, you might shake the rattle over the body part that most bothers you.) Keep focusing on your healing and the positive benefits for you, your family, and friends.

Rattling is an old shamanic technique used to shake up energy and move it away. It is a very powerful form of energetic healing that can cause some discomfort emotionally and physically. If you have an ailment that has been with you for quite some time, don't try to remove it all at once. Go slowly. Rattle for five minutes a week, building up to longer and deeper time periods of dispersal of energy. Go with your intuition and if something hurts, stop rattling. You might feel fluctuations in your body or your emotions. This is normal! But, if you start to become distressed or overworked, if you begin to hyperventilate or experience trouble breathing or if you begin to feel sharp pains, stop rattling immediately and move on with the ritual. Do not stop the ritual mid-way, as that may cause further damage to your body and/or mind.

Once you have completed the rattling session, blow out the candle that represented your ailment. If you feel you have eliminated the ailment with just one rattling session, great! Bury or burn the candle. If you feel you may need more sessions to fully uproot the ailment, save the ailment candle, along with your healing candle. As the healing candle burns on the table, wrap yourself in the white sheet and lie down. Ideally, the light from the healing candle should be shining on you. Breathe deeply and visualize white healing energy all around you and within you. The white sheet represents the healing energy from the universe, from the Great Spirit, from the God and Goddess, from the angels and faeries, from your ancestors. By wrapping yourself in the white sheet, you are filling any energetic holes created when the rattle dispersed the harmful energy. You are filling these energetic gaps with pure white healing light. Listen to your music and relax for a few minutes. When you feel ready, sit up, blow out the healing candle, and remove the white sheet. Your healing ritual is complete. Store your ritual items in a safe place so you can use them again.

CHAPTER EIGHT

Goddess Mantras for Growth

GROWTH: MINING THE PAST FOR A BETTER FUTURE

When we as humans talk about growth, there is always an element of bettering oneself—getting bigger, becoming better, gaining more. We discuss the growth charts of our children. We worry about our individual emotional growth and personal path to our goals. We work on growing our nest eggs and retirement funds. In short, growth is about measuring where we are now and comparing that to where we once were and where we someday hope to be. It is a constant judgment that, in truth, can become wearying. After all, what's wrong with where we are now?

Nothing. Absolutely nothing. In fact, I would like to boldly state that you are exactly where you are simply because you are exactly where you are. Confusing, I know, but bear with me. Consider the fact that all of our past actions and experiences led each of us to this exact moment in time. To you, reading these words, and me, writing them down. If any aspect of your life in the past had been different, you might never have picked up this book. You might never have thought that growth was possible. You might not have married your significant other or pursued your current career. You wouldn't be living your life, this life. Oh no, you'd be living someone else's life.

Our present actions and conditions are direct descendents of our past. We cannot undo the past. It is there, it has happened, and it cannot be changed. Our conscious minds may forget about the past, but we can never outrun or outmaneuver it. It simply keeps stride, subconsciously shaping all of our thoughts and feelings, actions and reactions, words and deeds. Our experiences, both good and bad, have brought us to this exact moment in time, infiltrating our present as quickly and thoroughly as any rampant virus. We may overcome the common cold in our body but the anti-virus cells remain, ever vigilant, forever on the lookout for intruders. Even though they may go into hibernation and may never be called on again, the anti-virus cells—the experiences and lessons learned—stay in our body, forever changed by one incident in the past.

So you have arrived here, at this moment at exactly the right time for you. Old or young, it doesn't matter, for you are on your life course and yours alone. No one can dictate your life. When I was a junior in college, I had a friend who took a year off from college. When her mother was shopping at the local grocery store, she ran into the mother of one of Chrissy's high school chums. This woman gasped when she heard Chrissy was not in schooling for a whole year. "But, how will she catch up?" she blathered, clearly distraught. And you know what Chrissy's mother said? She said, "Catch up to what?" She realized that Chrissy's life was her own and that she didn't need to follow a prescribed societal notion of life after high school. College can be done in four years or five years or eight years. Or maybe not at all. After all, it's your life.

Therefore, while our past guides our present, it does not define it. We can move beyond our experiences, our conditioning, our mental lapses and trigger points, to be exactly who we are and who we want to be. This is the essence of growth. It's not about being dissatisfied with your current life; rather, it's about crafting the life that you want to live, both now and in the future. Growth encourages you to throw away the notions, ideas, and actions that don't mean anything to you so you can create space for the things you love.

Growth gives you space to look at your past through the lens of your memories and decide which experiences served you and which ones did not. Granted, you can't remove the aspects of the past that were detrimental to you. After all, they are woven into the very fiber of your body, mind, and soul. However, you can lessen their negative impact by staring at them face-to-face and acknowledging their existence in your life. You can dig deep into your soft, squishy, inner core to see where these incidents have hidden their insidious ideas and where they currently manifest in your life. Perhaps you simply can't go to the movie theater due to a persistent fear of the dark that has haunted you since you were locked in the closet as a joke by your older brother. Maybe you believe you can't sing because your cousin told you so when you were twelve. Or perhaps you refuse to wear black after having experienced a tragic funeral at a young age. Whatever the past experience, we all have aspects of some event still affecting our lives.

But the important question is: how do we reduce the impact of a negative experience from the past? Some people like to symbolically "get rid" of such incidents by writing letters and burning them or burying objects that represent the experience. Unfortunately, the past can't be removed. It can be transmuted and changed, but it can't be forcibly lifted from the recesses of your memory. It's there and it's not going anywhere. So, the trick is to utilize this experience for the good of yourself, the good of your family, and the good of your community. With the singing example mentioned above, you might begin by singing along with the radio, when you know you are alone. Eventually, over time, you might graduate to singing along with the radio when other people are in the room. As you begin to understand that singing is an expression of the soul, an emotional release, a way to connect to others around you, you may decide to sing in your church choir or with a community theatrical group, attuning yourself to the world around you. And then, as you become more and more confident in your singing expression, you will be able to encourage others to sing, helping them move past fears of ridicule or censure.

At that point, you will have experienced growth. Not for the sake of change. Not in order to achieve and succeed. Not in order to accomplish a goal. Rather, your growth occurred as a natural expression of your past and your present. Beginning with one random comment from your cousin from your past, you were able to alter its effect on your present in order to create a more comfortable existence for yourself and for your community. Growth on an individual scale is fabulous, but true growth should exceed the limitations of the self. If you are really growing and integrating the past for the benefit of all, then you have tapped into the unconscious reality of *wyrd* or *orlog*. You are taking the threads of your past life and modifying them so they fit your current reality. That is the essence of true growth, the shaping of old individual experiences into new futures affecting all. Welcome the rebirth!

ENERGY RETURN

One of the most difficult aspects of growth is delving deep into our psyche in order to see the experiences of the past that are currently shaping our reality. It's messy. It's nasty and often deals with issues and problems that we'd just as soon forget. Sometimes looking at the past can bring up even greater traumas, negatively influencing our current lives. If this should happen to you, get the help of a trained professional that you trust. Your best friend will likely lend a sympathetic ear, but she won't know how to help you through the psychological pain. Find a therapist. Ideally, he or she should have some sort of spiritual or New Age focus in order to understand your need to integrate and utilize the past for positive benefits in the present. You can often find listings for such therapists at your local New Age shop or through a regional New Age magazine or newsletter.

After you have looked at past experiences that are negatively affecting your life, you might find yourself with feelings of bitterness or resentment toward the people who orchestrated those experiences. If you choose to dwell on them, these feelings can lead to self-pity and an attitude of martyrdom. This benefits nobody! Not the person in your past, not your community at large, and most certainly not you! Self-pity is just an excuse to wallow in the past and not take responsibility for your present and future. The past happened; you can't change it, but you do have control over your life in the present. Other people are to blame for experiences in your past but they cannot be held responsible for your present and future. Their control over you has ended. Don't give control back to them! It is time to realize your power and wield it for the good of yourself and of the world.

Coming into your power and reshaping your relationship with the past has far-reaching consequences. Before you begin your growth quest, you should be aware that growth in one aspect of your life usually influences other aspects of your life. Be prepared for alteration and change in all its many forms. Change can sometimes be unsettling, but know that in the long run, you are crafting a more fulfilling life for yourself. The bumps and bruises along the way will seem like nothing once your present and future reflect the things you love rather than the rippling images of the past.

HEQET
Egyptian Goddess of Childbirth and Resurrection

MANTRA

I am the resurrection.
The Breath of Life revives me.

Although a minor deity in the Egyptian pantheon, Heqet is a very powerful goddess who participates in major transition times in a person's life. Usually depicted as a woman with a frog head, a woman with a frog headdress, or an actual frog, she is the protector

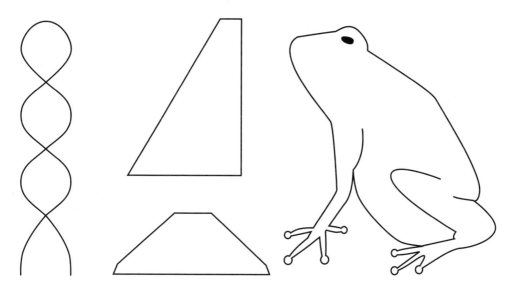

Figure 4: Name of Heqet in Hieroglyphs

and helper of women in the throes of childbirth as well as one of the guides who attends the soul (or *Ka*) after death. In the last sense, she is deeply entrenched in the notion of resurrection or re-birth, as the ancient Egyptians believed that the Ka was reborn in the afterlife. In the first, she perpetuates her role as goddess of fertility and creation.

Above all, Heqet is associated with the concepts of germination and birth. She is the beginning and the end of the cycle that brings life to the world. With her assistance, seeds sprout and babies are born. As the wife of Khnum, the god who molds human bodies on his potter's wheel, she gives the newly created child the breath of life before placing it in the mother's womb. Both Khnum and Heqet are visible on the birth colonnade of Hatshepsut in her Mortuary Temple at Deir el-Bahri in Egypt. This colonnade shows the mother of Hatshepsut (Ahmose) being led to the birthing room by Khnum and Heqet. They hold her hands and Heqet walks in the lead, turning her head as if to assess the condition of the expectant mother.[1]

Heqet continues to display her creative power in the story "Khufu and the Magician," which is found on the Westcar Papyrus and dates from the Second Intermediary Period, around 1500 BCE. In this story, Raddjedet, wife of a priest of the sun god Ra, is pregnant with triplets who are destined to become kings of Egypt. As her birthing time nears,

---

1. "Deri el-Bahri, Mortuary Temple of Hatshepsut."

she begins to experience difficulty, so Ra requests the aid of deities of childbirth and creativity. Isis, her sister Nephthys, the birthing brick goddess Meskhenet, and Heqet are dispatched to the side of the laboring mother-to-be. The four travel under the guise of musicians and dancers, with the god Khnum as their manager.

When they arrive at the house, they are immediately ushered into the birthing chamber. Isis and Nephthys flank the birthing woman, at her head and feet, while Heqet hastens the birth. Before each child is born, Isis commands they leave the womb and enter the room. After each birth, the child is cleaned and the cord cut, presumably by Nephthys and Meskhenet, since Heqet and Isis seem to be busy with the birthing mother. Meskhenet then presents the child to Khnum, who gives health to the baby.[2] All five gods have important roles to play in the birth of a child, but it is Heqet who works with the mother to bring the child into the world. She is in the thick of the birthing process, using her hands to guide new life into the world. Unlike Isis and Meskhenet, who provide encouragement and necessary implements for the birth, Heqet simply brings herself. It is not her voice or her tools that matter but her actual presence. Heqet is the midwife for the laboring mother-to-be, attending to the task at hand with her knowledge and skill. Heqet's unique role in this story (one of the few surviving stories of childbirth from ancient Egypt) has led some modern goddess-lovers to believe that some of Heqet's priestesses served as midwives. However, no tangible evidence has been found to verify this claim.

Heqet further cements her connection to fertility and creation with her totem animal, the frog, which appears along the swollen Nile in great numbers, heralding periods of grain germination and fruitfulness. To the ancient Egyptians, the frog came to represent growth, new life, and abundance, linking Heqet not just to human reproduction but to vegetation and grain production as well.

The frogs' connection to the Nile River in particular, and to water in general, further strengthens Heqet's relationship with fertility. Water is often equated to femininity, the Divine Feminine, and the organ that often defined women in the ancient past, the womb. Indeed, the frog (and its land-locked cousin, the toad) were often thought to be the manifestation of the goddess' uterus, which may have led to the belief of the "wandering womb" concepts found in Egyptian, ancient Greek, and Roman texts.[3] Several anthropomorphic statues with frog bodies and human heads have been found through-

---

2. Seawright, "Tales of Magic in Ancient Egypt."

3. Gimbutas, *Language of the Goddess*, 251.

out Europe dating from the fifth and sixth millennia BCE. These statues specifically mark the vulva of the frog-woman with a triangle, indicating her importance in reproductive activities and thus with the uterus and the vulva.[4] Belief in the fertile powers of frogs continued into the nineteenth century CE, where a frog was found next to the Madonna on a votive tablet and a tombstone of a frog with a flower bursting forth from its head mirrored a terra cotta figurine, nearly 8,000 years its senior.[5]

The flower depicted on both frog artifacts could have been a lily, often associated in ancient Egypt with birth and rebirth. Ancient Egyptian women commonly wore amulets of a frog sitting on a lily in the latter stages of their pregnancies.[6] The blue lily (or blue lotus) grows in abundance on the Nile River and is a symbol of regeneration and rebirth. Every evening, the flower closes its petals against the chilly night air and every morning it re-awakens, opening its blossom to the warm sun. As the lily sinks its roots in the mud and muck of the river bottom, it is also a potent reminder that life (the flower) springs from death (the decaying vegetation). Therefore, the blue lily is a flower of rebirth in the afterlife, as well as birth in this life. The blue lily is often depicted next to Osiris, the Egyptian god of resurrection. The four sons of Horus, who guard the canopic jars of the deceased, stand on Osiris' lotus. There is even a spell in the Egyptian Book of the Dead entitled "Making the Transformation of the Lotus," which was said over a dead body in the belief that it would assist in the journey of the Ka to the Land of the Dead.[7] A large, wall-sized image of Heqet is apparent in the Osiris Chapel or Suite in the Temple of Seti I at Abydos. In this scene, offerings are being made to Heqet, who, in this instance, is serving in her role as intercessor for the dead.[8] Frog amulets were also placed on dead bodies in the hopes that the resurrecting power of Heqet would aid the Ka in its final journey. Frog terra cotta lamps found in Egypt often have the words "I am the resurrection" stamped on them, further testifying to Heqet's restorative power.[9]

Heqet is a goddess of change, of movement from one phase of life to another. Birth, rebirth, creation, resurrection—Heqet holds power over them all, ushering souls into

---

4. Ibid., 252–253.

5. Ibid., 254.

6. Seawright, "Heqet, Frog Headed Goddess of Childbirth."

7. Santos. "The Magical Blue Lotus," 281–283.

8. Rome, "The Temple of Seti I and the Osireion at Abydos."

9. Budge, *Egyptian Magic*, 63.

new stages of existence. Heqet is the small, frog-shaped mother goddess who under-stands the complications of female anatomy. She breathes life into new bodies and helps those bodies as they exit the womb. As we each exit this life for the next, the same guiding hands are there to aid us in transitioning to our new existence. Ushered in or out of this mundane world, our bodies feel the gentle pressure of Heqet's stable, secure hands. She is the constant as we manifest on this plane or other planes of existence. Comfortable in the spiritual world and the material world, Heqet leads us to lives beyond our imaginations, from the womb world of water to the granular dirt of the Earth to the spiritual breeze of the Otherworld and back to the womb. Circular and cyclical, we can count on Heqet's support and assistance as we grow beyond our current boundaries, face our fears, and move forward.

Pathway to Heqet

When in Egypt, do like the Egyptians! Wear a frog amulet! But not just *any* frog amulet. (You knew there was a catch, didn't you?) Try to find a frog pendant that truly speaks to you and reminds you of the fertile and rejuvenating power of Heqet. The amulets of the ancient Egyptians were most likely made out of an organic material, such as wood, bone, ivory, or stone. And these, my friend, are not easy to find in the modern era. Silver frogs and silly frogs, dangling frogs and grinning frogs, there are numerous frog pendants on the market, but not many of them evoke the majesty of a goddess. Your best bet is to search on-line auction sites, pawn shops, second-hand stores, and antique shops for unusual frog jewelry pieces. If you are handy with beading, you can also create your own frog amulet necklace using semi-precious frog charms and beads. These can be found at your local beading shop or craft store. If you start to become desperate and you can't find or create a suitable amulet, consider purchasing a personalized Egyptian cartouche necklace. A cartouche is a name plate written in hieroglyphics. With this option, your amulet would have the added benefit of connecting directly to Egyptian culture and history. Cartouche pendants are fairly inexpensive (as low as $20) and you could have the word "Heqet" or "frog" written on it, in order to connect to the goddess.

Once you've purchased or crafted your Heqet amulet, make a pot of herbal tea using only flowers from the blue lotus in Egypt. You will have to buy these herbs on-line at a shamanic website or special order them through your local herb shop. Make sure that the blue lotus you purchase uses the scientific name *Nymphaea caerulea*; this is the plant associated with the Nile River. Other lotus varieties utilize other scientific names—you don't want those! While beautiful and sweet smelling, they do not connect to Heqet and the concepts of resurrection and rebirth.

Allow your herbal tea to cool and pour it into a bowl of your choice. You should be able to immerse your entire amulet in the tea. Place your amulet in the tea mixture and envision the essence of the blue lotus merging with the energy of your amulet. You are bringing together the two aspects of Heqet—Birth Mother and Rebirth Guide. If you are pregnant and wish to use this amulet to bring health and a positive birth experience to yourself and your baby, place your hands over the bowl and focus on your goal. Really see yourself and your baby whole and well. Visualize your perfect birth experience. Be sure to include as many details as possible, including the people who will be in the birthing room with you, the tools or implements surrounding you (such as birthing stools, tubs, massage oils), and the environment in which your baby will enter the world.

After steeping your amulet in the blue lotus tea, remove it and allow it to drip dry. This will seal in your intentions, as well as the effects of the blue lotus flower. (Rubbing with a towel will simply wipe the power of the blue lotus away.) Once dry, slip your Heqet amulet on and be prepared to connect with this fascinating, caring goddess as you strive for inner growth!

POMONA
Roman Goddess of Orchards and Fruitfulness

MANTRA
Life! Life!
Love! Love!
Sex! Sex!
Growth! Growth!

If you're looking for a goddess with a green thumb, look no further: Pomona is your girl! As the caretaker of orchards and flowering trees, Pomona works intimately with living plants, getting her hands dirty. She does not command from on high. Instead, she works directly with the soil and the mud, with the saplings and the ancient trees to entice sweet fruits from their barren branches. With knowledge and love, Pomona lives among her charges, caring for them and honoring them for the delicacies they offer to the world.

The story of Pomona was written down almost two thousand years ago by the noted Roman poet, Ovid, who focused on her courtship with the god of change, Vertumnus. Change, when shaped by Vertumnus, does not dissolve into chaos. Rather, Vertumnus oversees the changing of the seasons, the exchange of trade, the turning of a river channel, and, most especially, the "change in nature from flower to ripe fruit."[10] Being concerned with vegetation and fruit, Vertumnus is aptly suited to the fair Pomona, but she would have none of him. In fact, she was uninterested in any attachments to men, be they satyrs, fauns, or gods. By the time Ovid tells his tale, Pomona has already refused the proposals of Silvanus, a fertility god of wild fields and forests, and Priapus, a well-endowed god of gardens and livestock. She devotes her life to the care of her orchard. Through pruning and shaping the branches of her trees and providing water to thirsty roots and leaves, Pomona shows her love. With a pruning knife as her sacred tool, Ovid tells us that she knows exactly how to graft tree branches together in order to bolster a nursling and create richer fruit. In short, Pomona is completely content living by herself, in her orchard, without a man. But Vertumnus will not leave her alone.

As a god of change, Vertumnus has the ability to shift his appearance. He can assume any form he desires. As time passes and it becomes apparent that Pomona does not return the love of any man, Vertumnus begins to visit her grove in various guises. He shows up as a reaper with baskets full of corn, bringing in the harvest bounty. He arrives as an ox-handler, sweating after a day of plowing. He appears as a fisherman with rod, a soldier with sword, and an apple picker with a ladder. He strolls by as a dresser and pruner of vines and as a field hand fresh from bundling up the new mown hay. These disguises might represent the passage of time, as they correspond to seasonal activities. The reaper could be seen as signifying autumn, while the plowman could be spring, and the fisherman, summer.[11] They are not recalled by Ovid in any seasonal order, but the disguises may have been remnants of an older myth that is not remembered in all its totality. In any event, Vertumnus makes every excuse to visit the fair Pomona but, true to her first love (the orchard), she barely glances his way as she cares for her trees.

---

10. Kelley, *The Book of Hallowe'en*, chapter 4.
11. Ibid.

Finally, Vertumnus dons the grey hair, colorful kerchief, and staff of an old woman, a disguise that would have symbolized winter. Pomona invites the old lady into her orchard. Vertumnus enters and, after praising the orchard, immediately kisses Pomona, "as no true old woman would have done."[12] Using a metaphor of a vine and an elm tree, Vertumnus attempts to persuade Pomona that marriage is an amenable state. He further presses his case for marriage by relating all of his own virtues to Pomona, while still pretending to be the old woman. Pomona listens well to her elder, showing respect and deference, but she is unimpressed by the idea of marriage. Finally Vertumnus launches into a sad tale of unrequited love that ends badly for both man and woman. The man, who loves ardently, is spurned so frequently that he eventually takes his own life by hanging himself at the gateway of his love. The unmoved woman, upon viewing his funeral procession, turns into stone, the hardness of her heart spreading out to encompass her entire body, turning her into a statue.

Yet, even this story does not sway Pomona from her love of solitary life. With no further arguments and nothing left to say, Vertumnus throws off the dress of the old lady and appears to Pomona in all his glory, young, virile, and handsome. Ovid describes him as "the glowing likeness of the sun, when it overcomes contending clouds, and shines out, unopposed."[13] Overwhelmed by the godhood of Vertumnus, Pomona immediately feels passion for him and agrees to become his wife. Together Pomona and Vertumnus work side by side, tending the orchards and fruit trees of the world.

Throughout Ovid's tale, Vertumnus is regularly described as a "god," while Pomona is labeled as a "hamadryad" and a "nymph." A hamadryad is a female elemental spirit that is directly tied to one particular tree. She is charged with the care and protection of that tree and, should that tree die, the life force of the hamadryad dies as well. A hamadryad is a specific type of dryad (elemental tree spirit), and dryads are a particular type of nymph. A nymph is a broad term for a female nature spirit. They are usually depicted as living in forests, seas, lakes, or other natural settings. Nymphs, as the name suggests, are often highly sexual, serving as the consorts of satyrs and enticing the devotions and love of men, fauns, and even gods. It is obvious that while Pomona nurtures and provides like a goddess, she also teases and taunts with the best of the nymphs. She does, after all, have numerous suitors, play hard to get, and inspire deep devotion and

---

12. Ovid, *The Metamorphoses*, "Vertumnus Woos Pomona," Bk. XIV, 623–697.
13. Ibid.

passion. Her magic lies in the earthiness of the ground, of sex and fertility and growth and substance. The goddess Pomona lives and loves and lusts along with humanity. She is deeply rooted in the construct of Mother Earth and all the inhabitants of the planet.

Yet the terms "hamadryad" and "nymph" have their roots in Greek mythology, not Roman mythology. To the Romans, both Pomona and Vertumnus were listed as *numina,* or spirits of place. The worship of numina (*numen,* singular) was an important aspect of Roman religious life that varied slightly from the honoring of the more well-known nymphs and satyrs of Greek mythology. Numina were afforded a great place in Roman spirituality and represented a deeper well-spring of power. The childlike antics and one-track minds of the Greek nature spirits are subsumed by a presence that brings holiness to a physical object or place. The numina confer sacredness and bridge the human world and the world of the gods. Everyday objects and everyday places become holy, bringing religion out of the temple and into the fields and orchards.

Pomona had just such a sacred grove, called a *Pomonal,* which was located near Ostia, the ancient port of Rome. One of the fifteen flamina—Roman priests who kindled the sacrificial fires—was dedicated to her and was called the *Flamen Pomonalis.* It is generally believed that her main festival day was on November 1; Vertumnus had his festival on August 23. Since the growing season began in October for Mediterranean Italy, Pomona's festival focused on the turning of flower into fruit. Offerings to the deities and numina of fire and rain were given in the hopes of assuring a full and complete harvest. By comparison, the focus of Vertumnus' festival was thankful in tone and content. Since the harvest had already occurred, the offerings thanked the deities and numina for their aid in providing such a full and ready harvest. Together Pomona and Vertumnus assure a plentiful harvest for the people. As a giver of food and drink, Pomona is almost always depicted with a basket or cornucopia of ripe fruits. These symbols indicate her focus of ensuring a healthy, satisfying, and full crop.

By her very actions, Pomona shows her love and her caring. Pomona provides for the masses, giving healthy fruit—apples, dates, plums, pears—to the world. She shows the virtues of independent thought by living alone for so long and focusing on her personal interests and desires. At the same time, Pomona's innate fruitfulness reminds us that we are all sexual beings. We all are searching to make a connection with others, especially those of like mind. Pomona does not open her orchard gates to just anybody. Oh no! She waits for the opportune time and the right man to arrive, he who will complete her and aid her in her lifelong goal. Pomona teaches us that we can be true to ourselves while allowing others, who have our best interests at heart, into our lives. That is the recipe for growth toward a happy life. That is the recipe for a fruitful existence. Be true to yourself while opening your heart to love.

Pathway to Pomona

There is something about an apple that evokes deep-rooted feelings and emotions. We have so many superstitions and legends surrounding that blessed fruit. "An apple a day keeps the doctor away." It is the forbidden fruit from the tree of knowledge in the Garden of Eden. It lures us away from everyday life as the symbol of the mystical Island of Avalon and the five-seeded pentagram fruit of modern goddess-worship. The apple is far more than a delicious morsel; it is a gateway to the truth, the past, the Otherworld, the inner you. The apple, like Pomona herself, bridges the world of humanity with the world of the gods. It is a conduit of power and wisdom.

So, access that knowledge and eat an apple! While Pomona cares for all trees in her orchard, the apple is especially sacred to her. Her name is derived from the Latin word *pomum*, meaning "fruit." but the French word for apple, *pomme*, deliciously reflects her bounty. Apples, nuts, and grapes were especially present at her harvest festivals.[14] So, the next time you want to connect to the fruitfulness of the goddess Pomona, crunch into a sweet, firm apple. Even better, pick your own apples at a local orchard and then enjoy this healthy, satisfying snack. And, as you munch, consider the juiciness of your apple, so representative of Pomona's enticing beauty and her attraction to the opposite sex. Allow the tartness to tingle on your tongue and relish the sauciness of Pomona's demeanor in dealing with her erstwhile suitors, especially Vertumnus. Finally, enjoy the fullness of the apple, the way it quenches your thirst and fills your belly, so representative of Pomona's quest to be true to herself while opening her heart to love. The apple reminds us that we can indeed achieve our goals on our own terms, if we allow ourselves to grow and change. We can have it all!

---

14. Goddess Chess Blog, "The Goddess Pomona."

BLODEUWEDD
Welsh Goddess of Personal Growth and Change

MANTRA

I am the flower
And I am the owl.
I bend to my will.
(My will be done.)

There is nothing more difficult to accept than change. Daily life assumes a relaxing, natural rhythm and then WHAM! Something occurs to destroy your bubble of peace and security. We can thank Blodeuwedd (blo-DY-weth) for that. The goddess Blodeuwedd welcomes change, alteration, transformation, and variation. Not content with a devoted husband, a beautiful castle home, and a secure life, Blodeuwedd chooses the excitement of true love over the sanctuary of marriage. She realizes that a refuge can just as easily become a prison.

In *The Mabinogion*, the Welsh medieval mythological epic, Blodeuwedd is created by Math ap Mathonwy for his nephew, Lleu Llaw Gyffes. Lleu has been cursed by his mother Arianrhod with never having a human wife so he turns to his uncle, Math, a great magician, who crafts a woman out of flowers. Whether crafted from three flowers (those of the oak, broom, and meadowsweet) or nine flowers (those of oak, broom, meadowsweet, primrose, cockle, bean, nettle, chestnut, and hawthorn), it is obvious that Blodeuwedd is a being unlike any other in our world. As such, she lives outside the restrictions that humanity places on itself and, instead of succumbing to society's laws, bends society to her laws.

After her birth, Blodeuwedd is immediately married to Lleu and they settle into the castle of Tomen Y Mur in Wales. All seems well but, before long, Lleu decides to visit his uncle, leaving Blodeuwedd by herself. Left to her own designs, Blodeuwedd looks for something more than her hum-drum life as the wife of a medieval lord. She settles her sights on a hunter, Gronw Bebyr, who coincidentally happens to be hunting near Tomen Y Mur. Blodeuwedd invites Gronw and his men to spend the night inside her castle. (You see where this is going, right?)

Over dinner, Blodeuwedd and Gronw exchange glances and are immediately overtaken with love for each other. Their love is so sudden and so sharp that they sleep together that very night. For two days and nights, Blodeuwedd and Gronw live in an ecstasy of bittersweet love, constantly looking over their shoulders, hoping Lleu will not arrive home. With those acts of love-making, Blodeuwedd achieves a measure of satisfaction she has never felt before. She begins to realize her own power and her own ability to choose and act according to her own wishes. For two days, Gronw suggests that he should leave and Blodeuwedd counters with the phrase "Thou wilt not go from me."[15] Unbelievably, Gronw obeys, solidifying Blodeuwedd's newfound confidence in herself. On the third day, Blodeuwedd gives her consent to Gronw's departure but agrees with his plan to find out how to kill her husband so she may be free to marry her new lover.

The very day that Gronw departs, Lleu arrives home, blithely unaware of his wife's intentions. That evening, Blodeuwedd takes control of her marriage by refusing Lleu's amorous attentions. When her husband questions her about her obvious distress, she tricks him into telling her the arrangements and conditions necessary to kill him. (Remember, Lleu is the child of the goddess Arianrhod and thus no mere mortal.) Immediately, Blodeuwedd sends the instructions to Gronw and waits a year for Gronw to craft the killing spear. Once the year passes and the spear is made, Blodeuwedd, once again, takes control of her own life and tricks Lleu into constructing the scenario necessary for his death. (Lleu actually builds the necessary structures and demonstrates the necessary actions to kill him.) Naturally, Blodeuwedd had depended on Lleu's congenial nature, as Gronw is already in the necessary position to kill her husband. Throwing the spear, Gronw pierces Lleu with the poisoned tip. Blodeuwedd and Gronw then believe Lleu is dead, but he has actually shapeshifted into an eagle and flown away.

With Lleu gone, Blodeuwedd and Gronw are free to be lovers, and they move into Tomen Y Mur together. Blodeuwedd has followed her own mind and created her own reality. However, the outside world has its own set of rules and intrudes on the lover's nest. Gwydion and Math, relatives of Lleu, discover his transformation through their magics. They bring Lleu back to Math's castle, where they nurse him to health. Once whole again, the three men descend upon Tomen Y Mur, but Blodeuwedd has already fled to a nearby mountain. Alas, she is no match for the two magicians and one warrior. They catch up to her, and Gwydion changes her into an owl, a bird that is feared by all

---

15. Jones and Jones, *Mabinogion,* 59.

other birds. Gronw does not escape Lleu's wrath either, and ironically is killed by Lleu with a spear. Blodeuwedd's bid for independence and true self is thwarted. Or is it?

Through her relationship with Gronw, Blodeuwedd comprehends there is more to her character than she originally surmised. She has power but with that power comes awesome responsibility and a necessary acceptance of all sides of her complex personality. She is not all flowers and springtime and happiness. She has a strength of will and a personal agenda that goes beyond her role as Lleu's wife. She is greater than she imagined, more full and whole than her original flower-bride conception. Blodeuwedd is the owl as well, bringing midnight and darkness and death. Without her dalliance with Gronw, Blodeuwedd would never have thought to cuckold her husband and plan his death, despite the fact that these actions were always within her capabilities. Reaching into the dark places of her true self, Blodeuwedd unlocks her inner needs and desires and seeks to manifest them in her life.

Blodeuwedd teaches us that balance and transformation are necessary aspects of life. She grants us permission to accept our darker halves, to realize that we have power beyond that which we can comprehend. Fanciful, sexual, and lively, Blodeuwedd encourages us to live life to the fullest and to acknowledge our faults along with our positive attributes. We are all created of flowers and owls. If we only have the courage to change and unite our two halves, we will be amazed by our innate strength and power.[16]

Pathway to Blodeuwedd

Just as Blodeuwedd summoned up the courage to change her life for the better, so can you change to further your personal growth. Take a look at your life. A good, long look. And become aware of something that makes you unhappy. Perhaps it's your hair or your weight or your job or your family. Maybe it's all of these things but, for right now, just focus on one aspect. Choose the one thing that really frustrates you but doesn't appear overwhelming. Now, make the decision to change. That's right, take that one aspect of your life that upsets and frustrates you and alter it so it fits your agenda, your worldview, your will. Don't question your decision or your choice. Don't get bogged down in the details, just make the choice to change.

---

16. Much of the story of Blodeuwedd first appeared in *Goddess Afoot!*, 44–47. For more information and intimate workings with Blodeuwedd, Goddess of Personal Growth and Change, including a guided meditation and ritual, please see chapter 3 of *Goddess Afoot!*

Once you've chosen the aspect of your life, look at it rationally. How can you go about changing so that your life suits you better? Maybe you go to a new hairdresser or join a gym. Perhaps you make a pact to go to yoga every Monday or to buy a new outfit. You may choose to look through the want ads or take a college class. It doesn't matter what you decide to do as long as it propels you toward your goal of growth and change. It's time for you to act, to take charge of your life! It is yours! Not your boss'. Not your mother's. Not your children's or your husband's or your best friend's. *Your* life. What are you going to do with it?

RITUAL FOR GROWTH: WELCOMING THE POSITIVE

Suggested Ritual Days

Last Friday in April: U.S. National Arbor Day, as declared by the Arbor Day Foundation
May 18: Plant Conservation Day, as declared by the Association of Zoological Horticulture and Botanic Garden Conservation International

Items needed

a Chia pet
a sunny window

Whether you wish to create life in the womb, nurture a garden, or change your life situation, growth requires a willingness to move beyond the status quo. You have to leave your comfort zone and try something new. This can be difficult. It requires courage as you embark on a new adventure, a new way of life. You may flop and end up on a muddy patch of ground instead of a bountiful garden, but you'll never know unless you try. Chances are, there's a garden inside you just waiting for the opportunity to burst free. It will take work and commitment to nurture and sustain this garden, but your life will be much richer because of it. And don't forget—you'll have fun too!

On a day when you first feel the warming spring breezes, throw open your windows and breathe them in. Really allow the spring air into your lungs. Take deep belly breaths, totally filling your body with air. Hold your Chia pet in your hands while you do this. When you feel energized by the spring air, run outside (slamming the door behind you with reckless abandon) and frolic in your yard. Run around, skip, hop, gambol, swing, slide, and, in general, behave as though you are a second grader released from a long day of tedious math equations or reading assignments. This is your chance to remove the everyday drudgery and remember the exuberance of life, the freedom of growth and rebirth. Take as long as you'd like.

Before you fall down from exhaustion, settle yourself outside and prepare the first step in your Chia pet instructions. Hold the seeds in your hands and state your desire for growth. You can be as specific or general as you like; however, if you simply request "change," you never know what kind of change the universe will provide for you. After infusing the seeds with your intent, add water to them. As you add the water to the Chia seeds, think of all the positive aspects of your life that will help you to grow and achieve your goals. State aloud the names of your helpful friends and family members and all of your skills and positive qualities and characteristics. This is not the time to be modest! Go ahead and flaunt your stuff! When the time comes for you to stir the seeds, imagine that you are a part of the whirlpool of the cosmos, the spiral of time and space. You are connecting to the Otherworld, through a numinous Chia pet bridge.

Set your seeds aside for twenty-four hours. The next day, use your hands to spread your cosmically attuned, personally infused seeds on your Chia pet, really focusing on your goal. Every day, check the water level of your Chia pet, making sure to nurture and nourish your seeds. You are symbolically propagating and caring for your goals and life vision. As the seeds grow, so does your own personal growth.

Now, don't be dismayed if your Chia pet plant dies. This is simply a message to remind you to take time for your growth. Your growth is not stymied! You are not stuck! Instead, the death of your Chia pet can make you more aware of your own needs. Take some time to figure out why your Chia pet plant did not flourish. Is it because you didn't spend any time at home and thus ignored it? (This could indicate a refusal to carve out time for yourself.) Or did mold and mildew grow on your pet, destroying the seeds? (This message could indicate a toxic presence in your life, an attitude, past event, or even a person who is undermining your quest for growth and an authentic life.) Revisit the issue represented by the death of your plant and make the choice to change your concepts and ideas. Then, try again! Eventually your plant will thrive and so will you!

CHAPTER NINE
Goddess Mantras for Hope

HOPE: HUMANITY'S GIFT TO ITSELF

The darkest depths are sometimes difficult to look upon. We want to believe that we are all shining beacons of light-filled radiance. And we are; unique, beautiful, light, spiritual beings. But the light can also cast shadow. The shadow is part of the light; if we ignore the shadow, if we pretend it does not occur, we are missing a profound aspect of being human. The shadow is a masterful teacher if we do not allow it to swallow us whole.

My husband and I were talking about the movie *The NeverEnding Story* earlier today. This movie is one of my husband's favorites. He watched it again and again as a child. It's about a young boy Bastian who is picked upon by bigger bullies while dealing with his mother's recent death. Running from the bullies one day, he ducks into an old bookshop. You know the kind—dusty shelves, antique books, rickety desk with one lone lamp. One thing leads to another, and the boy "borrows" an old book from the man who runs the shop. He races to school, and through a strange series of events, decides to skip school and read the mysterious book.

The book describes the adventures of a mythical land that is being ravaged by a force, known as "the Nothing." The Nothing devours everything in its path, leaving—well, nothing behind. Literally, nothing. The land, the rocks, the people, the animals are all gone, as if they never existed in the first place. The princess of this mythical land calls upon a great hero from a nomadic people to stop the Nothing. His name is Atreyu and his greatest possession and dearest friend is his horse Artax. His happiest times are spent upon the back of his beloved horse. Atreyu accepts the charge to destroy the Nothing and sets out on his quest.

Lots of stuff happens but, in the beginning of the quest, Atreyu and Artax must cross the Swamps of Sadness. For me, *The NeverEnding Story* boils down to this one scene. Atreyu enters the Swamps of Sadness with his horse Artax, but he does not leave with him. As you can imagine (or perhaps you remember), Artax becomes overwhelmed with the sadness of the place. And this beautiful horse sinks down, down, down into the thick, goopy mud. Atreyu is beside himself with grief, just crying out the name of his beloved horse over and over again. I know it's a kids' movie, but this is truly a heart-wrenching scene.

This scene has always affected me because it is such a pure expression of grief. No cover-up. No soft lighting. No pretense. It is naked grief in all its raw purity, a sight rarely seen in modern society. The hero Atreyu is completely bereft without his horse, his companion, his friend. He feels as though his world is over and life is not worth living. He almost allows the struggle, the sadness, the grief to overcome him but he does not. Through force of will, he continues on through the Swamps of Sadness, not letting the darkness overwhelm him. And, just as he feels he can go on no longer, just as he begins to sink deep, deep, deep into the swamp, down swoops a joyous luck dragon with an infectious laugh who gives him the chance to fly.

And that, I think, is the hardest thing to remember about the shadow. It's not a forever thing. It's transitory. A process. A part of life but not the entirety of life. Eventually the shadow lifts, no matter how imperceptibly. *The NeverEnding Story* is really a movie about the journey into and out of the shadow. And how, in the end, we all have a part to play in the creation of our own world, in the creation of our own lives. For in the end, Atreyu cannot stop the Nothing. It devours all of the mystical land. Everything is gone. The only things left are one grain of sand and the fragile princess who holds it aloft. But the land can be saved, it can be restored, if only the young boy skipping class believes it can be. If Bastian believes he has the power to save the land and the right to wield that power, the land can be saved. "How?" he wonders. He is just a boy in a school attic, small and insignificant. But, in the end, he answers his own question . . . how can he not?

And it is this power, which comes from within, from the experience of battling and escaping the shadow, that allows us to rise above the darkness and shine with our inner light. This power grows into self-worth and self-love. However, in the beginning, it starts with a tiny, glowing bit of sand. Amidst the darkness we see a tiny glimmer. A shimmer. A spark. Hope.

ENERGY RETURN

Hope is a quintessential element of living on planet Earth, a right that humans enjoy far beyond the darkness that engulfs them at any given moment in time. We sing songs about it, write poems, watch movies, and engage in weekly television rituals in an effort to see its miraculous effects on others. This bolsters us and reminds us that hope is always there, always present, always waiting to lift us up. Hope is a wonder. Without it, humanity would be a far sorrier lot and our world would be a far sadder place to live.

But hope does come with a downside. (Hard to believe but true, nonetheless.) Inherent within hope is the choice to simply sit and wait and watch the world go by. In this instance, we wish for something, hope it will occur in our lives, pray to the Divine for guidance, but refuse to *do* anything to achieve our dreams. For whatever reason—fear, laziness, anger—we refuse to take control of our own lives. And hope should never be a replacement for action.

I am reminded of the story of the man in a flood. (No, not Noah with his arc but a different guy!) In this story, a man wakes up and realizes that his house is filling with water because of a flood. He climbs to the second story and prays to the Divine for help. A little old man rows by on a rowboat and asks the man if he wants to join him. He shouts back, "No, thanks! God [Goddess/Spirit/Ancestor/Buddha, take your pick] will save me." So the little old man rows by. The water continues to rise and, pretty soon, the man is balancing precariously on the roof of his house. A motor boat zooms past with a family of four in it. The pilot stops the boat and asks the man if he needs any help. The man on the rooftop shouts back, "No, thanks! God will save me." The pilot shrugs, guns his motor, and whisks away. The waters continue to rise and, before too long, the man on the rooftop is up to his head in water. A third boat, a shiny military issue overflowing with refugees, stops and a strapping soldier asks the man if he would like to board the vessel. The man answers, once again, "No, thanks! God will save me." The soldier works hard to convince the man to come into the boat but he refuses, clinging to his belief in the Divine, holding onto his hope. Eventually the soldier shrugs his shoulders and the boat motors away. The man is left by himself, with the rising waters. Eventually he finds himself in heaven (the Afterlife/the Otherworld/the Summerlands/take your pick), face to face with his deity-of-choice. The man asks the Divine why he (or she) didn't save him. The Divine answers, "Who do you think sent all those boats?"

So, by all means, allow the power of hope to drain away the darkness, but don't underestimate yourself! Don't allow yourself to sink into a lethargy of inaction, believing that hope will do all the work for you. It won't. Hope isn't a license for inaction. Think positively. Send out positive vibes into the world. But don't expect your dreams to manifest without some hard work as well.

DEMETER
Greek Sorrowful Mother Goddess

MANTRA

Darkness creeps.

Light ascends.

Wipe my tears,

O Demeter.

Although not listed among the twelve Olympian supreme gods who reside on Mount Olympus, Demeter is a (sometime) resident of that holy abode and she is a sister of Zeus, Hades, Poseidon, Hera, and Hestia. These six siblings compose the family of Cronus and Rhea, Titans who served as the creator-deities of the Olympian gods. The children of Cronus and Rhea are the starting point for all aspects of classical Greek mythology, especially Zeus, who single-handedly fathered the remaining seven of the twelve gods and goddesses.

It is interesting and a bit startling to realize that Demeter is not listed as one of the supreme Olympian gods. Perhaps this relates back to the fact that her worship is considered to be much older than the Hellenic patriarchal religion, having originated on Crete as part of the Minoan culture.[1] Or maybe the snub relates back to her country origins. As the goddess of grain and agriculture, it was not uncommon for her followers to worship her "in every humble act that made the farm fruitful."[2] Her temples were the field and the threshing-floor where, at any moment, she might appear and be present.

---

1. Leeming and Page, *Goddess: Myths of the Female Divine*, 66–67.

2. Hamilton, *Mythology: Timeless Tales of Gods and Heroes*, 47

Provider for her people, even of temper and full of love, Demeter was often called the "Good Goddess" by the ancient Greeks.[3]

Never married, Demeter still births three children from two different fathers, proving her power as a lusty, fertility goddess. One child, Plutus, is conceived at a wedding when she and the Titan Iasius (or Iasion) slip away from the party to lie together in a thrice-plowed field. This tryst suggests an ancient, undocumented fertility rite where priestesses of the corn and grain would have lain with a sacred king in order to secure a plentiful harvest.[4] When Demeter and her lover return to the wedding, stained with dirt and mud, Zeus immediately realizes the truth of their "innocent little walk" and kills Iasius with a thunderbolt in a fit of jealousy. Naturally, he has reason to be upset, since he is the father of Demeter's other two children—Dionysus and Persephone.[5]

While son Dionysus plays an important part in Demeter's life and myths, it is daughter Persephone who holds her heart. Their lives and souls are entwined as only a mother and daughter can be connected. Of the same blood and bone, possessing the same powers of growth and blossoming, interested in the same topics of nature and beauty, Demeter and Persephone flow together. Cavorting through the spring fields, they rejoice in the beauty and wonder of the world; they revel in each other's companionship. This idyllic lifestyle soon changes, however, bringing with it heartache, depression, anger, and sorrow.

One moment, all is well and Persephone is picking flowers in the fields with her friends and the next, she is gone, with only her echoing cry left. Hearing the scream, Demeter searches the whole world for nine days looking for Persephone. Some say she takes the shape of a bird as she flits here and there. Others that she simply acts like a bird, frantic with worry, quick-moving and jagged. She can find no news. Distraught, she drapes herself in black and, taking the shape of an old crone, retires to the city of Eleusis. There, sitting at the side of a well, looking like a most pathetic creature, the daughters of King Celeus take pity on her. They invite Demeter into their household to serve as a nursemaid for their baby brother. It is here, in Eleusis, where two seemingly

---

3. Ibid., 53.

4. Graves, *Greek Myths*, 93.

5. The mother of Dionysus is contested in Greek Mythology. Some writers say it is Demeter, others Persephone, and still others Io, Semele, or Dione. His father, however, is always the mighty Zeus.

insignificant events occur that are reminders of the elusive, yet pervasive, presence of hope.

First, Demeter, still in a deep depression, is accepted and made welcome by the king's lame daughter Iambe and the old dry-nurse Baubo. They give her barley-water freshened with mint (a drink often given to harvesters) and then proceed to tell humorous, lusty stories, complete with provocative and erotic hand motions and dancing. Baubo even pretends to be in labor and, after much groaning and carrying-on, produces Demeter's own son, Dionysus, from beneath her skirts! While this aspect of the story seems small, it is a reminder that when in the darkness of despair, it is easy to forget about all the things that you love and that make life worth living. Iambe and Baubo seek to remind Demeter of all the fun, frivolity, and lusty entertainment that is still in the world—as well as her other child, Dionysus. The world is the same, only Demeter's outlook on it has changed. Iambe and Baubo, then, are the small pin-pricks of light and love that reach our bruised hearts and souls when we are grieving. They let us know that the world awaits our return, when we are ready.

The second seemingly insignificant event takes place the night Demeter arrives at the palace of King Celeus. Having vented her anger on one of the king's poor helpless sons, Demeter seeks to repent by giving the gift of immortality to the newborn baby boy. While everyone sleeps, she places the baby in the fire, burning away his mortality. However, Metaneira, one of the women of the household (either the baby's sister or his mother), sees the baby in the fire and cries out. The spell is broken. Demeter pulls the baby out of the fire and hurls him onto the ground where, unfortunately, he dies. In symbolic terms, fire is often considered to be a transformative element. It is passionate and creative and always moving. It heals, often through change and (sometimes painful) growth. In my mind, at this point in the story, Demeter is working to accept the change that has been wrought in her life. She knows she can't change the past, so instead she is hoping to burn away the nasty residue of her loss so she can step forward into her future. The fact that the spell is broken and the baby dies shows that if you wallow in the past for too long, it will drag you down and you'll never escape from the grief. You'll never be reborn into your new, glorious self. Unfortunately, Demeter tried to move forward a little too quickly in the story. As the following episodes indicate, Demeter is not yet ready to let go of her past hurts.

After the night's disastrous events, another son of Celeus steps forward and relates to Demeter that his other brother had seen Persephone ten days ago, being taken underground by a man in a chariot. Armed with this new information, Demeter seeks out Hecate and together they march to the mountain of Helios, the sun god who sees everything. After much convincing, he tells them that Hades stole Persephone and brought her down to the Underworld, with Zeus' approval. Demeter is incensed! She quickly moves from bleak depression to crimson-wrapped rage. In her anger, she blights the land and refuses to let anything grow. Winter ravages the Earth and Demeter walks among her people, desolate and alone. Hunger grips the land, followed by starvation and death. But Demeter tells Zeus she will not bring prosperity to the land until her daughter is restored to her. Demeter's persistence is yet another aspect of hope, for Demeter has the courage to pursue what will make her happy. She will not settle for conciliatory gifts from Zeus. Her daughter was stolen from her; she will accept nothing but her return.

In the end, Demeter is rewarded for her determination. Persephone returns to her. Warmth and light revisit the Earth! Hope blooms in the hearts of all! However, the whole experience has marked the goddesses and the humans with whom they came in contact. Celeus, two of his sons, and another king who searched assiduously for Persephone are initiated into the Mysteries of Demeter, which become the much celebrated and secretive Eleusinian Mysteries. Demeter gives another of Celeus' sons the knowledge of agriculture and she instructs him to spread this knowledge around the world. Demeter is reunited with her daughter for eight or nine months of every year. And Persephone . . . well, Persephone is forever changed.

Pathway to Demeter

As an earth goddess, worshipped in the fields and on threshing-room floors, it makes sense to work with grains in order to get to know Demeter. Some of you may want to break out the yeast and bake bread. If so, great! Have at it! For those of us with few kitchen skills and little time, why not whip up a container of mint barley-water? It's nutritious, yummy, and a beverage said to have been consumed by Demeter. What more can you ask for?

The best thing about making barley-water is that it's really very simple. Get some barley, put it in some water, bring to a boil, and then simmer. When it's all done simmering, strain out the barley with cheesecloth or a fine strainer, add the fresh mint, and set aside until cool. Once cool, remove the mint and refrigerate before serving. The amount of water you'll need and the length of time to simmer depends on the type of barley you choose. Hulled barley is the most nutritious, but it's also the most chewy. Luckily, you'll be straining it out of your drink so you won't need to worry about your teeth! Alton Brown of "Good Eats" on the Food Network recommends using 2 quarts water to 1 cup hulled barley and simmering it for 30 minutes. Since he's an expert, I'll bow to his superior knowledge. He also suggests using lemons and honey in your barley-water. While I think those would be lovely suggestions, your goal is to connect with Demeter with this sacred drink. Add honey if you must, but I'd stay away from the lemons. (By the way, Alton recommends ¼ cup honey.)

Any time you feel overwhelmed and need to remember the pleasant aspects of life, reach into your refrigerator and drink some barley-water. Think of Demeter and how sad and depressed she was feeling when Iambe and Baubo gave her this drink. Know that Demeter feels your pain and understands the darkness of depression and the entrapping power of rage. She is here for you, for all of us, and she truly cares.

PERSEPHONE
Greek Queen of the Dead

MANTRA

I grow, I shift,
A second skin gift.
I am much more,
Greater than before.

Perhaps you're thinking after the re-telling of Demeter's ancient myth that I am completely crazy to find hope in the story of Persephone's abduction. And you might be right. After all, Persephone is stolen away from her mother, possibly raped by the lord of the Underworld, and then, because of these occurrences, cannot fully return to her old life. Instead, she has to spend three months (some sources state four months) in the darkness underground, as the queen of the dead. Hope? Where's the hope in all that?

It's important, when looking at Persephone's evolution, to really delve into the intricacies of the story. In other words, there's a lot more going on in the myth then can be gleaned at first glance. When we meet Persephone at the beginning of the myth, she is a child, in actions and demeanor if not in actual age. Her name is Kore (Core), which means "maiden." She is completely wrapped up in her mother's life. She is the "spirit of grain," while Demeter is "giver of grain."[6] Kore is so integral to the birth of the crops and the growth of the land that she is seen as an *aspect* of Demeter, the "barley-mother." In other words, Kore has no personality, no interest, no true life outside of her relationship with her mother. She is one with her mother, which, of course, leaves her no room for herself.

When Persephone chooses to leave the company of her friends (the water nymphs known as the Okeanides) on that fateful day, she is seeking out an individual path, different from her mother. Seeing a wondrous, glowing flower, Persephone is immediately drawn to pluck it. It is a narcissus of silver and purple, made by Zeus just for the purpose of luring Kore away from her companions. Robert Graves, in *The Greek Myths*, postulates that the flower is actually a three-petaled fleur-de-lys or iris, sacred to the goddess-as-three and used in the sacred wreaths of Demeter and Persephone.[7] If this is so, the flower may indicate Kore's secret wish to move beyond the maiden role that she is required to portray as the daughter of Demeter. In one re-telling of this fateful moment, Kore is described as stealing "toward it [the flower], half fearful at being alone, but unable to resist the desire to fill her basket with it . . ."[8] Any number of sexual innuendos could be read into that sentence, beginning with Kore's anxious anticipation and ending with her desire to have her "basket" filled.

Reaching toward the flower, without knowledge but ever mindful, Kore doesn't even get one finger on a petal before the Earth opens up around her. From a vast and dark chasm, Hades, lord of the Underworld, springs forth on his gold chariot, pulled by snorting, mutinous black-coated horses. He pulls Kore to himself, holding her body against his, and descends deep into the Underworld, closing the chasm behind him. The only things left of Kore on the Earth are her screams.

The story does not describe Kore's transformation into Persephone. We do not know what awaited Kore down in the dark land of the dead. We do not know how she felt or what she endured. At one point in Demeter's story, during her nine-day search, it is said that Hecate, the old crone goddess, heard Kore's voice crying out, "A rape! A rape!" However, when Hecate went to investigate and to help the young goddess, she found no one

---

6. Jordan, *Encyclopedia of Gods*, 135.
7. Graves, *Greek Myths*, 288.
8. Hamilton, *Mythology: Timeless Tales*, 87.

and nothing. Rape is a common activity among the male gods of Greek mythology. It is possible that Hades forced himself upon Kore. However, she never bore a child to Hades and, in some versions of the myth, Zeus secretly begot a son on Persephone before she was taken down to the Underworld.[9] With all these suggestions and considering her ultimate transformation into the yearly resurrection goddess, it is a good bet that Kore was deflowered sometime during her foray into the Underworld, moving her from her maiden aspect into that of woman.

When Zeus finally grants Persephone's freedom in response to Demeter's endless winter, he sends Hermes to fetch her from the Underworld. When the messenger of the gods arrives in the Underworld, he finds Persephone sitting next to Hades, shrinking away from him. She longs for her mother's arms and the warm touch of the golden sun. As Hermes delivers his message, Persephone jumps off the seat, eager to leave the dark Underworld and return to her former life. But Hades does not wish her to go. Outwardly acquiescing to his brother's orders, he begs Persephone to think well of him and generously offers her a pomegranate seed. It is uncertain in the myths whether Persephone is duped by his outward demeanor and eats the seed of her free will or if he forces the seed upon her. It may be that she ate the seed of the pomegranate behind Hades' back at some earlier time during her stay in the Underworld.

In any event, she eats the red fruit of the dead, of wisdom and knowledge, and forever gives up her maidenhood, further moving away from her enmeshed relationship with her mother. Persephone is Kore still, just a wiser, more worldly version of her former self. She has found her own sovereignty, separate from her mother. She has become complete unto herself. Persephone is driven in a chariot up out of the darkness, into the light, by Hermes, who takes her directly to her mother's temple. Demeter and Persephone, overcome with joy at the reunion, embrace each other. They sit and talk about the events that have befallen them since they were separated. When Persephone tells her mother about the pomegranate seed, Demeter's sadness is renewed, for Zeus had stated that Persephone could be with her mother *only* if she had not eaten any of the food of the Underworld. Holding her daughter close, Demeter decrees that, without her daughter, she will not remove the curse she has placed on the Earth.

Zeus, seeing that a compromise is needed but unwilling to offer it himself, enlists the aid of his mother, Rhea. Rhea descends to the temple of Demeter and suggests that

---

9. Graves, *Greek Myths,* 90 and 118.

Persephone spend most of her time with her mother, on the green, good Earth. But, since she has tasted the food of the dead and been forever altered, she must return to the realm of Hades for one-third of the year. Demeter and Persephone agree, but Demeter refuses to allow food to grow while she is separated from her beautiful daughter; every year she must see her daughter die, so she will cause the crops to die as well.

In truth, Persephone does die every year as the winter rolls in, for she returns to the underworld and her role as Queen of the Dead. Once married to Hades, she can never return to the merry naiveté of her youth as Kore. She is forever changed from her abduction and original encounter with the forces of the Underworld. Persephone returns in springtime to revel in the glories of her youth, to remember the beauty of spring and her connection to her mother. She is happy and pleased. However, Persephone can never shake off the aura of the Underworld and her title as queen of the dead. The memory of death hangs with her. No longer settled in the hip pocket of her mother, Persephone branches out to welcome a different aspect of herself. Innocent Kore still resides within her, but she has been strengthened and tempered by life. Learning from her choices, Persephone is able to offer gentleness, compassion, and care to those who pass into the realm of the dead. She has a purpose and a life that is true to her past and to her present and future. She is Persephone, "the maiden whose name may not be spoken."[10]

Pathway to Persephone

Sometimes it's hard to let go of the past and be hopeful about the future. We see the unwelcome change all around us, feel the shift in our souls, but still, we want to hang on to the familiar. This is a normal human reaction to unplanned transformation. (When is transformation ever truly planned?) However, using the spirit of hope to release the old and make way for the new will speed up the transformation process, allowing you to push past the difficult times to a welcoming period of freedom. And you can do this with the wisdom of the snake.

The snake is sacred to Persephone. Demeter placed her in a cave guarded by snakes, and she was impregnated by Zeus when he took the form of a snake. The snake, by its very nature, is a wonderful symbol of movement and growth. As a snake sheds its skin, it gives itself room to grow bigger and bigger. You want to remove the old aspects of your life that are holding you back from your growth. In essence, you want to shed your

---

10. Hamilton, *Mythology: Timeless Tales,* 54.

skin in order to transform. Utilizing the symbolic power of the snake and its connection to Persephone, you too can wiggle free of the restraints in your life.

First you need to get a snakeskin. This is actually easier to do then you think! Snakes are very accommodating creatures, and when you put a call out into the universe, they often will answer. So, don't be surprised if a snakeskin suddenly shows up in your garage or in the bushes by your front door. If the snakes in your area are hibernating for the winter, go on down to your local pet shop and ask them for a snakeskin. If they don't have one handy, they'll be able to tell you when they should have one available. It'll probably only be a few weeks and it'll probably be free. Most pet stores just throw the skins away!

Once you've acquired your snakeskin, check your calendar. On the next waning moon (when the moon is getting smaller between the full and new moons), hold on to your snakeskin and pour all of your feelings into it. Don't leave anything behind, really focus on your transformation and all the pain, anxiety, and upheaval you are feeling. Allow the emotions to leave your body through your fingertips, entering the paper-smooth snakeskin. When you feel you've released all that you can, go outside and bury the snakeskin beside a tree. You might consider burying a gift with the snakeskin, such as tobacco, cornmeal, or sage. You have now given over your attachment to the past to the energy of the snake and the care of the goddess Persephone. Feel free to perform this snakeskin release ceremony as many times as you need, even if the moon is in a different phase of its cycle. It will help you to move through your transformation with more ease and grace. In Persephone, we find hope even in our darkest times by remembering that the pain we are in is necessary for our transformation.

SUNNA
Norse Light-Bringer of Hope

MANTRA
Shining, bright,
Here comes the sun.
Arise!
A new day is here.

Our sun is approximately 4.5 billion years old and will probably live for another 4 to 5 billion years.[11] Since humans have been on planet Earth, the sun has hung in the sky, brightening our days, giving life to our plants, regulating our weather, and warming our lives. The ultimate symbol of hope, the sun rises every day on our eastern horizon, burning away the darkness of night. She brings light and joy into our lives with her bountiful, giving energy. After all, the sun is the catalyst that spurs the growth of vegetation on our planet. In fact, we exist because of her and because of a lucky fluke of nature that placed us in the exact right spot to benefit from her powerful presence. The sun is the constant in our lives that sustains our planet and assures our survival.

In Norse mythology, the sun is a woman, which differs greatly from traditional Greco-Roman, Egyptian, and Middle Eastern myths that give the sun a male persona. These are the myths with which we are most comfortable. After all, if the moon, with her fluctuations and watery emphasis, is female, then the sun, with his assertiveness and fiery ways, must be male. Or must he? To the northern peoples, the Norse of Scandinavia and the Celts of Britain and Ireland, the sun did not hold the same intense strength and power as the sun of the southern lands. In Greece, Egypt, and the Middle East, the sun baked the land, destroying crops and drying up lakes and riverbeds. The sun gave life or destroyed life, depending on the time of the year. In the north, the sun loses some of its intensity. While it still helps the plants to grow and flourish, it does not burn them during the hot months. Instead, the sun melts away the cold and ice of winter, revealing a burgeoning Earth underneath the snows. The sun loses its negative qualities, becoming a nurturing, nourishing entity, not unlike a mother feeding her children. Is it any wonder that the Celts and the Norse related the orb of the sun with the Great Goddess?

The Norse sun goddess is Sunna (SOO-na), daughter of Mundilfaeri, sister of Mani, wife of Glen. She is a human who rose to the rank of goddess with the help of the Norse gods. Sunna's father, Mundilfaeri (whose name means "Axis Mover"[12]), thought his children so beautiful that he named them Sun and Moon, respectively. The gods were unhappy with this proud father's choice of names and seeking to punish him, took hold of Sun and Moon and threw them up into the sky, where they became one with their namesakes. Therefore, Sunna drives the chariot of the sun and Mani, her brother, is the driver of the chariot of the moon. Both children of Mundilfaeri are hastened in their

---

11. High Altitude Observatory, Earth and Sun Systems Laboratory.
12. Schmitt, "Sunna and Mani."

flight across the sky by two wolves, named Skoll and Hati, who run at the heels of their horses, trying to devour the sun and the moon.[13] During an eclipse, it is said that Skoll and Hati take bites out of the sun and moon, heralding the death of these celestial orbs during the Norse end of the world, known as Ragnarok.

During Ragnarok, most of the Norse gods die in battle, fighting the legions of fire giants and dead men, led by the god Loki and his offspring, Hel (the Norse goddess of the Underworld), Jormungand (the world serpent), and Fenrir (the iron-jawed wolf). Ragnarok destroys the current incarnation of the world, allowing the rebirth of a new and brighter Earth, with the sons and daughters of the gods taking the place of their fallen parents. For Sunna, the wolf finally catches up with her, dousing her light by swallowing her. Skoll is descended from a giantess named Jarnvidiur, who births giants in wolf form in the Ironwood Forest. Born from this family, a wolf known as Moongarm "will swallow heavenly bodies and spatter heaven and all the skies with blood. As a result the sun will lose its shine . . . ."[14] He is known as "sun's snatcher in troll's guise" and the sun is described as "dark . . . for summer's after."[15] Yet, all is not lost. Like the other gods, at the end of Ragnarok, the sun still shines on the planet. Before her death, Sunna gives birth to a daughter, as beautiful as her mother, and "she shall ride, when the powers die, the maiden, her mother's road."[16]

One contemporary scholar of Norse myths has concluded that Sunna holds the powers and attributes of a mother goddess, as compared to a warrior goddess, maiden goddess, or crone goddess. In *Goddess of the North,* Lynda C. Welch postulates that since the Norse viewed the sun as a mature woman, capable of giving birth, the sun radiates with classic mother goddess attributes, such as the "mother's ability to provide nourishment to sustain her children."[17] While this is true from a modern goddess-spirituality viewpoint, there is little evidence to support that the medieval Norse categorized their goddesses into a maiden-mother-crone continuum. The fact that we cannot historically

---

13. Sturluson, *Edda,* 14–15.

14. Ibid., 15.

15. Ibid., 15. Further evidence of the sun's demise can be found on pages 52 and 53. It is interesting to note that Sturluson, in his list of acceptable alternative phrases or names for the word "wolf," does not list Sunna's chaser Skoll. He also does not record Moongarm, although Mani's pursuer Hati makes the list, page 164.

16. Sturluson, *Edda,* 57.

17. Welch, *Goddess of the North,* 151.

link Sunna to a maiden-mother-crone triple goddess structure does not lessen her impact as a mature, mothering goddess. She is a mother, not only to her surviving daughter but to all the medieval Scandinavians who relied on her warming rays for food and to all of us, in the present day, who need her to survive.

Sunna's role in Ragnarok, as the birthing mother and the dying sun, also shows her affinity to be present at times of transition and to ease the burden of new experiences for humankind. Despite being eaten by a ravaging wolf, Sunna is still able to birth a daughter who will continue in her mother's footsteps and shine the healing, growing, fertile rays of the sun on the world. While dying, Sunna gives birth to her own daughter and to humanity's only hope of continuing life on planet Earth. The last activity of her existence puts her on the threshold of this world and the Otherworld twice—during death and during birth. Sunna's demise at Ragnarok and her neither fully-human nor

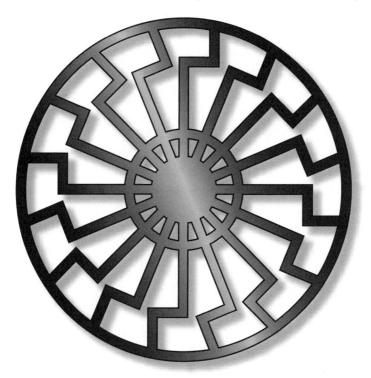

Figure 5: The Sunwheel

fully-goddess lineage demonstrate her familiarity with transitory periods, with an ability to aid those undergoing such changes and alterations.

The inclusion of Sunna in the Second Merseberg Charm is undoubtedly by design, rather than by happenstance. Sunna seems an odd choice to include in a charm to heal a horse's leg until one looks at the tale of Baldr's funeral and the fact that he replaces his father among the gods after Ragnarok. Baldr, like Sunna's daughter, survives to aid and guide humanity after the destruction of the world as we know it. Both of them heal the world, knitting together the fragmented pieces of life after the chaos of Ragnarok. By birthing her daughter, Sunna performs the ultimate healing. She gives the Earth the light necessary to survive utter destruction. The sun survives, gifting the world with her life-giving rays.

Healing, mothering, guiding, the sun shines on all of us from on high. Sunna, sun goddess of the northern lands, is much more than the growing, warming sun's rays. She is a symbol of hope, a beacon of light shining through the dark times of despair and desperation. She heals our broken bones and our fragmented psyches with the gentle touch of a mother. Present at times of change and transformation, Sunna offers her support and comfort to us during difficult transitions. And she gives us the ultimate offering, her newborn daughter, who will continue her mother's work, bringing the light of the sun to all of us here on Earth. Generous and selfless, Sunna cares for all her children, feeding us, warming us, and shining on high with boundless energy and devotion. For humans, Sunna has always hung in the sky, nurturing our planet Earth, nurturing ourselves. May we always feel her distant love, embraced by her light.[18]

Pathway to Sunna

There is nothing more uplifting than spending a day outside in the sun. Whether it's cleaning up the yard, taking a walk, or relaxing by the pool (or beach), the sun has the ability to relax, rejuvenate, and restore our emotions, our mental attitude, and our sense of self. It really is hard to be negative when basking in the rays of the sun. Part of this is chemical. We receive the powerful nutrient Vitamin D from the sun. Vitamin D helps the body to produce serotonin, a neurotransmitter critical to emotional health. Low

---

18. Much of the story of Sunna first appeared in *Goddess Afoot!*, 248–254. For more information and intimate workings with Sunna, Light-Bringer of Hope, including a guided meditation and ritual, please see chapter 13 of *Goddess Afoot!*

Vitamin D levels or a Vitamin D deficiency can contribute to depression and a negative outlook on life. Vitamin D is often prescribed to people who are affected by the cold and dark of the winter months. This "seasonal depression" is linked to the lack of sunlight, and thus the lack of Vitamin D, in their body.[19] Therefore, when needing a boost of energy and hope, just look to the sun!

While soaking up the sun's rays, I recommend listening to a fun, bouncy, sunshiny song. There are many from which to choose: "Here Comes the Sun" by the Beatles, "Sunshine" by the Partridge Family, "Walking on Sunshine" by Katrina and the Waves, "You are My Sunshine" by Jimmie Davis, or "Pocketful of Sunshine" by Natasha Bedingfield are great examples. My personal favorite (and I'm dating myself here) is "It's a Sunshine Day" by the Brady Bunch.[20] It is impossible not to smile when listening to this song. From the beginning moments of whiny, rock-anthem 1970s guitar to the groovy mellow bridge, which asks "Can't you dig the sunshine?" this song is peppy, positive, and eminently danceable. So, download it onto your MP3 player, cruise around town, and enjoy the unflappable Bradys. Re-live the nostalgia. Share your memories with your children or somebody else's children! Celebrate the sun!

RITUAL FOR HOPE:
CRAFTING H.O.P.E.

Suggested Ritual Days

The first Wednesday in April: National Day of Hope, as proclaimed by the U.S. Congress and founded by the Childhelp organization

November 8: Day of Hope, as founded by the Four Seasons Hotel on the island of Maui, Hawaii

Thanksgiving Day: A Day of Hope, a program founded by students at the California State University, Stanislaus

---

19. "Diet for Depression," WebMD: Depression Health Center.

20. You can find this song on YouTube or on the album *It's a Sunshine Day: The Best of the Brady Bunch* from Amazon.com. You can purchase the whole album or simply download an MP3 for cheap money. While you're there, check out their song "Time to Change." It is perfect for working with Persephone and the transitions in life! Maybe the Bradys were on to something . . .

Items needed

random pictures from magazines, the internet, or from your digital camera
large sheet of poster board
a glue stick
colored marker pens
sparkly stickers
scrapbook decals
any fun, crafty items you love
a fire of some sort

Hope springs from our humanity. It is undefeatable, indefatigable, present in even the most heinous of conditions. Whether lost in the slums of India or in the darkest jungle of the psyche, every single person needs hope in their lives—the belief that people care, that they are necessary and worthy, and that difficult circumstances can be overcome and conquered. How do we experience the presence of hope in our lives? Through the wisdom, caring, and touch of others. We, our individual selves, give each other hope. Through our actions, words, and thoughts, we can be the light that pierces the darkest gloom of our fellow human beings. For this ritual, I'd like you to consider the following acronym for the word *hope*:

H: help
O: out
P: people
E: everywhere

And this includes yourself. If you are performing this ritual during a dark time in your life, be willing to receive the generosity and love of others. They do it because they care. And, if you're currently feeling good and positive, perform this ritual for all the people who may not be in such a happy space. Decide for yourself which type of ritual you'd like to perform and then gather your materials and sit down in a calm and relaxed space.

Begin to flip through your pictures and see them as connecting to each other. Begin placing them, in groups, on the poster board. Do you happen to have a picture of a contemplative young woman? Maybe you place her next to a photo of your favorite garden space, at the edge of a cliff at the Grand Canyon, or sitting next to a group of friends. Do whatever feels right to you at the time. Don't second guess yourself. You are working on allowing the colors and shapes and emotions of the pictures to flow through you. If you've gathered a lot of scenic pictures of the Earth, place them together in a style that resonates to you. Don't worry if they overlap each other or hang off the poster board. Maybe you notice that you have a lot of pictures of children. Put them together. Don't feel like you've got to cover every square inch of your poster board. Allow yourself some room to move things around and manipulate the scene.

Once you've got the general idea of the design, begin to glue down one "vignette" at a time. Allow your hands to work while your mind wanders. What are you feeling while you glue down this section? What memories are you thinking of? What old hurts are resurfacing? With your marker pens, begin to make notes on your board. Write well-known expressions, family mottos, phrases of songs, book titles. Make a note (literally) of whatever comes to mind. Don't be neat and tidy about it. Consider this poster board to be your own urban canvas for the graffiti of your soul. Continue gluing all the sections of your HOPE board, using your markers to add personal touches. Feel free to add the stickers or scrapbook decals at any time.

When you have finished, step back and look at the beautiful montage you have created. It is probably colorful, with glorious, emotional pictures that highlight all your personal thoughts. What a wonder you have created! What a wonder you are! With your finished poster board in hand, sit down outside in the sunshine and consider exactly what your personal canvas is telling you. Are you most concerned with the lives of children, animals, or the poor around the world? Do you care deeply for the environment, survivors of sexual abuse, or those in need of education? What does you poster say about you and how does it affect your life? Take some time to really contemplate the answers to these questions and decide what, if any, actions you wish to take to care for others and be a source of hope.

Right about now, you're probably ready for an all-out diatribe and call to action, but that's not my style. Nobody can tell you what's right for you. Perhaps you really need to focus on your inner needs. Perhaps contemplating the plight of the world is simply too big for you right now—that is totally fine. Healing starts with the self. Honor your space. When we heal ourselves, we begin to heal the world. Hope starts with one person and grows one person at a time. Feel the light of hope within you and watch as it ignites the hope in others.

Having contemplated the message you sent yourself on your urban canvas, safely burn your poster board in a fire. Allow the fire to completely destroy the actual physical object.

But don't worry, it's not gone for good! It still resides inside you and in the ethers to which it returns. The fire is the shining power of hope to transmute and alter the negative things in your life and around the world. It is the first step in allowing hope into your life and into the lives of others. Feel the warmth, see the light of the fire as it burns bright and true. Feel the hope. It burns within you.

Chapter Ten

Goddess Mantras for Spirituality

SPIRITUALITY: IT BEGINS WITH YOU

When the word *spirituality* comes up in conversation, most people run and hide. "Eek," they think, "another religious fanatic seeking to convert me." They expect the traditional persuasive tactics and words of manipulation. We've heard them before. Come to my temple/church/coven/grove/mosque (insert religious setting of choice here). Learn about the truth/the way/the light/the beginning of days/the end of the world (insert religious philosophy of choice here). Open to communication with the spirits of nature/the angels/God/Yahweh/Jehovah/Allah/Buddah/the Goddess/the Great Spirit (insert religious divinity of choice here). Come! Repent! Convert! Accept! Love! Fear! (Insert religious mantra of choice here!) It's enough to give anyone a bit of a headache.

But the funny thing is, no matter what religious setting, philosophy, divinity, or mantra subscribed to, most people are spiritual beings. Most people believe in something bigger than themselves, something beyond the confines of everyday reality. There seems to be a fundamental human need for a connecting universal force that guides, aids, and even punishes us as we live our lives.

No one really wants to talk about the wrathful side of deity. It's so much more comforting to discuss love for all and world peace and joy and happiness and bunnies and flowers and rainbows and bubbles. But the truth is that every religion has its boundary markers for accepted behavior. The Wiccan Three-Fold Law states that whatever you do comes back to you, magnified three times. So, if you do something nasty, you're going to get slammed with nasty stuff. Hello bankruptcy, divorce, and life-threatening illness. The Buddhist concept of Karma tells you that if you do something impure or unclean in this life, you're going to pay for it in your next incarnation. Welcome to life as a worm! The Christian idea of the afterlife explains that if you go against the precepts of God and your fellow man during life, you're going to pay for it after death. Greetings from the eternal fires of hell! Not very uplifting images.

In reality these boundary markers have little to do with spirituality and everything to do with religion. Religion is a documented set of rules and regulations, philosophies and beliefs concerning spirituality that a designated group has agreed to and (in most cases) written down. Religions have dogma, or unwavering concepts that cannot be refuted or proven. They just are. If our particular dogma doesn't work for you, doesn't make sense, or seems out of touch with reality . . . tough! Move on to another religion. There is little room for individuality or fluidity in many religions, as the core truths cannot be changed.

The same cannot be said about spirituality. Spiritually is as unique as every human being on the planet. It is our own connection to the greatness beyond ourselves. We may view it as a man, a woman, an insect, a tree, or a lightning bolt. We may see it in the wind, the waves, the cross, the star, or the moon. But these images are mere human constructs for the mind. We, as spiritual beings, unite with something far bigger than these human trappings. We search for energy, for power, for life and understanding in our spiritual quests. We seek the beginnings of ourselves, which may still be evolving. And we look for the end, which may be happening even as we live each wondrous, glorious moment.

I'm talking about the spirit of ourselves. No one knows for sure if we have a spirit, a soul, an essence, or a vibration all our own. We know we are ourselves. Completely different and whole from every other living being on the planet, and yet connected with all other things. We know we are here, in this moment. We know we have crafted our lives from our circumstances, from our skills, and from the opportunities before us. But we don't scientifically *know* if we have a separate energy being that inhabits our body and moves on once the body decays. We think so. There are many near-death incidents that report a floating sensation, of being able to look down and see the corporeal body below. Pregnant women relate dreams or sensations that indicate the passing of a soul or spirit into the fetus in the womb. But these are all unsubstantiated claims that science cannot prove. But neither can science refute them. A scientific study done in the Netherlands in 2001 found few mitigating Earth-bound links between patients who experienced near-death experiences. In other words, there were no common medical factors that could be calculated and analyzed to explain the feelings and sensations of the patients. The near-death experiences just happened, randomly.[1] No one knows why.

One of the commonalities in near-death experiences is the inclusion of light. We always hear the refrain that these people were "pulled toward the light." Light includes all the colors of the spectrum (indeed, colors are by definition just one vibration of light waves as a whole). Light can move atoms, causing heat. It is at the heart of quantum mechanics and quantum physics, science that focuses on the very small elements that make up the atom and then separates those into even smaller particles. These small particles do not follow the rules and laws set forth in traditional physics, which was created when studying the large scope of the universe. Thus, quantum physics is, at a very basic level, a science based on probability and chaos. In other words, no one really knows for sure what will happen and why. Everything is possible.

We, as human beings, are crafted from these intensely small particles—atoms, electrons, protons, neutrons, quarks, and gluons. (And, no, I didn't make up those last two!) They are a part of us, just as they are a part of the trees, the planet, the streaking comet, the Milky Way Galaxy, and the universe. When looked at from that vantage point, we, as humans, are tiny. On a universal scale, when compared to galaxies, we are as big as the smallest quantifiable particle in an atom. Yet, if we are the quark or even the tiny gluon of the universe, we are created from the same matter and energy as the biggest planet or solar system. On the most basic level, at the very core of ourselves, we are the same. Do we, perhaps, simply return to this most basic form when we "see the light?" Could this microscopic interconnectedness be at the heart of our quest for spirituality? Is the Divine simply a human manifestation of the aspect of ourselves that we can feel and sense, on a subatomic level, in other beings and objects? Are we, in fact, God?

Who's to say? But the truth of the matter is that humans feel an abiding need to reach beyond the confines of this material world, toward something that is greater than themselves. Called divinity, spirit, or energy, the essence is experienced internally, is intangible, and cannot be measured or weighed. Perhaps it is a molecular bridge or connection to other people and things. Perhaps it is an old man in the sky or a bountiful triple woman. Perhaps it is a rabbit on the moon or a spirit within a tree. Whatever "it" is, it begins with each individual. It begins with you. Without you, there is no point here on Earth for the light to descend upon. There is no anchor to hold fast the streaming

---

1. French, "Dying to Know the Truth," *The Lancet*, 2010–2011.

possibilities and truths. We, as humans, create change in the world and the universe, just as the quarks and swirling electrons create change in the atom. Nothing is standing still.

So, when exploring spirituality, it is important to remember our authentic selves as we are a reflection (via tiny molecules) of the Divine. Embrace your spiritual form. Agnostic. Christian. Buddhist. Wiccan. Moslem. Druid. Atheist. Each of these is a true manifestation of humanity, of spirituality, of light, of electrons, of truth. We are the truth of ourselves. We are the truth of the Divine.

ENERGY RETURN

There are few negatives to focusing on and improving your spirituality. After all, you're not wishing to gain anything except enlightenment. But, therein lies the hidden trap in the attainment of spiritual connection. Spirituality, by its very nature, moves us outside of our world. We wish to learn about our spirit guides and power animals. We seek the truth of life and the continuance of the soul after death. We yearn to feel a union with a presence bigger than ourselves, not found on the planet Earth.

With our minds and hearts occupied with the essence of the Divine, it is easy to ignore the very nature of life on Earth. The lessons of this world and the sheer beauty of material existence become overshadowed with matters that are far beyond human comprehension. We obsess over mystical knowledge and sacred wisdom and Divine light. It fills our every waking thought. All other pursuits become less interesting, less powerful, less fulfilling. Our quest for spiritual enlightenment becomes so encompassing that we forget to look around us for the very things we seek. We disregard the body we currently inhabit. We cannot see the wonderful family and friends who reside in our individual life spheres. We are blinded by the light of spirituality.

Therefore, when reaching for spiritual enlightenment, for a link to the Divine, it is extremely important to continue to focus on this reality, on this life. Buy an engagement calendar and honor your body by remembering those doctor and dentist appointments. Talk with your children, significant others, and friends so you remain a part of their everyday lives. Eat well and on a regular basis. Continue to work toward that promotion at work. Treat yourself to a fancy pocketbook, a new pair of shoes, or that big-screen TV. In short, don't allow your spiritual quest to isolate you from the people and places and earthly goals that mean something to you. Don't cut yourself off from this material plane. If you've ever felt the hug of a child or the devotion of a loving dog, you know that spiritual beauty can be found in the simplest things just as easily as it can be found in profound esoteric texts and enchanted meditation.

THE PLEIADES
Greek Goddesses of All Time and Space

MANTRA

Seven Sisters, we,
Arise from the Sea.
Illume Above
Transform Below
Flying Sweet and Free.

The Pleiades are a star cluster, a home for aliens, a set of sisters, a set of mothers, a flock of hens, a marketplace, a group of birthing women, a storehouse, a group of orphans, a granary, a set of water nymphs, and the physical location of Jehovah God's throne. These Divine entities have been known throughout history, marked and commented upon by cultures as diverse as the Aztecs, the aboriginal Australians, the Norse, Persians, Ukrainians, Celts, and the Lakota, Kiowa, and Blackfoot Native American tribes. They form an important part of Indian astrology, helped named a Japanese car manufacturer (Subaru), and were even mentioned in the Bible. There are as many stories about this star cluster as there are cultures around the world. They are a universally felt presence on planet Earth and, as such, connect the world to a higher level of existence. Whether it be goddesses, aliens, or an all-powerful male god, humans have drawn inspiration and enlightenment from these powerful seven stars for years.[2]

The Pleiades, star cluster M45, form a part of the Taurus constellation. In the night sky, they are followed by the Orion Nebula and the Sirius binary star system, giving them the illusion of "being chased" by the hunter and his dog, respectfully. (This interpretation of the circular movement of the Pleiades comes from Greek and Roman mythology. Other

---

2. Pleiade Associates, "The Pleiades in Mythology."

Figure 6: The Pleiades Constellation

cultures see the dog as caring for the stars, in a surrogate mother role.) The Pleiades are 425 light years (or 130 parsecs)[3] away from Earth and can usually be seen in the sky in late spring, summer, and early autumn in the Northern Hemisphere. Their rising (in late April or early May) and setting (in late October or early November) corresponds almost exactly to the harvesting and plowing seasons of ancient Greece and Rome, where they were written about as seasonal indicators.

The Greek poet Hesiod writes about the Pleiades numerous times in his book *Works and Days*. He tells Greek farmers to begin their harvest "when the Pleiades Atlagenes [born of Atlas] are rising" and to plough "when they are going to set."[4] He continues to utilize the Pleiades as a seasonal indicator by warning against sea travel when they are hidden from view, in late October or early November. "But when the Pleiades and Hya-

3. Anglo-Australian Observatory, "The Pleiades."
4. Evelyn-White, *Hesiod: Works and Days*, 383–404.

des [their sisters in the sky] and strong Orion begin to set, then remember to plough in season. But if desire for uncomfortable sea-faring seize you; when the Pleiades plunge into the misty sea to escape Orion's rude strength, then truly gales of all kinds rage."[5] Hesiod shows us that the ancient Greeks used the Pleiades star cluster to mark the best times for sea travel and agricultural labor. Almost seven hundred years later, the Roman poet Virgil echoed Hesiod's advice concerning the Pleiades' role in agriculture in *Georgics,* and Valerius Flaccas, a contemporary of Virgil, continues to perpetuate the use of the setting of the Pleiades as a warning against sea travel in his book *Argonautica.* So, whether working by land or by sea, in ancient Greece or in ancient Rome, the Pleiades were a useful cluster of stars to observe.

This connection to the seasonal changes of planet Earth comes as no surprise to those who are familiar with the story of the Seven Sisters, known collectively as the Pleiades in Greek mythology. Daughters of Atlas and the oceanid (ocean nymph) Pleione, they are nymphs themselves, intimately connected to nature and the workings of planet Earth. Like many nymphs, they enjoy spending time outside in the wilds of nature and are often found in the company of Artemis. Born on the mountain of Kyllene, the Pleiades were known as oreiades, or mountain-dwelling nymphs. Yet their collective name derives from the Greek word *peleiades*, which means "flock of doves," or from their mother's name, *Pleione*, which means "sailing queen." The daughters of Pleione would then be known as the "sailing ones." By their birth location, parentage, collective name, and innate characteristics, the Pleiades connect to the essential elements of nature. They are tied to the element of earth through their mountainous birth and their father Atlas, who is charged with holding the Earth on his shoulders. The element water enters their lives through their mother Pleione, the ocean nymph. The Pleiades relate to a third element, air, by their association with the word *peleiades* (flock of doves). And, the elemental connection can be extended to the element of fire, since, as stars in the sky, they are actually bright burning balls of gas.

The fire association continues in the individual stories of the Pleiades. These sisters are most well-known for their lovers, husbands, and eventual offspring. The Pleiades are passionate spirits of nature, often pursued by gods, giants, and mortals. They have sexual encounters with Zeus, Ares, and Poseidon; are wives of mortal kings; and give birth to gods, goddesses, and founders and kings of cities. Through the myths, it is not

---

5. Ibid., 618.

the Pleiades themselves that have power, but rather their relations and intimates. The Pleiades are conduits of power, channeling it to those of their choosing.

The most well-known of these sisters is undoubtedly Maia, mother of the god Hermes. Maia is said to be the oldest of the Seven Sisters and also the most beautiful. Tired of being pursued by erstwhile suitors, Maia lived by herself in a cave on Mount Kyllene, where she was born. One night, while she was sleeping, Zeus snuck into her cave and made love to her, resulting in the birth of the messenger god Hermes. At his birth, Maia swaddled him and laid him on a winnowing fan. But, true to his quickness and mercurial nature, Hermes grew up at an astonishing rate, and when Maia's back was turned, he snuck away to seek adventure. The myths relate his stealing of Apollo's herd of sacred cows, which he led back to his mother's cave. He then invented the lyre and lulled Maia to sleep. When Apollo stomped into the cave and demanded the child be tried for theft, Maia came to the defense of her son, pointing at his swaddled form and claiming that the charge was absurd. (We know, of course, that Hermes was tricking his sweet mum, and he had, in fact, taken the cows.)[6] Maia's love of children and just ways shows themselves once again when she serves as surrogate mother for Arcas, Zeus' son by Callisto, after Callisto had been changed into a bear by Hera and (eventually) raised to the heavens by Zeus to form the constellation of Ursa Major.

While Maia might be the most popular of the Pleiades, the brightest of the Sisters is Alcyone, whose name means "queen who wards off storms."[7] She, alone of the Pleiades, stands by herself as a goddess separate from her sisters.[8] There is some confusion as to her exact story because there is another demi-goddess in Greek legend of the same name. Over the years, their two stories have become entwined, utilizing the same symbols and meanings. The Alcyone of Pleiades fame is known to have indicated good sailing weather (and thus, protection from storms) due to the seasonal time of her rising in the night sky. Alcyone had a son by Poseidon, named Anthas, who founded the cities of Anthea and Hyperea.[9] The Aeolians, who were known for their sailing, knew the goddess by the name Alcyone and had a queen by the same name. The queen Alcyone (who

---

6. Graves, *Greek Myths,* 63–64.

7. Ibid., 749.

8. Many would claim that Maia is a separate Goddess as well but, in the myths, she is continuously referred to as a "nymph," not a "Goddess."

9. Graves, *Greek Myths,* 323–324.

may or may not be an incarnation of one of the Seven Sisters) also protected sailors. After her husband, Ceyx, died and she committed suicide by jumping into the sea, they were both changed into kingfishers, birds that were thought to hold magical powers to ward against sea storms. Whether these stories are about the same goddess or not, Alcyone holds the power of protection and defense, especially in connection with the sea.

Like her sister Alcyone, a third member of the Pleiades, Electra, was connected to the sea and the ocean. Under the guise of an ocean nymph, Electra gave birth to the Harpies and the goddess Iris by Thaumus, a Greek sea god whose name means "wonder." Both the Harpies and Iris serve as messengers for the Olympian gods—Iris mainly for the goddess Hera, and the Harpies mainly as agents of retribution for any human being who has wronged the gods or humanity. There is another semi-divine deity called Electra who birthed Dardanus, the founder of Troy. It is unclear whether these two characters are the same woman, but it is likely, since both are oceanids. Many classical texts state that the Pleiade Electra hid her face out of sadness when the city of Troy was destroyed. Robert Graves believes that this aspect of her story shows the mythological explanation of the disappearance of a star in the night sky during ancient times.[10] Perhaps this is also why she is known as "dark-faced."[11]

Ovid, however, claims that it is the sister Merope who refuses to shine brightly in the night sky because she alone fell in love with a mortal.[12] Merope is the wife of Sisyphus, founder of Corinth and all-around sly and nasty fellow. He waylaid travelers and killed them for their goods and even chained up the god of death Thanatos so the dead could not reach the Underworld. There is no reason given in the classic texts for Merope's inexplicable love for such a devious man. Perhaps she enjoys living on the darker side of life or perhaps Aphrodite worked her love magic and emotionally enslaved Merope to a less-deserving man. Whatever the reason, Merope births four children with Sisyphus: Glaucus, Ornytion, Thersander, and Almus. Perhaps, after being raised to her vantage point in the night sky, Merope changes her mind concerning her choice of husband and this is why she blushes and is less visible to the naked eye. In any event, she is the sister who best understands human frailties and mistakes, regrets and poor choices. She is

---

10. Ibid., 154.

11. Hesiod, *The Divination by Birds to Idaean Dactyles.*

12. Ovid, *Fasti: Book IV."*

bound to her past actions and can never fully express herself or experience true freedom.

Of the Seven Sisters, Taygete is the most wild and free. She travels almost exclusively with the goddess Artemis, as a member of her chaste retinue of nymphs. When Zeus aggressively pursued Taygete (much to her chagrin and distaste), Artemis sought to hide her by changing her into the shape of a doe. However, Taygete's new form did not fool Zeus, who simply changed into a stag and made love to her anyway. Nine months later, their son Lacedaemon, founder and king of Sparta, was born. After giving birth, Taygete hanged herself on Mount Amyclaeus, which from that point on was known as Mount Taygetus.[13] Taygete teaches us that we have to be true to our inner spirit, while still weathering the ups and downs of everyday life.

The last two sisters of the Pleiades are known only by their lovers and children and have no stories attached to them. Celaeno was a lover of Poseidon and bore him two sons, Nycteus and Lycus, who became regents and rulers of Thebes. Her sister, Sterope or Asterope, was seduced by Ares, Greek god of war. With him, she bore a son, Oenomaus, who became the king of Pisa. Despite being relatively ignored by the classical writers, Celaeno and Sterope are still important enough to have drawn the attention of these two important Olympian gods. One doesn't catch the attention of Ares or Poseidon by hiding one's true greatness. By staying true to themselves, they reach greater heights through recognition and personal fulfillment.

In fact, all of the Pleiades celebrate their true elemental natures, connecting with forest, sea, and mountain as they dally with gods and mortals alike. Yet, their greatest challenge occurs when they are pursued by the giant Orion. Orion is a great hunter and one day, he saw the Seven Sisters and their mother Pleione in the forest. He became consumed with need and chased after them. Mother and daughters fled from Orion for seven years but, still, he was undeterred. Finally, they beseeched the aid of the gods, who turned them into doves and then into stars. Of course, this story hinges on the fact that the Pleiades were virgins, which we know is not true, since they birthed numerous dynasties in Greek mythology.[14] Yet, this is the only surviving story to explain the reasoning for the goddesses' ascent into the heavens.

---

13. Graves, *Greek Myths,* 473.
14. Ibid., 152.

In my mind, the Pleiades are connected to starlight because they are a force that is a part of but greater than the cyclical nature of planet Earth. Having loved and lost in their Earth-bound lifetimes, the Pleiades were lifted to the heavens by the ideals of classical philosophers. Having intimately known the elements of earth, water, and air, they needed to expand their physical constructs to include a fire element that still related to their Earth-bound selves. As star cluster M45, the Pleiades guided the ancient Greeks and Romans in agricultural and seafaring pursuits. Their ascent into the night sky indicated the correct time for these activities. Therefore, even 425 light years away, their presence was felt on the Earth. Even now, when we have twenty-four-hour weather reports and rotating space satellites, the Pleiades are still a force of mystery and power. Some people believe that the Seven Rays of Manifestation originate in the Pleiades and that UFOs and aliens live within their nebulous light. Who can say? The truth is, the spiritual draw of the Pleiades is absolute and has lasted for more than 2,000 years on planet Earth. How can so many people possibly be wrong?

Pathway to the Pleiades

Beautiful, earthy, sensuous, and divine, the Pleiades celebrate life even as they look beyond this earthly plane to the far reaches of space. As goddesses of balance, of the celestial and the material, of the spiritual and the mundane, the Pleiades recognize that the Divine can be felt in all aspects of life. The birth of a child, the touch of a lover, and the pain of separation all evoke a deeper meaning and message when the Divine is seen to reside within them. The experience is the essence of the Divine just as the Divine is within the essence of the experience.

With that in mind, it is time to transcend this limited reality by focusing upon it. Sounds complex, doesn't it? It is actually much easier than you can imagine, as long as you have a few simple tools and the right mindset. The first thing you need to do is locate some kick-butt music. It really doesn't matter what music you use, as long as it gets you up off the couch and dancing across the floor. Different music is going to resonate with different people, so really take your time to pick the right music for you. I personally like the song "Navras" by Juno Reactor from the movie *The Matrix Revolutions* or, if you have positive memories of *The Sound of Music* from your youth, you could try Gwen Stefani's "Wind it Up." As a lover of all things faerie, I also feel the power of the drumming and folk-sound of the song "Awakening" by Elvendrums[15] on their album *Gateway to Faerie*. All of these songs make me want to dance and strike a deep, mystical chord within my core. This is the feeling you are looking for when you select your music. Don't go for the most popular or most available music. Pick the song that you feel with your body and soul.

Now that you've got your music, it's time to pick a tool of power. You don't necessarily need a "dance item" but it serves as an extension of yourself, pushing you beyond your ordinary senses. Your "power tool" lifts you outside of yourself, allowing you to focus on something other than your feet or arms or head. In short, your item will help you to overcome any nervous or self-conscious feelings you may be experiencing. As a woman, I tend to gravitate toward the diaphanous, see-through scarves created by Doorway Publications[16] in their "sacred symbols" series. I also love to use tambourines or zils when dancing. However, your dance tool can be anything that calls to you. Swords (non-sharpened), staffs, rattles, and drums are all possible tools that will help you escape this current reality. Look around your house and use your imagination.

Once you've collected your dance music and your tool of power, it's time to get your groove on! Pick a time when you will be alone in your house. I personally like to dance at night but any time is fine for this exercise. Clear a good-sized space in your living room or bedroom, creating a mini dance floor. If you like, turn off the lights or tie on a blindfold to allow yourself to go within. At the very least, close your eyes, but make sure you have enough space and familiarity with the room to avoid hurting yourself! Now turn on the music and move. Don't think. Don't question. Don't judge. Just move to the music, allowing it to surround you, motivate you, and encapsulate you. Surrender to the notes, to the driving drum beat, to the soaring vocals. Feel the music in your blood. It sustains you. It supports you. It is a part of you. You *must* move. The music gives you no other option. And so the song and you continue, separate, yet entwined. Together and independent, you reach beyond your possibilities and embrace the Divine.

You can do this exercise for as long as your body holds out or for only one song. It's completely up to you. You can do it once a day, once a month, or only one time in your life. But, whatever you do, try it! It sounds silly but, by stepping outside of your comfort zone, you truly tap into your own power and your connection to the Divine.

---

15. www.elvendrums.com
16. http://www.doorwaypublications.com/

ISIS
Great Egyptian Goddess of Magic and Motherhood

MANTRA

Giving Rise
To waters, full
O, Isis.

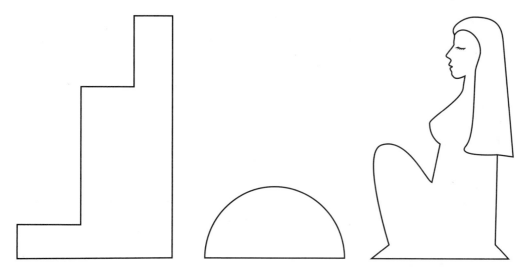

Figure 7: Name of Isis in Hieroglyphs

Vibrant, powerful, and loving, the Egyptian goddess Isis is as alive today as she was thousands of years ago in the sands of Egypt. Pick up a book on Egypt, peruse a New Age jewelry case, or simply utter the name "Isis" and you are immediately assailed with images of a winged goddess with a crown of power, sometimes kneeling, oftentimes seated on a throne with her suckling son. There was even a television show based on the power and mystery of Isis. The 1970s spawned the cult classic Saturday morning kids' show *The Secrets of Isis*, which was re-released on DVD in 2007 to much individual, if not critical, acclaim. What is it about Isis that appeals to so many people in so many different ways?

Isis is the preeminent goddess of Egypt. Often known by the title "Lady of Ten Thousand Names," Isis assumed many of the characteristics and attributes of older Egyptian goddesses. Originally seen in paintings as a goddess with a throne on her head due to the fact that her hieroglyph means "Mistress of the Throne," over time she began to wear the sun disc and horns of Hathor as a crown. As a human woman, Isis wears a queen's headdress, with the uraeus or cobra on her forehead. [17] During the height of Rome, Isis is seen on coins minted in Alexandria, Laodicea, and Greece. On these coins, her headdress changes once again, reflecting the temperament and understanding of the goddess within the varying cultures. On the coins, Isis often wears a lotus blossom or lotus blossom coronet on her head, the horns of Hathor with the sun disc and two plumes rising above (possibly combining her with symbolism from the goddess Ma'at), or the kalathos, which is a type of basketlike headgear. [18]

It should not be surprising that Isis is found on coins from the Mediterranean world, for she was adopted and accepted as a deity by many cultures outside of Egypt. She had a temple in Rome and was one of Rome's most important deities. Although a "foreign" goddess, Romans embraced her because of their reliance on the grain that came from her native homeland, Egypt. Her cult became fully integrated into Roman life and influential senators and noblewomen followed and worshipped her ways. [19] The far-reaching expanse of the Roman Empire ensured that Isis was known around Europe. There was even a Temple of Isis located on the River Thames in England!

In the modern era, Isis is a central goddess-figure in the spiritual group the Esoteric Order of the Golden Dawn, which was conceived in 1887. Wishing to gain a deeper understanding of the Western Esoteric Mysteries (of which Egyptian teachings are only one part), the three creators of the Golden Dawn founded the first Temple dedicated to Isis-Urania in London in 1888. Since that time, the appeal of Isis has remained strong in the Golden Dawn tradition. [20] The Golden Dawn *Invocation to Isis* is a beautiful, poetic tribute to a deeply magical, mystical goddess.

Isis, as a divine female figure, has been transplanted far from her original time and place, proving that her appeal is far-reaching, touching something deeply embedded in the human psyche. In my mind, Isis' popularity stems from the many events in her life that run the gamut of human experiences and emotions. Despite adversity, Isis still

---

17. Seawright, "Isis, Sister of Nephthys, Mistress of Magic."
18. Welch, "The Sign Language of Roman Coins: Isis, Goddess of the Nile."
19. Ibid.
20. Golden Dawn Research Center.

emerges strong, confident, and caring. She is the ultimate Mother Goddess. Yet, don't expect her to be one-dimensional. Isis has been known to wallow in the mud, trick unsuspecting gods, and even hide her divine nature in order to achieve her goals. And she always seems to accomplish just what she sets out to do, while still remaining true to her inner self.

One of the legends of Isis explains how she gained the power of the Great Sun God Ra, who created all the heavens and the Earth and all the beings upon the Earth. In this story, Isis is a human woman who was favored by Thoth, the magical god of books, words, wisdom, and intelligence. Thoth has already taught Isis the magic of incantations and charms and talismans, but Isis is still just a woman. She longs to be a goddess, saying, "Cannot I by means of the sacred name of god make myself mistress of the Earth and become a goddess like unto Ra in heaven and upon the Earth?"[21] With these words, Isis gets an idea. She crafts a snake out of mud created by the drool and spittle of Ra, who, as an old man, likes to enjoy his earthly creation by walking around in human form. Isis sets the snake in Ra's path and he is bitten. Immediately overcome with terrible pain, Ra cries out to his fellow gods to aid him but none have the power. Then Isis emerges and offers to help Ra, but he needs to tell her his name. She states this is because, "whosoever shall be delivered by thy name shall live."[22] Ra deflects Isis' request at first but the pain soon becomes too intense to bear; he consents to having Isis "search into me, and that my name shall pass from me into her."[23] It is important that Isis joins with Ra in order to learn his divine name. Ra never utters it out loud. Rather, Isis gains her divinity by knowing Ra's name through her joining with the Great Sun God. The concept of "becoming one" with a male deity is vital to Isis' character and her role as a fertility goddess. It is the central theme of her most popular and well-known myth, the story of Isis and Osiris.

In this myth, Isis is the lover (and sister) of the god Osiris. They sit together upon the throne of Egypt, guiding the Pharaohs and manipulating the seed growth of the plants of Egypt. Jealous of his brother's power, Set, the dark god of the Egyptian pantheon, crafts a coffin built to house his brother Osiris. By either murdering him, setting him in the coffin, or tricking him into stepping into the coffin himself, Set effectively

---

21. Budge, *Egyptian Magic,* 137.
22. Ibid., 140.
23. Ibid., 141.

kills his brother Osiris and drops the coffin into the waters of the Nile River. The coffin floats to the Phoenician city of Byblos, where it is encased in a tamarisk tree that is magically enhanced and grows very fast. The king of Byblos becomes enamored of the magic tamarisk tree and orders it cut down and made into a column for his palace. This is done and the column emits a sweet smell unlike any other in the world.

Isis, hearing of the sweet smell and the magical growth of the tree, goes to Byblos as a simple serving woman, disguising her goddesshood. She attaches herself to the royal family, serving as a nurse for Queen Astarte's new baby boy. Falling in love with the boy, she seeks to give him immortality by holding him in the household fire. Astarte happens upon Isis in the midst of this magical transformation and cries out, disrupting the goddess' concentration and plunging her baby boy back into mortality. When Isis reveals her divine nature, Astarte forgives her the transgression and gives her the palace column, which hides Osiris' coffin. Isis retreats back into the swamps of Egypt.

In the swamps, Isis brings Osiris' body back to life just long enough to conceive the child Horus, eventual ruler of the Egyptian deities. The details of how Isis gave Osiris life vary due to the many versions of the story. In one tale, Isis and her sister Nephthys turn into kites—birds of prey similar to falcons—and fan the breath of life back into Osiris' body with their light-filled, shining wings. Another account of the legend has Isis wandering over Egypt searching for the lost pieces of her husband's body after it had been cut apart by her brother Set. Isis finds all the parts of Osiris' body except the phallus, which she creates from mud (or gold). Reassembled and reanimated by the artisanship of Isis' hands, Osiris once again comes to life and the couple spends an amorous, passionate evening together, conceiving Horus. In this version, Isis is said to perform funerary rites at each spot where she found a body part, erecting steles to mark the place of burial. By this, she hoped to confuse Set and make him think that Osiris was no longer a threat, either in death or life.

Most stories of this myth combine the aspects of both the bird and the dismemberment, either relating that she fanned Osiris to life and then gathered his body parts, or gathered his body parts and then fanned him to life. Either way, she brought her husband back from the dead and conceived life.

To the ancient Egyptians, death and life and rebirth were intertwined aspects of the same transitory period of existence. The fact that a fertility goddess such as Isis brought her husband back to life in order to become impregnated with a child symbolizes her magical ability to shepherd souls after death to another existence in the Afterlife. Being intimately connected with death, rebirth, and life through the mystery of Osiris, Isis becomes one of the intermediary goddesses between this world and the next. Her name is even intoned during numerous aspects of the funerary rites of the deceased, usually in conjunction with amulets of power that were placed on the body before burial.[24]

Yet, Isis is called upon not only for spiritual rebirth but for physical birth as well. In the story "Khufu and the Magician," which is found on the Westcar Papyrus and dates from the Second Intermediary Period (around 1500 BCE), Isis plays an important role in one of the few surviving birth stories from ancient Egypt. In this story, Raddjedet, wife of a priest of the sun god Ra, is pregnant with triplets who are destined to become kings of Egypt. As her birthing time nears, she begins to experience difficulty, so Ra requests the aid of deities of childbirth and creativity. Isis, her sister Nephthys, the birthing brick goddess Meskhenet, and Heqet are dispatched to the side of the laboring mother-to-be. They travel under the guise of musicians and dancers, with the god Khnum as their manager.

When they arrive at the house, they are immediately ushered into the birthing chamber. Isis and Nephthys flank the birthing woman, at her head and feet, while Heqet hastens the birth. Before each child is born, Isis commands he leave the womb and enter the room. She calls each child by name, drawing him out of the mother with the power of her voice.[25] After each birth, the child is cleaned and the cord cut, presumably by Nephthys and Meskhenet, since Heqet and Isis are busy tending to Raddjedet. Meskhenet then presents the child to Khnum, who gives health to the baby. All five gods have important roles to play in the birth of a child, but it is Isis who, as a goddess of fertility and of magical incantations, literally pulls the child from the transitory life of the womb into the warmth of Ra's light here in the mundane world. The womb is but one step forward from the realm of the dead, the realm of her husband Osiris, just as it is but one step backward from the realm of the living, the realm of her son Horus. Isis is the link between these two states of being and, as such she is able to usher in the birth of a baby as easily as she shepherds out the soul of a deceased loved one.

When birthing a child, the womb and the embryonic fluids inside are sometimes rather romantically known as the "waters of life." One's "water breaks" directly before giving birth, expelling, in an obvious symbolic metaphor, any doubt that this experience is a

---

24. Ibid., 43, 44, 59, and 115.
25. Seawright, "Tales of Magic in Ancient Egypt."

false alarm. Is it any wonder then that Isis, as a fertile, birthing goddess, was thought in ancient Egypt to bring fertility, not only to individuals, but to the land itself? Her temple on the island of Philae was thought to be the source of the waters of life that allowed the Nile to rise and the grain to germinate.[26] In fact the flooding of the Nile River each year was said to be caused by the tears of Isis, who was lamenting the death of her beloved husband. Even today, the night of the flooding of the Nile River is called by Muslims "The Night of the Drop," a name that originated with Isis' sorrow as "The Night of the Tear-Drop."[27] Isis is also connected to the star Sirius, which appears in the Egyptian sky around the time of the yearly flooding of the Nile River.

The Romans converted the euphemism of the "waters of life" and encapsulated it into the physical representative of the *situla,* a fancy bucket or urn. Isis' image is often preserved in statues and on coins holding a situla in her hand. It is possible that the situla served as a reminder of Isis' fertile, life-giving powers. The ceremonial water container might have been a way to symbolize the rising water of the Nile and its ability to fill the channels and ditches of the fields, thereby bringing life to the seeds.[28] Isis, once again, is seen to be the Mother of Egypt, providing sustenance for her children.

And, of course, the popular image of Isis suckling her son Horus emphasizes Isis' role as provider for her people. The fertile goddess gives birth and then, with her own milk and her own tears, feeds her children. It is her body that nourishes us, her fluids that allow the plants to grow and the children to be full. (For, as we know in modern times, the correlation between a well-fed mom providing plenty of breast milk and a healthy child with a plentiful supply of food is inescapable.) This image of Isis and Horus is closely linked to the early Christian paintings of the Madonna and child, depicting Jesus on Mary's lap. Although Isis' fertility is toned down in the Christian version (no exposed breasts allowed), the implication is still clear: the divine son born of the divine mother, together bringing life to us all, both in this world and the next.

Isis is a far-reaching, fascinating goddess whose worship, rites, and stories extend beyond this brief introduction to her powers. As a goddess connected to birth, death, and rebirth, Isis spans our entire existence on and beyond the planet Earth. She is concerned with issues that sustain us in the here and now and expand our sensibilities in

---

26. Anderson, "Philae."
27. Goddess Gift, "Isis Egyptian Goddess of Magic and Giver of Life."
28. Welch, "The Language of Roman Coins: Isis, Goddess of the Nile."

the hereafter. Wife and mother, Isis knows the sorrow and joy, the anxiety and happiness of life on Earth. She feels for us and extends her compassion. The fertile life-giver, the provider, the protector, the lover, Isis touches all aspects of our lives, our emotions, our thoughts, and our feelings. She is seen in the star Sirius, in the annual flooding of the Nile, in the flight of the kite, and in the depictions of the Madonna and child. Great and powerful, yet caring and compassionate, Isis mothers us as only she knows how, with power, strength, and a clear, steady voice.

Pathway to Isis

In many of Isis' myths, she is shown using her voice in order to alter the course of events in her life. In the "Seven Scorpions," she draws poison out of a boy stung by scorpions. In "Khufu and the Magician," her voice encourages three babies to leave the womb of a pregnant mother. In another story (which I call "The Day the Sun Stood Still"), Isis' cries stop the movement of the sun in order to heal Horus, with the help of Thoth. Indeed, her spoken word power stems from that powerful god, as Thoth taught her the correct words and pronunciations of the magical talismans and incantations. It is said that Isis "was strong of tongue, and uttered the words of power which she knew with correct pronunciation, and halted not in her speech, and was perfect both in giving the command and in saying the word."[29]

In today's world, how many of us are strong in speech? How many of us are comfortable with our words and our ability and right to voice them? Isis teaches us that we all have something meaningful to say, if we just accept our Goddess-given right to do so. All we have to do is learn to open up our throats and allow our divine voices to come out. So, with that in mind, let's sing!

As with the Pleiades exercise, the choice of song is up to you. Choose something that has meaning to you personally and moves you emotionally. It would be best if it contained a powerful, life-affirming, self-confidence boosting theme, but it's not strictly necessary. I like songs that showcase strong, assertive women and are a little brash and edgy. Pink's "U + Ur Hand" or "Centerfold" (bonus track) from her album *I'm Not Dead* come to mind. Sometimes you can find the best grrl power songs on the soundtracks of movies designed for a teenage audience. Check out the *Freaky Friday*, *Josie and the Pussycats*, or *Bend It Like Beckham* soundtracks. (The movies aren't half-bad either!) As a lover of all things faerie,

---

29. Budge, *Egyptian Magic*, 129.

I also have a particular affinity for the song "Trees" by the group Lovehammers, on their debut album *Marty Casey and Lovehammers.*

Once you've chosen your song, pick a time when you are alone in your house or apartment and CRANK IT! That's right, blast the volume so loud that the windows rattle and the birds outside rise off their tree branches in consternation. (It is best not to do this at midnight, especially if you live in an apartment building or in a very close neighborhood. However, if you happen to live in a frat house, sorority house, or college dormitory, by all means—feel free to *share* with your fellow students!) Listen to your song several times. Try not to *do* anything but listen. This is going to be difficult for most of us because there always seems to be so much to do and so little time in which to do it. But refrain from paying bills or flipping through the newest issue of your favorite magazine or planning supper. You might consider mowing the grass while listening to your song but only if you don't have to think about it very hard. Same goes for dusting or cleaning the kitchen floor.

After listening to your song and learning the words, the time has come to sing. That's right, sing. Open up those unused vocal chords and allow sound to come out. It doesn't really matter how you sound (that's why the music is so loud!). The point is to remind your psyche, your throat, and your inner self that you have a divine voice and you can use it! For good or ill. Don't whisper the words to your song. You know them! Belt them out at the top of your voice! Sure, you may sound like a bullfrog in heat, but who cares? You're alone. Nobody's listening, except you and Isis and maybe the birds outside your window; they're not judging you, so stop judging yourself! Remind yourself that your voice matters, whether you're singing or waiting in line at the grocery store or requesting a raise from your boss. You matter! The universe has been waiting to hear your own unique, individual song. Don't let it down by giving up and swallowing your words. It doesn't matter if people like what you say; the point is that *you* think your words are important and necessary. And they are. Just ask Isis, goddess of powerful, magical incantations. She supports your vocal abilities by showing just how powerful a woman, a man, a human can become. Follow her example and grow into a fuller, more radiant, more successful, and more vocal you.

RHIANNON
Welsh Great Queen and Triple Goddess

MANTRA
Through time and space
Rhiannon and me
Rhiannon (your name) Rhiannon (your name) Rhiannon (your name)
Rhiannon

Rhiannon is an imposing figure, regal in stature and in personality. Goddess of regeneration and the Underworld, patience and change, enchantments and sleep, fertility and death, she is a paradox, a maze, a labyrinth of inner worlds and outer realities. She is the faerie goddess of the sacred mounds and the worldly goddess of plain speech and quick action. She is as comfortable aiding us with materialistic goals as she is with spiritual achievements or emotional commitment. She truly is the goddess for all occasions and for all people, regardless of age or life path.

Modern devotees of the Divine Feminine (the universal or Great Goddess) often divide her energy into three distinct life phases—maiden, mother, and crone. They see these phases in the passing of human life, as well as in the movement of time through the seasons, and in the cycle of the moon phases. Whether or not you personally agree with this cosmological construct, it is a pervasive part of the modern goddess movement. Notice the phrase *modern Goddess movement*. The triple goddess, as assigned to the roles of maiden, mother, and crone, is a modern perception of ancient triple-aspected goddesses (such as Brigid, Morrighan, Hecate, etc.) whose three aspects were often sisters of similar age. There is a correlation between the maiden-mother-and crone goddess and the Greek Moirae and Roman Parcae, who were personifications of Fate and Time and thus represented past, present, and future. For this reason, they are sometimes thought to be a youth, a mother, and a hag. However, in classical texts, all three were depicted as ugly, old women, sometimes even sharing one eyeball.

Throughout classical and medieval literature, the goddesses are often depicted as fertile. They give birth. They fertilize the soil. They help and aid the growth of babies, plants, and our inner selves. As "mother figures," they either begin as maidens and flourish into mothers, or they begin with a birth that allows them access to inner states of being and the wisdom of the crone. It is rare to find a goddess who passes through all three stages of the modern Triple Goddess. Such is the power of Rhiannon. In *The Mabinogion*, a Welsh medieval mythological epic, we see her at three distinct stages of her life: as virginal maid, a new mother, and an older crone. Rhiannon is the "Great Triple Goddess," who incorporates the cycles of the moon into herself in order to experience all stages of a woman's life.

We first meet Rhiannon as a beautiful maid on horseback, as she gently and calmly rides through the countryside. Her future husband, Pwyll is reclining on a sacred mound and, seeing Rhiannon in her ornate golden gown, immediately falls under her enchantment and must talk to her. For two days in a row, he sends one of his men to apprehend Rhiannon, but even though her horse looks to be walking slowly, neither man can catch her. The faster they ride, the farther away Rhiannon appears to be. Her displacement of time and space is key to understanding Rhiannon's connection with the realm of the faeries. When working with faeries, it is not uncommon for time to speed up or slow down. Faeries are also known to distort the landscape, sometimes leading humans astray by manipulating the environment.

Despite Rhiannon's obvious Otherworldly powers, Pwyll does not give up easily. On the third evening, after dinner, he saddles his own horse and waits for Rhiannon to show up. She does and at first glimpse, he rides after her. The magic of Rhiannon's horse stays true; as Pwyll rides faster, Rhiannon grows farther away. Confounded and wanting very badly to meet this maid, Pwyll calls out to Rhiannon, asking her to stop and talk with him. She does, answering, "I will, gladly, and it had been better for the horse hadst thou asked this long since."[30] Here we get a glimpse of Rhiannon's strong, forthright personality. She is no meek, medieval maid.

Rhiannon waits for Pwyll to ride up to her and then, removing a veil from across her face (another symbol of the Faerie and the Otherworld) she fixes him with her gaze. The fact that she looks Pwyll directly in the face indicates, as does her plain-spoken words, that she believes herself to be his equal. She tells Pwyll that she has been riding here to talk with him because she is being given in marriage to a man she does not like. She explains, in true modern feminist fashion, that she would rather marry Pwyll, as long as he will have her. Pwyll, overcome by her beauty and spirit, does not even ques-

---

30. Jones and Jones, *Mabinogion*, 10.

tion this unusual way of contracting a marriage. Instead, he agrees immediately and sets up a tryst for them to meet at her father's court in a year and a day.

Rhiannon's behavior shows her innate power as she takes matters into her own hands, creating her life on her terms. Her straightforward conduct continues when Pwyll arrives at her father's court in a year and a day. Rhiannon has prepared a feast for his coming and all in the household and in Pwyll's war-band feast well. Rhiannon's marriage occurs exactly as she had planned, when suddenly an auburn-haired, well-dressed youth arrives. He addresses Pwyll and requests a boon or favor of him.

Pwyll, not always the brightest of men, agrees magnanimously, without thinking. Rhiannon is horrified; the man is her ex-suitor Gwawl. But Pwyll has already committed to honoring Gwawl's request and cannot refuse without losing his good reputation. Gwawl, obviously a tad more intelligent than Pwyll, asks for Rhiannon's hand in marriage, as well as a feast. Pwyll is shocked into dumb silence and turns to Rhiannon with a blank expression on his face. True to her personality, Rhiannon offers no comfort to her husband-to-be. Instead, she tells him, "Be dumb as long as thou wilt. Never was there a man made feebler use of his wits than thou hast."[31]

However, it is obvious that Rhiannon loves Pwyll for his emotional commitment to her, not his intelligence. When she suggests to Pwyll that he has to honor Gwawl's request, he says, "Lady, I know not what sort of answer that is. I can never bring myself to do what thou sayest."[32] But Rhiannon has a plan. She asks Pwyll to give her to Gwawl but to arrange the feast for a year and a day hence. On that day, Pwyll is to arrive at the court dressed as a beggar, holding a magical bag that Rhiannon has given him.

The year passes and the marriage feast for Gwawl and Rhiannon is laid and all eat well. Pwyll comes to the feast, according to plan, dressed as a beggar and holding Rhiannon's magical bag. He asks that his bag be filled with food scraps. Food is placed in the bag but it seems to never get full. Gwawl wonders out loud at the marvel of this bag and Pwyll says that it will never be full unless a true land-holding man treads down the food with both feet. Rhiannon goads Gwawl into volunteering to tramp down the beggar's food and, as soon as both feet are in the bag, Pwyll pulls up the sides and calls in his war-band. As every member of Pwyll's retinue enters the hall, they hit the bag with a

---

31. Ibid., 11.
32. Ibid., 11.

foot or a stick. Before too long, Gwawl gives up his right to Rhiannon and Pwyll makes her his bride.

Pwyll's love for Rhiannon is tested in the fourth year of their marriage, as Rhiannon makes the transition from maiden to mother. On May Eve that year, Rhiannon gives birth to a baby boy. Exhausted from the birth and surrounded by six waiting women, Rhiannon falls into a deep sleep. One by one, the serving women also fall asleep. By the hour of midnight, no one is watching the baby. Both May Eve and the time of midnight are intricately connected to Faerieland, as they are considered "between-times"—times outside the normal course of time and space. May Eve is a date neither of spring nor of summer; midnight is a time neither of today nor of tomorrow. Therefore, it is no surprise that the baby disappears, possibly taken by the faeries as many new mothers feared in the medieval era.

The maidservants wake up before Rhiannon and discover the baby missing. Nervous that they shall be blamed and severely punished, they decide to kill a puppy and smear his blood all over Rhiannon and all over the hearth where the baby rested. Then, they plan to feign disgust when Rhiannon wakes up, telling her that she killed her son in her sleep and that they could not protect him due to her unnatural strength. It is in this section of her life story that Rhiannon becomes associated with dreamtime and dream magic, yet another Otherworldly experience.

When Rhiannon awakes, she is confronted by the scurrilous lies of the maids. She denies any wrongdoing and promises the servants, "You will come to no hurt for telling the truth."[33] The maids do not trust her, however, and stick with their original story, blaming Rhiannon. Pwyll, caught between his love for his wife and his love for his baby boy, is told by his advisors and chieftains to "do away" with Rhiannon. However, Pwyll has too much love for his wife. Instead, he orders her to do penance for seven years. (Seven has long been considered a magical number and is yet another connection to the land of faeries.) Rhiannon must meet all travelers at the horseblock to the castle and explain the crime for which she is being punished. Then, she must offer to serve as their horse, carrying each and every visitor on her back to the court. Rhiannon, knowing her innocence but unable to prove it, shows unearthly patience and willingly agrees to the penance.

---

33. Ibid., 16.

About halfway through her seven years' penance, a farmer arrives at court with a boy who looks remarkably like Pwyll. The farmer explains that on May Eve, several years ago, he battled a demon that tried to steal his newborn colt. He ran after the demon and when he returned to the barn, stumbled across a baby boy. He points to the boy, saying that he believes the boy he found is actually Rhiannon and Pwyll's son. The entire court agrees and Rhiannon is cleared of any wrongdoing. The entire court is in a frenzy of happiness and joy. Amid the gleeful chaos, Rhiannon exclaims, "Between me and God, I should be delivered of my care if that were true."[34]

With those words, Rhiannon evokes her mother right to name her child. Taken from the first sentence Rhiannon said when hearing her son had returned, the child is named Pryderi, which means care, worry, or anxiety in Welsh.[35] By speaking her mind, Rhiannon has reinstated herself as the chieftain's wife and a woman of authority. Her power, inside herself and inside the community, is greater after undergoing her terrible ordeal. While at the horseblock, she had to find her own inner strength, as she was emotionally and physically alone in the world, shunned and mistreated by the people she loved. Suffering through her penance changed Rhiannon, allowing her to grow in influence and supremacy, as well as in patience, modesty, and serenity. She knows she can survive anything.

Rhiannon's newfound power is tested when her son, all grown-up, arrives home from Bran's ill-fated attack on Ireland to retrieve his sister Branwen. Pryderi is only one of seven men (again that number) who survive the battle. After arriving back on The Island of the Mighty (a.k.a. England and Wales), he travels across the country from London with Manawydan, his companion and fellow warrior. When Manawydan complains that he has no land and no place to lay his head, Pryderi suggests that he marry his mother, Rhiannon, since she is a widow (Pwyll has died by this time) and has possession of his father's lands in Dyfed. Manawydan agrees to meet with Rhiannon and see if they are compatible.

Rhiannon's enchantments are still strong, despite the fact that she is no longer young. When they sit down to talk, Manawydan's "heart grew tender towards her, and he admired in his heart how he had never beheld a lady more graced with beauty and comeliness than

---

34. Ibid., 19.
35. Ibid., 19.

she."[36] Rhiannon's beauty does not diminish with age and is another bond to the faerie folk of old. Folk tales tell of faeries living hundreds of years, yet possessing the physical attractiveness of youth. Whether through glamoury, faerie magic, or really good genes, Rhiannon is still a gorgeous woman. Manawydan falls under Rhiannon's otherworldly charms and, after only one evening, contracts with Pryderi to marry her.

After the marriage feast, Rhiannon and Manawydan are out riding with Pryderi and his wife, Cigfa, when the entire countryside changes. A peal of thunder shakes the ground, a strange mist covers the four riders and Dyfed no longer looks like Dyfed. The houses, the people, the flocks of animals, and the towns are completely different. The four have been transported to another realm. And suddenly, the chieftain and his family must support themselves doing physical jobs such as making shoes, shields, and saddles.

In the midst of this strange occurrence, Pryderi and Manawydan happen upon an unusual *caer*, or fortress. Pryderi, ever the adventurer, goes inside and becomes trapped by touching a golden bowl next to a fountain. Manawydan, older and more cautious than Pryderi, refuses to enter the caer and returns home to Rhiannon, who is appalled that her husband left her son to fend for himself. With shades of her younger, irrepressible, out-spoken self, Rhiannon proclaims, "Faith! A bad comrade hast thou been, but a good comrade hast thou lost."[37] Without a second thought, Rhiannon races to the caer, enters the castle, finds her son, touches the golden bowl, and is also trapped inside the caer! Luckily, Manawydan proves himself worthy of her love by solving the riddle of the caer and freeing Pryderi and Rhiannon.

Although Rhiannon's part in this story is very small, it is of importance. Here is a goddess who, as an older woman, still retains her vital spark of life and her innate beauty of spirit and of body. Her sense of self has not diminished with time, rather it has become more definite and well defined. As one of the few women in *The Mabinogion* who actually ages, Rhiannon is a role-model for the modern woman. Strong and agile, fleet of mind and foot, her age does not impede her. She is comfortable with herself and does not hide her inner greatness, no matter her age, position, or life task.

As shown in *The Mabinogion*, Rhiannon truly is Maiden, Mother, and Crone. In all three stages of her life, she talks quickly, thinks quickly, and acts quickly, yet has an

---

36. Ibid., 36.
37. Ibid., 40.

amazing capacity for acceptance and patience. Loyalty, honor, and truth are Rhiannon's sacred gifts, as are gentleness and forgiveness, both of yourself and of others. Rhiannon is of the mind and as such, responds to plain-spoken words and actions. However, her capacity for love is vast and she will willingly take on the burdens of others in order to protect them and save them from disgrace.

Rhiannon is a goddess of growth and survival, weathering unspeakable heartache and misery in order to emerge stronger, courageous and whole. Yet her innate spunky, even faerie-like, nature does not react well to self-deceit. She asks you to come to her open and vulnerable and she will help you with your life path, healing emotional wounds and giving you words of power when you have need. Her power, like yours, comes from life experience.[38]

Pathway to Rhiannon

In today's modern world of huge televisions and slick magazines and digital pictures, it becomes easy to accept the modern concept of beauty. Youth is beauty. Slimness is beauty. Perfection is beauty. Musculature is beauty. The icons of beauty (and, thus, of success) are movie stars, rock singers, super models, and star athletes. We all strive to attain the golden panacea of beauty with styling products, expensive makeup and facial creams, body wraps, and athletic trainers. As we grow older, we color our hair, tuck our tummies, and lift our faces in order to appear to be something we are not so we can fit into society's concept of beauty. We all want to be considered beautiful, don't we?

There's nothing wrong with wanting to look and feel beautiful. But there's something warped about a society that refuses to acknowledge the many facets and the infinite variety of beauty. When we deny our own innate beauty, we deny our own ability to grow and give to the world. We weaken our self-confidence and self-esteem, lessening our ability to make positive, life-affirming decisions and changes in our lives and in the world around us. Beauty—like divinity—comes from within. If we are beautiful on the inside, then others will see us as beautiful. If we are ugly, self-deprecating, self-conscious, and jealous on the inside, then others will see us as those rather ugly things. Some of the most beautiful people in the world are not supermodels, movie stars, or star athletes.

---

38. Much of the story of Rhiannon first appeared in *Goddess Alive!*, 256–261. For more information and intimate workings with Rhiannon, Great Queen and Triple Goddess, including a guided meditation and ritual, please see chapter 14 of *Goddess Alive!*

They are those people who love themselves and whose love for themselves shines out to encompass all they meet. They are the skipping children, the smiling grandmothers, the open-hearted teachers or coaches.

So, let's turn off those televisions and close those magazines and remember to love the body we're in—every wrinkle and gray hair and love-handle. Rhiannon is beautiful and divine in all of her phases of life, just as we all are. Take some time every day to remind yourself that you are beautiful and loved. Every morning, after washing your face and brushing your teeth, look at yourself and say, "You are beautiful." Say this three times for each of Rhiannon's life phases—Maiden, Mother, and Crone—or say it seven times for the faerie number that consistently appears in her stories. If you feel awkward, start by saying it just once. The number of times really doesn't matter as long as you say it out loud with conviction. Remember, Rhiannon uses her voice and is not shy to speak plainly and succinctly, while still harboring love and devotion. See this time as a daily devotion to yourself. After all, you've done wonderful, incredible things in this world. You are a wonderful, incredible, beautiful human being. Honor the Divine in you by reminding yourself of that fact!

RITUAL FOR SPIRITUALITY:
WHAT DO YOU WANT TO DO?

Suggested Ritual Days

December 31: World Spirituality Day, as declared by the Integrative Spirituality Movement

The first Thursday in May: The National Day of Prayer, as recognized by the government of the United States

The first Thursday in May: The National Day of Reason, as declared by numerous secular, humanist, atheist, and rationalist groups

You can perform this ritual on any days of importance that are specific to your particular religion or spiritual path. Secular holidays (like Valentine's Day, Veterans Day, and St. Patrick's Day), snow days, the equinoxes and solstices, the first day of the month, the last day of the month, stormy days, sunny days, and your birthday are all powerful times throughout the year that can be used to access and work with your personal spirituality. The options are limitless!

Items needed

an album of your favorite music
cleansing or energizing room spray (such as Florida water or a vibrational essence myst)
a pen
several pieces of paper

Sit down in your favorite space and begin to listen to your album. Spritz the spray around the room (making sure to mist yourself as well) and begin to connect to the source of the Divine within. You can do this through dance, meditation, grounding and centering, yoga, singing, or by simply "being." Don't feel obligated to stay in your chair. Get up and move if you feel so inclined!

Once you feel connected to the Divine, sit down and answer the following questions. Don't think about them. Don't agonize over the right answer. There isn't one. You are simply figuring out the type of ritual that relates to your spirituality at the present moment. Spirituality shifts, just as our emotions and moods shift. What moves us on a deep level and connects us to the Divine source changes on a daily, possibly even hourly, basis. Every time you wish to honor your spirituality, you need to tap in to its exact frequency *at that given moment in time.* Your spirituality begins and ends with you and your perception and connection to the Divine. No one can tell you how to honor your spirituality. You have to do that for yourself.

THE QUESTIONS

1. Today, I feel_____.

2. When I close my eyes, I see the color(s) _____.

3. When I open my eyes and look around, I predominately see the color(s) _____.

4. Out of the four elements of earth, air, fire, and water, today I feel most drawn to
   _____.

5. Out of the three aspects of above, below, and within, today I feel most connected to
   _____.

6. Out of the two constructs of light and dark, today I feel most connected to
   _____.

7. Out of all the animals in the world, today I feel closest to _____.

8. Out of all the mythological and fantasy creatures in the world, today I feel closest
   to _____.

9. Today my favorite piece of jewelry is _____.

10. Right now, the weather is _____.

11. Right now, I wish the weather was _____.

12. If I could be anywhere in the world or the universe, throughout time and space,
    I would most like to be _____.

13. If I could be doing anything right now, I would be _____.

14. Looking at my items of spiritual power, today I am most inclined to pick up and
    hold _____.

15. Today my favorite memory is _____.

16. Right now, I am hungry for _____.

17. Right now, I am thirsty for _____.

18. Right now, my deepest wish is _____.

19. Right now, my immediate goal is _____.

20. Right now, I am grateful for _____.

After answering the questions, read through them and see if you see any similarities. For instance, you might find that the room you're sitting in has a lot of red colors, your favorite piece of jewelry is an amber pendant, you feel most connected to the element of fire, and you wish the weather was warm and sunny. This would indicate that you may wish to experience heat of some sort in your spiritual ritual, possibly utilizing a candle, hearthfire, or campfire. Perhaps you are hungry to spend time with your best friend, thirsty for acknowledgement in the workplace, while realizing that your deepest wish is to become a Reiki Master Healer, and your immediate goal is to make more money so you can attend an upcoming class or workshop. These answers would show you that your workplace is not supporting your ideas of success (personal or material) and that you need to look outside the workplace for new ideas.

The questions that don't seem to fit into the pattern are also important, as they represent individual interests and influences that could be cultivated, if you choose. A random frog or water influence might indicate a need for change or mutability. A rose quartz might show that you are not loving yourself enough to pursue your goals, or it might show you that you need to open up to a new love in your life. Read the answers to the questions by yourself. Only you know what they mean to you. Do not consult a book—any book—until after you have fully analyzed the answers and come to your own conclusions.

Now that you've ascertained your present mindset, needs, passions, goals, interests, and influences, you can craft a ritual specific to your own spirituality. Go with your gut. It doesn't need to be flashy or fancy or two hours long. A five-minute ritual performed from the heart has much more impact than an hour-long celebration that you copied word-for-word from a book or from the internet. Remember, this is *your* ritual designed to work with *your* Divine connection. Trust your intuition and enjoy the spiritual experience!

Bibliography

Adams, J. M., and H. Faure, eds. "Europe East to 40 degrees E (the Urals), and including Asia Minor." *Review and Atlas of Paleovegetation*. Quaternary Environments Network (Q.E.N.), Oakridge National Laboratory, TN, 1997. http://www.esd.ornl.gov/projects/qen (accessed February 2009).

Afrodesign Studios. "West Africa." http://www.afrodesign.com/west-africa-a-14.html (accessed February 2009).

Anderson, Joan A. "Philae." Baltimore City College. http://users.erols.com/bcccsbs/Africa/toisis.htm (accessed February 2009).

Anglo-Australian Observatory. "The Pleiades." Steven J. Gibson, Arecibo Observatory. www.naic.edu/~gibson/pleiades/ (accessed February 2009).

Ann, Martha, and Dorothy Myers Imel. *Goddesses in World Mythology*. New York: Oxford University Press, 1993.

Apeadu, Nan. "The African Indigenous Religion." International Center of Cultural Studies USA, Proceedings of First International Conference and Gathering of Elders. http://iccsus.org/1stConf/310.html (accessed February 2009).

Auden, W. H., and P. B. Taylor, "The Lay of Hyndla." *Norse Poems*. Faber and Faber, Ltd. Norse Mythology Source Texts. home.Earthlink.net/~wodensharrow/hyndluljodh .html#norse (accessed February 2009).

Beckwith, Martha. *Hawaiian Mythology*. New Haven, CT: Yale University Press, 1940. Available online at www.sacred-texts.com/pac/hm/index.htm (accessed February 2009).

Bellows, Henry Adams, trans. *The Poetic Edda*. Princeton, NJ: Princeton University Press, 1936. Available online at http://www.sacred-texts.com/neu/poe (accessed January 2008).

Best, R. I, Osborn Bergin, and M. A. O'Brien, eds. "Lebor Gabala Erenn." *Irish Texts Archive.* www.ancienttexts.org/library/celtic/irish/lebor.html (accessed February 2009).

Bharati, Swami Jnaneshvara. "Meaning of 108 beads on a mala." SwamiJ.com Traditional Yoga and Meditation of the Himalayan Masters. www.swamij.com/108.htm (accessed February 2009).

Brown, Michele. "The Lessons of Juan Camargo Huaman—Peruvian Shaman." *Sacred Hoop* magazine, Issue 3 (1993). www.rahoorkhuit.net/goddess/goddess_quest/pacha _mama.html (accessed February 2009).

Budge, E. A. Wallis. *Egyptian Magic.* Avenel, NJ: Wings Books, 1991.

Carrasco, David. "Uttered from the Heart: Guilty Rhetoric Among the Aztecs." *History of Religions,* v39 i1 p1. (August 1999). Available online at www.mexicauprising.net/ guiltyrhetoricamongtheaztecs.html (accessed February 2009).

Carroll, James. "Who Was Mary Magdalene?" *Smithsonian Magazine* (June 2006). www. smithsonianmag.com/history-archaeology/magdalene.html?c=y&page=8 (accessed February 2009).

Catholic Youth Networking. "Blessed Jacinto and Francisco: The Fatima Prayer." www .catholicyouth.freeservers.com/prayers/fatima.htm (accessed February 2009).

Chamberlain, Basil Hall, trans. *The Kojiki.* Read before the Asiatic Society of Japan in 1882, reprinted 1919. Available online at www.sacred-texts.com/shi/kj/kj023.htm (accessed February 2009).

Cross, Tom P., and Clark Harris Slover, eds. and trans. *Ancient Irish Tales.* New York: Henry Holt and Company, 1936. Available online at www.ancienttexts.org/library/ celtic/ctexts/lebor5.html (accessed February 2009).

De Marchi, John. *The Immaculate Heart: The True Story of Our Lady of Fatima.* New York: Farrar, Straus and Young, 1952.

"Deri el-Bahri, Mortuary Temple of Hatshepsut." Hosted by Tripod. ib205.tripod.com/ hatshepsut_temple.html (accessed February 2009).

"Diet for Depression." WebMD: Depression Health Center. (August 2, 2004): http:// www.webmd.com/depression/guide/diet-recovery?page=2 (accessed February 2009).

Evans, Dyfed Lloyd. "Sulis." *Nemeton: The Sacred Grove.* www.celtnet.org.uk/gods_s/ sulis.html (accessed February 2009).

Evelyn-White, Hugh G., trans. *Hesiod: Works and Days*, 1914. Sacred Texts.com. www .sacred-texts.com/cla/hesiod/works.htm (accessed February 2009).

Fairgrove, Rowen. "What We Don't Know About the Ancient Celts." *The Pomegranate,* Issue 2 (Lammas 1997). www.conjure.com/whocelts.html (accessed February 2009).

French, Christopher C. "Dying to Know the Truth: visions of a dying brain, or false memories?" *The Lancet,* Vol. 358, Issue 9298 (December 15, 2001). www.thelancet .com/journals/lancet/article/PIIS0140-6736(01)07133-1/fulltext (accessed February 2009).

Geddes-Ward, Alicen, and Neil Geddes-Ward. *Faeriecraft.* Carlsbad, CA: Hay House, 2005.

Gimbutas, Marija. *The Language of the Goddess.* New York: Thames and Hudson, 1989.

The Gnostic Society Library. "The Gospel According to Mary Magdalene." www.gnosis .org/library/marygosp.htm (accessed February 2009).

The Goddess Chess Blog: Chess, Goddess, and Everything. "The Goddess Pomona." 25 November 2007. oddesschess.blogspot.com/2007/11/goddess-pomona.html (accessed February 2009).

Goddess Gift. "Amaterasu, Goddess of the Sun; Uzume, Goddess of Mirth and Dance." www.goddessgift.com/goddess-myths/japanese_goddess_Amaterasu.htm (accessed February 2009).

———. "Isis, Egyptian Goddess of Magic and Giver of Life." www.goddessgift .com/goddess-myths/egyitian_goddess_Isis.htm (accessed February 2009).

Golden Dawn Research Center: The Esoteric Order of the Golden Dawn, home page. www.golden-dawn.org (accessed February 2009).

Graves, Robert. *The Greek Myths.* New York: Penguin Putnam, 1992.

Gray, Elizabeth A., trans. *The Second Battle of Mag Tuired.* Sacred Texts.com www .sacred-texts.com/neu/cmt/cmteng.htm. (accessed February 2009).

Gray, Martin. "Bath, England." Sacred Sites: Places of Peace and Power. www.sacredsites .com/europe/england/bath.html (accessed February 2009).

Hamilton, Edith. *Mythology: Timeless Tales of Gods and Heroes.* New York: New American Library, 1969.

Hamilton, Virginia. *Bruh Rabbit and the Tar Baby Girl.* New York: The Blue Skye Press, 2003.

Hesiod. "Hesiod, the Homeric Hymns and Homeria: The Divination by Birds to Idaean Dactyles." The Astronomy Fragments, Fragment #1. Online Medieval and Classical Library. http://ling.lll.hawaii.edu/faculty/stampe/Oral-Lit/Greek/Hesiod/frag1.html (accessed February 2009).

High Altitude Observatory. Earth and Sun Systems Laboratory at the National Center for Atmospheric Research. http://www.hao.ucar.edu/Public/education/basic.html (accessed February 2009).

Holy Bible: The New International Version. Grand Rapids, MI: Zondervan, 1984. www.biblegateway.com (accessed February 2009).

Housman, A. E. "XII" *Additional Poems* (1939). Available online at http://www.kalliope.org/digt.pl?longdid=housman2002021312 (accessed February 2009).

Illinois State Museum. "Mammoths." www.museum.state.il.us/exhibits/larson/mammuthus.html (accessed February 2009).

Johnson, Kirk. "Venus in Pompeian Gardens." (January 1, 2000). Hosted by Suite 101. www.suite101.com/article.cfm/garden_design/31002/1 (accessed February 2009).

Johnson, Richard. *Tom a Lincoln*. London: H. Brugis, 1682. Hosted by The Camelot Projects at the University of Rochester. www.lib.rochester.edu/camelot/TAL.htm (accessed February 2009).

Jones, Gwyn, and Thomas Jones, trans. *The Mabinogion*. Rutland, VT: C. E. Tuttle, 1996.

Jordan, Michael. *Encyclopedia of Gods: Over 2,500 Deities of the World*. New York: Facts on File, 1993.

Keating, Geoffrey. *The History of Ireland (Book I and II)*. Cork, Ireland: CELT (Corpus of Electronic Texts), 2006. http://www.ucc.ie/celt/published/T100054.html (accessed February 2009).)

Kelley, Ruth Edna. *The Book of Hallowe'en*. Boston: Lothrop, Lee & Shephard, 1919. Available online at www.sacred-texts.com/pag/boh/boh06.htm (accessed February 2009).

King, Karen L. *The Gospel of Mary of Magdala: Jesus and the First Woman Apostle*. Santa Rosa, CA: Polebridge Press, 2003. Excerpt available online at www.beliefnet.com/story/134/story_13458_1.html (accessed February 2009).

Koleman, Carol. "Profile of a Goddess: Ama-No-Uzume." *Catalyst: Healthy Living, Healthy Planet*. Volume 28, Number 7. www.catalystmagazine.net/component/content/article/31/35-profile-of-a-goddess-ama-no-uzume (accessed February 2009).

Krensky, Stephen. *Anansi and the Box of Stories*. Minneapolis, MN: Millbrook Press, 2008.

Larbi, Rev. Dr. Emmanuel Kingsley. "The Nature of Continuity and Discontinuity of Ghanaian Pentecostal Concept of Salvation in African Cosmology." *CyberJournal* #10 (July 2001): www.pctii.org/cyberj/cyberj10/larbi.html (accessed February 2009).

Leeming, David Adams, and Jake Page. *Goddess: Myths of the Female Divine*. New York: Oxford Universary Press, 1994.

Lila. "Pachamama." The Order of the White Moon. www.orderwhitemoon.org/goddess/Pachamama.htm (accessed February 2009).

Lilinah. "Diety Temple, Room One." 'Asherah (Hebrew). Qadash Kinahnu: A Canaanite-Phoenician Temple. www.geocities.com/SoHo/Lofts/2938/majdei.html (accessed February 2009).

Lost in Space (film). Dir. Stephen Hopkins. Perf. William Hurt, Mimi Rogers, Heather Graham, Lacey Chabert, Jack Johnson, Gary Oldman, Matt LeBlanc. New Line Cinema, 1998.

MacAllister, R. A. S. *Lebor Gabala Erren*. Dublin: Irish Texts Society, 1956.

Meplon, Anne. "Gem Guide: Amber." Maha Lakshmi Jewelry. www.annemeplon.com/gemguide.htm (accessed February 2009).

Merriam-Webster Inc. *Merriam-Webster Dictionary*. www.m-w.com/dictionary (accessed February 2009).

Monaghan, Patricia. *The New Book of Goddesses & Heroines*. Minneapolis, MN: Llewellyn Publications, 2002.

Moss, Robert. "A Mirror for the Sun Goddess: A Myth Story of Soul Recovery from Japan." www.mossdreams.com/mirror%20for%20sun%20goddess.htm (accessed February 2009).

New American Standard Bible. La Habra, CA: The Lockman Foundation, 1995. www.biblegateway.com (accessed February 2009).

Obenewaa, Nana Amma. "The President's Accident: Obenewaa Scoffs at the Spinning and Yarning for a Nation's Sympathy." Ghana Home Page. (November 22, 2007): www.ghanaweb.com/GhanaHomePage/NewsArchive/artikel.php?ID=134368 (accessed February 2009).

O'Connell, John. "Our Lady of Fatima." *The Catholic Faith.* San Francisco: Ignatius Press (May/June 1998): www.catholic.net/rcc/Periodicals/Faith/1998-05-06/fatima .html (accessed February 2009).

O'Neill, Patt. "Mama." *Glossary of Terminology of the Shamanic and Ceremonial Traditions of the Inca Medicine Lineage at Practiced in the United States.* www.incaglossary .org/M.html (accessed February 2009).

Osei-Adu, David. Ghana. "Puberty Rites." Ghana Home Page. (February 23, 2003): www.ghanaweb.com/GhanaHomePage/tribes/puberty_rites.php (accessed February 2009).

Ovid. *Fasti: Book IV.* A. S Kline, trans. Available online at www.tkline.freeserve.co.uk/ OvidFastiBkFour.htm (accessed February 2009).

———. *The Metamorphoses.* "Vertumnus woos Pomona." A. S. Kline, trans. Available online at www.tkline.freeserve.co.uk/Metamorph14.htm (accessed February 2009).

Patel, Samir S. "A Sinking Feeling." *Nature* Vol. 440 (April 6, 2006): www.scidev.net/ uploads/File//pdffiles/nature/tuvalu.pdf (accessed February 2009).

Permutt, Philip. *The Crystal Healer: Crystal Prescriptions That Will Change Your Life Forever.* New York: CICO Books, 2007.

Pleiade Associates, Ltd. "The Pleiades in Mythology." http://www.pleiade.org/pleiades _02.html (accessed April 2009).

Roman-Britain.org. "Aquae Sulis." www.roman-britain.org/places/aquae_sulis.htm (accessed February 2009).

Rome, Peter. "The Temple of Seti I and the Osireion at Abydos." TourEgypt. www .touregypt.net/featurestories/setiabydos.htm (accessed February 2009).

Ruffinelly. *The Little Shepherds of Fatima.* Pamphlet attained outside Fatima, Portugal, in 1970s. Publisher unknown, located at Alibris, #8347915319

Sakura Designs. "What is a Mala?" www.buddhistmala.com/store/mantra.html (accessed February 2009).

Santos, Michelle. "The Magical Blue Lotus." *Llewellyn's 2006 Herbal Almanac.* St. Paul, MN: Llewellyn Publications, 2005.

dos Santos, Sr. Lucia. "The Message of Fatima: Congregation for the Doctrine of the Faith." *L'Osservatore Romano English Edition*, special insert (28 June 2000): www .ewtn.com/fatima/apparitions/Third_Secret/Fatima.htm (accessed February 2009).

Schmitt, Dirk. "Sunna and Mani: An Investigation into the Sun and Moon in the Germanic Folkway." *Assembly of the Elder Troth.* www.aetaustralia.org/articles/ ardssunnamani.htm (accessed February 2009).

Scott, Michael. *Irish Folk and Fairy Tales Omnibus.* London: Warner Books, 1995.

Seawright, Caroline. "Heqet, Frog Headed Goddess of Childbirth." TourEgypt. www .touregypt.net/featurestories/heqet.htm (accessed February 2009).

———. "Isis, Sister of Nephthys, Mistress of Magic." Egyptology. (May 7, 2001): www .thekeep.org/~kunoichi/kunoichi/themestream/isis.html (accessed February 2009).

———. "Tales of Magic in Ancient Egypt." (April 24, 2001) Egyptology: www.thekeep .org/~kunoichi/kunoichi/themestream/egypt_magic.html (accessed February 2009).

Shakespeare, William. "Venus and Adonis." Available online at www.online-literature .com/shakespeare/330 (accessed February 2009).

Simpson, Liz. *The Book of Chakra Healing.* New York: Sterling Publishing Company, 1999.

Skye, Michelle. *Goddess Alive!* Woodbury, MN: Llewellyn Publications, 2007.

———. *Goddess Afoot!* Woodbury, MN: Llewellyn Publications, 2008.

Spade, Beatrice. "Roman History." Colorado State University at Pueblo. http://faculty .colostate-pueblo.edu/beatrice.spade/rome.htm (accessed February 2009).

Springs. "Hawaiian Goddess Hina." Powers That Be. www.powersthatbe.com/goddess/ hina.html (accessed February 2009).

Squire, Charles. *Celtic Myth and Legend.* London: Gresham Publishing Company, 1905. Sacred Texts.com. www.sacred-texts.com/neu/celt/cml/cml20.htm (accessed February 2009).

StarSpirit International, Inc. "Akan Culture and Protocol." www.starspirit.com/akan _culture.php (accessed February 2009).

Sturluson, Snorri. *Edda.* Rutland, VT: Charles E. Tuttle, 2002.

Sulzberger, Ann. "Ara Pacis Augustae." The Institute of Classical Architecture and Classical America. www.classicist.org/resources/historic-plaster-cast-collection/catalogue/greek-020/ara-pacis-augustae/ (accessed February 2009).

Symbols.com. "Symbol 20:18, The Heart Symbol." HME Publishing. www.symbols.com/encyclopedia/20/2018.html (accessed February 2009).

Thompson, Vivian L. *Hawaiian Myths of Earth, Sea, and Sky.* Honolulu, HI: University of Hawaii Press,1966.

The Tibetan Monks of Deprung Gomang Monastery. "Sand Mandalas, Sacred Art." Deprung Gomang Monastery Tour. www.gomangtour.org/mandala.html (accessed February 2009).

Took, Thalia. "Tlazolteotl." A-Muse-ing Grace Gallery. http://www.thaliatook.com/AMGG/tlazolteotl.html (accessed July 2009).

University of Oxford. "Discovery of Oldest Human Decorations—Thought to Be 82,000 Years Old." (June 5, 2007) Physorg.com www.physorg.com/news100272567.html (accessed February 2009).

Venefica, Avia. "Spiritual Meaning of Numbers." What's-Your-Sign.com. http://www.whats-your-sign.com/spiritual-meaning-of-numbers.html (accessed February 2009).

Welch, Bill. "The Sign Language of Roman Coins: Isis, Goddess of the Nile." *What I Like About Ancient Coins.* Hosted by Forum Ancient Coins. www.forumancientcoins.com/moonmoth/reverse_isis.html (accessed February 2009).

———. "The Sign Language of Roman Coins: Leaning on the Handy Column." *What I Like About Ancient Coins.* Hosted by Forum Ancient Coins. http://www.forumancientcoins.com/moonmoth/reverse_securitas.html (accessed February 2009).

Welch, Lynda C. *Goddess of the North.* York Beach, ME: Weiser Books, 2001.

Westervelt, W. D. *Legends of Maui: A Demi-God of Polynesia and His Mother Hina.* Honolulu, HI: The Hawaiian Gazette Co,1910. Available online at www.sacred-texts.com/pac/maui/index.htm (accessed February 2009).

Witcombe, Christopher L. C. E. "Venus of Willendorf." Sweet Briar College, Virginia. (2005): witcombe.sbc.edu/willendorf (accessed February 2009).

Wood, Nicholas Breeze. "Wind Power." *Sacred Hoop Magazine* issue 53 (2006).

World Culture Encyclopedia. "Akan Religion." Advameg Inc. www.everyculture.com/Africa-Middle-East/Akan-Religion.html (accessed February 2009).

Yiadom, Queen Boakyewa I. "We Believe That the Earth is God's Gift to Us." *African Traditional Religion*. afgen.com/queen.html (accessed February 2009).

Ziehr, Joseph. "Ame-no-Uzume no Mikoto." Shimbutsuto: A Website for the Study of Japanese Religions. University of Wisconsin–Eau Claire. www.uwec.edu/philrel/shimbutsudo (accessed February 2009).